SHORTLIST

San Francisco

WHAT'S NEW | WHAT'S ON | WHAT'S BEST

www.timeout.com/sanfrancisco

Contents

Published by Time Out Guides Ltd
Universal House
251 Tottenham Court Road
London W1T 7AB
Tel: + 44 (0)20 7813 3000
Fax: + 44 (0)20 7813 6001
Email: guides@timeout.com
www.timeout.com

Managing Director Peter Fiennes
Financial Director Gareth Garner
Editorial Director Ruth Jarvis
Deputy Series Editor Dominic Earle
Editorial Manager Holly Pick
Assistant Management Accountant Ija Krasnikova

Time Out Guides is a wholly owned subsidiary of Time Out Group Ltd.

© Time Out Group Ltd
Chairman Tony Elliott
Financial Director Richard Waterlow
Group General Manager/Director Nichola Coulthard
Time Out Magazine Ltd MD Richard Waterlow
Time Out Communications Ltd MD David Pepper
Time Out International MD Cathy Runciman
Production Director Mark Lamond
Group IT Director Simon Chappell

Time Out and the Time Out logo are trademarks of Time Out Group Ltd.

This edition first published in Great Britain in 2008 by Ebury Publishing
A Random House Group Company
Company information can be found on www.randomhouse.co.uk
10 9 8 7 6 5 4 3 2 1

Distributed in US by Publishers Group West
Distributed in Canada by Publishers Group Canada

For further distribution details, see www.timeout.com

ISBN: 978-1-84670-086-6

A CIP catalogue record for this book is available from the British Library

Printed and bound by Firmengruppe APPL, aprinta druck, Wemding, Germany

The Random House Group Limited supports The Forest Stewardship Council (FSC), the
leading international forest certification organisation. All our titles that are printed on
Greenpeace approved FSC certified paper carry the FSC logo. Our paper procurement
policy can be found at www.rbooks.co.uk/environment.

Time Out carbon-offsets all its flights with Trees for Cities (www.treesforcities.org).

San Francisco Shortlist

The **Time Out San Francisco Shortlist** is one of a new series of guides that draws on Time Out's background as a magazine publisher to keep you current with what's going on in town. As well as San Francisco's key sights and the best of its eating, drinking and leisure options, the guide picks out the most exciting venues to have recently opened and gives a full calendar of annual events. It also includes features on the important news, trends and openings, all compiled by locally based editors and writers. Whether you're visiting for the first time, or you're a regular, you'll find the *Time Out San Francisco Shortlist* contains all you need to know, in a portable and easy-to-use format.

The guide divides central San Francisco into eight areas, each of which contains listings for Sights & Museums, Eating & Drinking, Shopping, Nightlife and Arts & Leisure, with maps pinpointing all their locations. At the front of the book are chapters rounding up these scenes city-wide, and giving a shortlist of our overall picks in a variety of categories. We include itineraries for days out, plus essentials such as transport information and hotels.

Our listings give phone numbers as dialled within San Francisco. From elsewhere in the country, dial 1, then 415 (or 510 for a Berkeley number), then the phone number. To call a venue from outside the US, use your country's exit code followed by the number given (the initial 1 is the US country code).

We have noted price categories by using one to four $ signs ($-$$$$), representing budget, moderate, expensive and luxury. Major credit cards are accepted unless otherwise stated. We also indicate when a venue is NEW.

All our listings are checked, but places do sometimes close or change their hours or prices, so it's a good idea to call before visiting. While every effort has been made to ensure accuracy, the publishers cannot accept responsibility for errors that this guide may contain.

Venues are marked on the maps using symbols numbered according to their order within the chapter and colour-coded according to the type of venue they represent:

❶ Sights & Museums
❶ Eating & Drinking
❶ Shopping
❶ Nightlife
❶ Arts & Leisure

Map key	
Major sight or landmark	
Hospital or college	
Railway station	
Parks	
River	
Interstate	🛡
US Highway	🛡
State or Provincial Highway	①
Main road	—
Airport	✈
Church	✚
Area name	CASTRO

Time Out San Francisco Shortlist

EDITORIAL
Editor Ros Sales
Researcher Miranda Morton
Proofreader Kieron Corless

DESIGN
Art Director Scott Moore
Art Editor Pinelope Kourmouzoglou
Senior Designer Henry Elphick
Graphic Designer Gemma Doyle
Junior Graphic Designer Kei Ishimaru
Digital Imaging Simon Foster
Advertising Designer Jodi Sher
Picture Editor Jael Marschner
Deputy Picture Editor Katie Morris
Picture Researcher Gemma Walters
Picture Desk Assistant Marzena Zoladz

ADVERTISING
Commercial Director Mark Phillips
International Advertising Manager
Kasimir Berger
International Sales Executive
Charlie Sokol
Advertising Sales (San Francisco)
Anil Shah
Advertising Assistant Kate Staddon

MARKETING
Head of Marketing Catherine Demajo
Marketing Manager Yvonne Poon
**Sales & Marketing Director, North
America** Lisa Levinson
Marketing Designers Anthony Huggins,
Nicola Wilson

PRODUCTION
Production Manager Brendan McKeown
Production Controller Caroline Bradford
Production Co-ordinator Julie Pallot

CONTRIBUTORS
This guide was researched and written by Robert Avila, Marke Bieschke, Kimberly Chun, Jeanne Cooper, Matt Markovich, Miranda Morton, Mark Taylor, Cyrus Shahrad and Bonnie Wach. Thanks also to all other contributors to *Time Out San Francisco*.

PHOTOGRAPHY
All photography by Hans Kwiotek, except: page 13 Daniel Wedick; page 19 Val Atkinson; page 33 Cindy Chew; page 34 John N Lee; page 35 Dejan Cabrilo/Licensed under Creative Commons Attribution 2.5 license; page 38 John Western; pages 48, 62, 63, 71, 144 Elan Fleisher; page 68 Dirk Lindner; page 145 California Academy of Sciences; page 173 The Westin Hotel, San Francisco.

The following images were provided by the featured establishments/artists: pages 36, 55.

Cover photograph: Golden Gate Bridge. Credit: Pictures Colour Library.

MAPS
JS Graphics (john@jsgraphics.co.uk).

About Time Out

Founded in 1968, Time Out has expanded from humble London beginnings into the leading resource for those wanting to know what's happening in the world's greatest cities. As well as our influential what's-on weeklies in London, New York and Chicago, we publish more than a dozen other listings magazines in cities as varied as Beijing and Mumbai. The magazines established Time Out's trademark style: sharp writing, informed reviewing and bang up-to-date inside knowledge of every scene.

Time Out made the natural leap into travel guides in the 1980s with the City Guide series, which now extends to over 50 destinations around the world. Written and researched by expert local writers and generously illustrated with original photography, the full-size guides cover a larger area than our Shortlist guides and include many more venue reviews, along with additional background features and a full set of maps.

Throughout this rapid growth, the company has remained proudly independent, still owned by Tony Elliott nearly four decades after he started Time Out London as a single fold-out sheet of A5 paper. This independence extends to the editorial content of all our publications, this Shortlist included. No establishment has been featured because it has advertised, and no payment has influenced any of our reviews. And, for our critics, there's definitely no such thing as a free lunch: all restaurants and bars are visited and reviewed anonymously, and Time Out always picks up the bill. For more about the company, see www.timeout.com.

Don't Miss

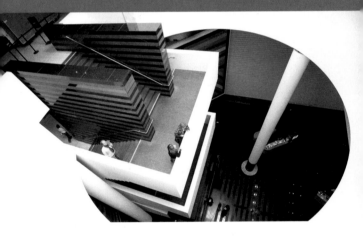

Museum of Modern Art p12

WHAT'S BEST
Sights & Museums

Size, as they say, isn't everything. But what San Francisco lacks in geographical stature, it more than makes up for in cultural largesse, with more eye-popping architecture, postcard-worthy landmarks, cutting-edge art institutions and museums than most cities three times its size. Spend any time wandering through its nooks and crannies and you'll quickly see how the city has earned its monikers Paris of the Pacific and Athens of the West.

While the dotcom industry hit meltdown in the last decade, there was no equivalent slowdown in the steady stream of new and revitalised cultural attractions that make San Francisco such a fascinating place to live or visit.

A changing cityscape

Nearly 20 years after the 7.1 Loma Prieta earthquake shook loose a chunk of the Bay Bridge (p86), a new eastern span is finally coming to fruition. Mired in bureaucratic red tape and cost overruns, with plans scuttled several times, the grey, utilitarian Oakland leg of the bridge is slowly being replaced by a sweeping, white single-span suspension design. With the skyway and approaches nearing completion, attention is at last focusing on the signature suspension tower – scheduled to open sometime in 2013, with a price tag hovering around $6 billion.

Though the bridge might be the most showy addition to the San Francisco skyline, it's not the biggest. The Transamerica Pyramid (p58), once the definitive exclamation point on the city's skyline, is quickly being eclipsed in 2008 by a series of larger, more imposing structures. The obelisk-like One Rincon Hill condominium tower – the first of two skyscrapers currently under construction next to the Bay Bridge – looms some 641 feet above the Bay. Recently approved plans for the Transbay Transit Center, a combination office/residential/retail complex and train/bus terminal, include a rooftop park the length of five football fields and an 80-storey highrise tower, which will give San Francisco the dubious distinction of having the tallest building on the West Coast. The Millennium Tower, a 645-foot blue-glass homage to luxury living, will offer penthouses with showstopping views and amenities that include a residents-only dining room serviced by celebrity chef Michael Mina.

On the coveted Embarcadero waterfront, two new sister restaurants – the first two privately owned buildings to be constructed from the ground up on the waterfront in a century – opened to much fanfare in early 2008 and are set to become landmarks. Epic Roasthouse and Waterbar (p60) are the creations of designer and restaurateur Pat Kuleto, and acclaimed chefs Mark Franz, Parke Ulrich and Jan Birnbaum.

This building boom is being offset, quite literally, with construction that addresses San Francisco's carbon footprint. Using 'green', 'sustainable', and 'local' as their guiding principles, a slew of new projects are looking to lead the way against climate crisis and global warming.

San Francisco's development is not all about big-money prestige projects. In 2007 children and

S H O R T L I S T

Best new
- California Academy of Sciences (p142)
- Contemporary Jewish Museum (p75)
- Koret Children's Quarter (p142)

San Francisco icons
- Alcatraz (p101)
- Coit Tower (p96)
- Golden Gate Bridge (p158)

Best museum architecture
- California Academy of Sciences (p142)
- Contemporary Jewish Museum (p75)
- De Young Museum (p142)
- San Francisco Museum of Modern Art (p75)

Best green spaces
- Golden Gate Park (p141-5)
- The Presidio (p156)
- Marina Green (p153)

Best shoreline
- Ocean Beach (p141)
- Crissy Field (p157)

Best murals
- Balmy Alley (p107)
- City Club of San Francisco (p97)
- San Francisco Art Institute (p105)
- Coit Tower (p96)

Best art collections
- California Palace of the Legion of Honor (p159)
- De Young Museum (p142)
- San Francisco Museum of Modern Art (p75)

Quintessential SF experiences
- A visit to Alcatraz (p101)
- Crossing the Golden Gate Bridge (p158)
- A ride in a cable car (p50)

Cable car on Nob Hill p9

parents hailed the renovation of America's first municipal playground in Golden Gate Park. Renamed the Koret Children's Quarter (p142), the new playground pays homage to the Bay Area landscape, with sea caves, tidepools and the like. Planners also restored the historic carousel, and the death-defying cement slides.

Museums

On the other side of the park, across from the de Young Museum (p142), which received a complete makeover from Tate Museum architects Herzog and de Meuron in 2005, workers are putting the finishing touches on a new building for the California Academy of Sciences (p142). When it opens in the autumn of 2008, the natural science museum, aquarium, and planetarium, designed by Italian Pritzker Prize-winning architect Renzo Piano, will be housed in what is to be the world's 'greenest' museum

– an environmentally sustainable building that contains a rainforest, a coral reef, and a living roof supporting some 1.7 million plants.

Separated by a grand concourse and bandshell (which are also undergoing renovation), the two museums will serve as the cultural jewels in the green crown of Golden Gate Park. And it is not just their collections that are flagships: both feature restaurants that are a departure from typical museum cafés. The Café de Young, overlooking a whimsical sculpture garden, offers seasonal fare from small family farmers and artisanal producers, made with ingredients grown within 150 miles of the kitchen. The new restaurant and café at the Academy of Sciences will be run by acclaimed chefs Loretta Keller and Charles Phan and will feature local, organic, and sustainable cuisine.

The rehabilitation of these venerable establishments is focusing new attention on all the city's cultural institutions, and attracting a fresh influx of major exhibitions in 2008. The de Young museum, which holds a vast collection of American art, is scheduled to show works and installations by renowned glass artist Dale Chihuly from June. In February 2009 the museum hosts Warhol Live, a look at Pop Art figure Andy Warhol's influence in the world of music and sound.

The de Young's sister museum, the Legion of Honor in Lincoln Park (p159), whose collection emphasises European and decorative arts, presents Annie Leibovitz: A Photographer's Life, 1990-2005, opening in May 2008. The exhibition of some 200 photographs by the visual chronicler of the rich and famous, includes celebrities, war photos, and personal pictures of private family life. In November 2008, the Legion brings the Biblioteca Reale drawings of Leonardo da Vinci to the United States for the first time. Dating from about 1480 to 1510, the works traverse the arc of Leonardo's career. Both the de Young and the Legion are free to the public the first Tuesday of each month.

Across town, the Museum of Modern Art (p75), with its distinctive red-brick building and huge circular skylight, is the second-largest US museum devoted to modern art. It presents a retrospective of works by Frida Kahlo from June until September 2008, including 50 paintings, and photographs that once belonged to Kahlo and husband Diego Rivera. Many of these have never before been published or exhibited. There is also a particular interest in Rivera in San Francisco as he painted several striking murals around town during the 1930s (box p97). Admission to MOMA

is half-price every Thursday from 6pm to 9pm, and free the first Tuesday of every month.

Around the corner, the new Contemporary Jewish Museum (p75), with a design by famed New York architect Daniel Libeskind, features a blue-steel cube jutting out of a 1907 brick power-substation. It opens its doors on 8 June 2008, and its first exhibition will be In the Beginning: Artists Respond to Genesis, exploring a range of responses to the creation story.

The Asian Art Museum (p71), located across from City Hall, is also a draw for its architecture as well as its collections – a dramatic, modern blending and repurposing of a soaring beaux arts building by architect Gae Aulenti (Musée d'Orsay) that formerly housed the main public library. After its move from Golden Gate Park to the Civic Center in 2003, the museum became one of the largest museums in the western world devoted exclusively to Asian art. Its holdings include nearly 17,000 Asian art treasures spanning 6,000 years of history. Several major travelling exhibitions come to the Asian in 2008-9, including Afghanistan: Hidden Treasures from the National Museum, Kabul from October 2008 until January 2009, a collection of archaeological treasures that explore the rich cultural heritage of ancient Afghanistan from the Bronze Age through the first century AD. In February 2009, the Asian presents The Dragon's Gift: The Sacred Arts of Bhutan, a rare look at some of the most sacred and beloved Buddhist arts from the sovereign nation of Bhutan. In addition to reduced admission on Thursdays after 5pm, the Asian Art Museum is free the first Tuesday of each month.

Nopa

WHAT'S BEST
Eating & Drinking

You've heard of walking contradictions. When it comes to restaurant trends, San Franciscans are dining contradictions. They delight in trying new cuisines, but also want ingredients to be locally sourced; they despise restaurant chains, but flock to second and third outposts opened by famous chefs; they spend more on dining out than residents of other US cities, but favour rustic cuisines and informal settings. Yet while they love the buzz of communal tables and sharing small plates, they also adore the exclusivity of small, intimate restaurants with few seats. The net result is that there really is something for everyone in this city.

One recent trend means that it is becoming easier to eat in some of the city's best restaurants for less money. High-end notables, such as the Civic Center's stellar Jardiniere (p72) and South Beach's wine-oriented Bacar (p86), have remodelled their interiors to include attractive lounges with less expensive bar menus.

Table talk

Communal tables – like lounge seats, they're generally for those without reservations – have been around for a while at the city's staunchly European joints. But it took trendsetters like Town Hall (p82) and Nopa (p134) to popularise them – to the benefit of singles and visitors, who

SAMOVAR | TEA LOUNGE

organic seasonal food and artisanal fresh crop tea

Create Peace, Drink Tea

www.samovartea.com

have an excuse to strike up conversations with strangers – and now they're found in a number of recently opened hot spots. Among them are Orson (p80), the mod, film-focused New American restaurant from Elizabeth Falkner, creator of the wildly popular Citizen Cake (p138); and Perbacco (p59), a stylish home for Piedmontese cuisine with Ligurian and Provencal touches, tasting plates and a bar menu.

Speaking of small plates, twists on tapas keep popping up like Starbucks in the suburbs. While Colibri (p52) and Cortez (p66) serve more traditional Latin American small plates to Theatre District patrons, Bin 38 (p154) in the Marina emphasises Wine Country cuisine, and Coco 500 (p86) serves vibrant Med-inspired plates. And while Chinese restaurants that serve dim sum are legion, one Japanese establishment that offers something other than raw seafood or sushi rolls on small plates is the new O Izakaya Lounge (p136). Part of the remodelled Hotel Kabuki, O Izakaya is a sleek, Japanese sports bar with grilled meat skewers (pork belly, chicken thighs, beef loin), beer-battered tempura mushrooms and onion rings, and shared plates of duck breast and New York strip, among other hearty choices.

With good cause

The idea of seasonal food and sustainable agriculture and aquaculture first took root at Alice Waters' legendary Chez Panisse (p163) in Berkeley back in the '70s, but it has really taken off in recent years. The latest efforts to be heralded for environmental reasons as well as culinary concerns include Frisée (p121), the brainchild of brothers

DON'T MISS

SHORTLIST

Dining with a view
- Beach Chalet (p143)
- Boulevard (p62)
- Greens (p154)
- Waterbar (p60)

Great food, laid-back atmosphere
- Nopa (p134)
- Salt House (p82)
- Town Hall (p82)

Old-school Americana
- St Francis Fountain (p114)

Outdoor dining
- Beach Chalet (p143)
- Café Claude (p51)
- Foreign Cinema (p111)
- Park Chalet (p143)

Cal-Ital
- Chez Panisse (p163)
- Perbacco (p59)
- Zuni Café (p73)

Eco-eating
- Chez Panisse (p163)
- Frisée (p121)
- Millennium (p67)

Special occasions
- Chez Panisse (p163)
- Gary Danko (p104)
- Jardinière (p72)
- Michael Mina (p52)
- Waterbar (p60)

Outdoor drinking
- Medjool Sky Terrace (p113)
- Park Chalet (p143)
- Savoy Tivoli (p98)

Coolest cocktails
- Absinthe (p138)
- Alembic (p127)
- Catalyst Cocktails (p80)
- Slanted door (p64)
- Top of the Mark (p90)

Tiki kitsch
- Tonga Room & Hurricane Bar (p90)

EAT HAMACHI **WAKAME** HYPE PINOT NOIR **WINE**
RISING SUN **BINCHO TATAKI** SPLURGE **DAIGINJO**
SINGLE MALT **JAPAN** DAIGINJO FUN **CHAMPAGNE**
DRINK **MAMASAN** WAKAME SALAD **SINGLE MALT**
TORO **SPLURGE** SEXY DRINK **FUN** FLYING V SUSHI
JAPAN DRINK SUSHI **SAMURAI** COCKTAIL **LOUNGE**
ENJOY **MUSIC** FUN WINE NIGORI **SAKE** OMAKASE
SUSHI FUN **SEXY** DAIGINJO EAT **YAMATO** BINCHO
WHISKY **CHATEAU MARGAUX** TORO SUSHI GINJO
SAMURAI DRINK WAKAME **SINGLE MALT** SALAD
BINCHO TATAKI **RISING SUN** SPLURGE **DAIGINJO**
WINE **KAPPA MAKI** PINOT NOIR SASHIMI **NIGORI**
CHATEAU MARGAUX **SASHIMI** MUSIC **HYPE** SEXY
EAT HAMACHI **WAKAME** HYPE PINOT NOIR **WINE**
YAMATO DAIGINJO EAT BINCHO SUSHI FUN **SEXY**
WINE NIGORI **SAKE** OMAKASE ENJOY **MUSIC** FUN
JAPAN SINGLE MALT DAIGINJO FUN **CHAMPAGNE**

SAKE
DYNAMITE MUSSEL MALBEC JAPAN
MUSIC **MAMASAN** DRINK **JUNMAI**
SUSHI
NIGORI SAKE **SUNOMONO** FUN
DRINK OMAKASE FUN PAPASAN
WHISKY PINOT NOIR COCKTAIL
WHISKY
JUNMAI **OMAKASE** HYPE
WALOO LOUNGE SASHIMI
IZAKAYA
MAMASAN **CHAMPAGNE**
YAMATO THUNDER BIRD
SINGLE MALT **DAIGINJO**
NIGHTLIFE
SPLURGE WHISKY
TORO PINOT NOIR
JAPAN **FUN** GINJO
SAN FRANCISCO HYPE **EAT** SEXY ENJOY **DRINK**

TSUNAMI
1300 Fulton st
415-567-7664
NOPA District

NIHON
1779 Folsom st
415-552-4400
Mission District

Brett and Nathan Niebergall, who offer organic salads and cheeses, low-calorie soups, grilled meat and seafood from eco-friendly sources, and biodynamic and organic wines. Millenium (p67), in the Tenderloin's Hotel California, has one of the best all-organic wine lists in the US, and puts a lot of creative verve into its vegetarian menu. The chic and intimate Fish & Farm (p67), meanwhile, tries to source ingredients from no more than 100 miles away, while the Acme Chop House (p86) at the ballpark – sister restaurant of the sustainability-conscious and upmarket Jardinière – uses organically raised meat.

Cheers!

San Franciscans have long been known for their adventurous palates, but their tastes in alcohol are also proving ever-more wide ranging.

When it comes to beer, old-timer Magnolia (p130) is a constant favourite. A focal point for hippie culture during the '60s, it is now known for its home-brewed beers,

including a selection of cask ales. Over in Golden Gate Park, the idyllically situated Park Chalet (p143), also brews its own beer. Back in the Haight, Toronado (p131) has a massive, ever-changing selection of draught beers, including Belgian imports.

Whisky's the watchword at Alembic (p127), a decidedly non-hippie hangout in Haight-Ashbury that prides itself on microbrews and speciality spirits – including a globe-trotting list of gins, vodkas, rums and brandies – paired with hipster bar snacks (devilled duck's eggs, prosciutto-wrapped dates with goat cheese) and upscale comfort food (macaroni and cheese with Gruyere, mini lamb burgers with harissa aioli). Tequila fans need look no further than South of Market's Tres Agaves (p87), which serves rustic cuisine from the Mexican state of Jalisco with artisanal tequilas, margaritas made with fresh-squeezed lime juice and other agave-inspired libations. Restaurants all over the city have jumped on the speciality cocktail bandwagon. Absinthe (p138) in

St Francis Fountain p15

supper**club**

657 harrison street
415.348.0900

If you are looking for an ordinary restaurant then supper**club** is not for you...

But if you are up for a full night out and a unique experience, then supperclub is the place to be. You don't eat "a la carte" at supperclub. Instead, we serve a five-course surprise menu as you relax on oversized beds and enjoy the DJ, VJ, art and performances in very special surroundings. After dinner the best national and international DJ's will play their tunes and make you want to party!

Are you up for it?

www.supperclub.com

Waterbar

Hayes Valley can truly live up to its name now that the eponymous spirit has been legalised in the US. Its remarkable spirits selection and world-class cocktails may incorporate the Green Fairy, but the mixmasters here have also taken classic drinks and recreated them with up-to-date, premium ingredients. Meanwhile, if you must go sober, Coco500 (p86) offers a 'no-jito' mojito and other teetotaller concoctions alongside high-octane drinks made with small-batch spirits and organic ingredients.

Yet for all the sake-tinis and pomegranate gin fizzes being shaken or stirred in the city's bars and restaurants, there is also a noticeable trend in wine bars – and dining rooms with wine bars attached – with more on the way. At Bin 38, for example, the samll plates are designed for pairing with suggestions from the extensive wine list in mind. While at the hidden-away Hotel Biron (p139) in Hayes Valley, accompaniment to the list of 80 wines by the bottle and around 35 by the glass is kept simple: tasting plates of artisanal cheeses.

Do it again

Uber-restaurateur Pat Kuleto may have created a big splash with his new duo of Waterbar and Epic Roadhouse (p60), where swanky looks and Bay views are matched with New Orleans-inspired steakhouse fare and sustainable seafood respectively. But he isn't the only San Francisco restaurateur with an expanding empire. Expected to open in 2008 are two new restaurants by Franck LeClerc of Café Claude (p51): Italian-flavoured Cinque (next door to Claude, off Union Square) and French-rustic Gitane (nearby). At the time of writing, the people behind Town Hall (p82) and the Salt House (p82) were readying a South of Market fish shack called Anchor & Hope, while chefs Gary Danko and Michael Mina, famed for their ultraluxe eponymous restaurants (p104 and p52), were each preparing to open a second establishment – Danko's in Ghirardelli Square, Mina's in a new downtown high-rise. Don't count on prices to be small, even if the plates turn out to be.

City Lights p100

WHAT'S BEST
Shopping

Be ready to browse and ready to ramble when it comes to tackling San Francisco's wild and woolly, quirky and cool, ever-changing shopping scene. Though it recently welcomed both Barneys (p53) and Bloomingdale's (p53) to Union Square, sports its share of malls, and is riddled with Starbucks, Gaps, and other chains, the City by the Bay has effectively championed independent business owners and barred big boxes such as Home Depot and Walmart from its limits.

State of independence

Independently owned shops are generally the way to go here – apt in a town that's proud of shopping locally and thinking globally. Recent trends include a startling number of Anthropologie-esque, Franco-centric boutiques, such as Nest (p152), which mix women's clothing and imported tchotchkes such as kitchen ware and toiletries. Also springing up are a host of carefully edited gift stores – such as Lavish (p140) – carrying a mix of women's clothing, lifestyle bits and pieces, stationary, and infant items, with a curatorial eye toward the perfect bridal or baby shower gift.

Pacific Rim pop mania is in full force at Japanophile T-shirt, toy, and art book emporiums buttressed by manga sensibilities and vinyl figurine collectors' aesthetics: Giant Robot, Super 7, and Park Life (all p132). Meanwhile, a slew of nouveau fine art/arts and crafts spaces that combine gallery

exhibitions, artifacts and/or artwork, fashion, and curiosities have sprung up. Stores like Needles and Pens (p116) and the Curiosity Shoppe (p115) draw customers interested in new design.

Food and drink can also be a labour of love in this city. The San Francisco institution that is the Graffeo Roasting Company (p100) roasts its beans on the premises; the Red Blossom Tea Company (p93) has been in the business for more than two decades, and San Francisco also has the US's first shop devoted entirely to sake (True Sake, p140).

Neigbourhood watch

These small stores and boutiques are scattered throughout the city. Thankfully San Francisco's gridlike layout and generally solid public transportation system make getting around easy. But to save shoe leather, it's a good idea to focus on specific neighbourhoods.

Union Square – flanked by Saks Fifth Avenue (p57), Neiman Marcus (p56), Macy's (p54), Levi Strauss & Company, Niketown, Gucci, and Tiffany & Company -- and adjacent designer-laden arteries like Maiden Lane, with Marc Jacobs (p54), Chanel (No.155) and Helmut Lang (No.120), are the spots to hit for international designers' current collections. Upscale shoppers in search of women's fashion will also want to check out the boutiques lining Union Street in the northern part of the city, but the incursion of chains here has been hotting up of late. So be sure to also stop at the sister Marina/Cow Hollow-area of Chestnut Street, and even better, roll down the other side of Pacific Heights, to blossoming upper Fillmore Street, with its lively mix of Marc by Marc Jacobs (No.2142), Jonathan Adler (p151), and Shu

SHORTLIST

Best for vintage clothing
- Buffalo Exchange (p132)
- Painted Bird (p117)
- Schauplatz (p116)
- Ver Unica (p140)
- Wasteland (p132)

Best for books
- Adobe Bookshop (p114)
- City Lights (p100)
- Stacey's (p61)
- Kayo Books (p69)

Best for music
- Amoeba Music (p131)
- Grooves Vinyl Attraction (p140)
- Medium Rare Records (p123)
- Ritmo Latino (p116)

Best for local designers
- Diana Slavin (p53)
- Minnie Wilde (p115)
- Lemon Twist (p137)
- Rag Co-op (p137)

Best for Japanophiles
- Giant Robot (p132)

Best for Afrophiles
- African Outlet (p139)

Best for jewellery
- Five & Diamond (p115)
- Gallery of Jewels (p151)
- Macchiarini Creative Design (p100)

Best for children
- Cotton Sheep (p139)
- Laku (p115)

Best boutiques
- Behind the Post Office (p132)
- Brown Eyed Girl (p51)
- Dylan (p156)
- MAC (p140)
- Nest (p152)

Shops with history
- City Lights (p100)
- Gumps (p54)
- Macchiarini Creative Design (p100)

Brown Eyed Girl

Uemura (No.1971), as well as independent retailers Zinc Details (p152), Erica Tanov (p151), Brown Eyed Girl (p151) and more.

Make sure to check out the Mission's quirky, hipster-friendly scene, which includes the Burning Man-inspired Five and Diamond (p115), fun 'n' spunky Therapy (p117), as well as local designers such as Minnie Wilde (p115). Also essential: the spiritual birthplace of SF's countercultural cool, the Haight-Ashbury, with its teeming vintage fashion shops, urban fashion flavour (check the skateboarder-fave RVCA's flagship store at Haight and Ashbury), and footwear emporiums for women and men alike.

Meanwhile, fully emerging 'hood Hayes Valley, with its clutch of local designer boutiques (including RAG, and Lemon Twist, both p137), upscale children's fashion, and eclectic eateries, now rivals North Beach's Grant Street for old-world charm and new-school style.

Going local

Looking for a local creation? San Francisco's designer scene is small but feisty. Stop in at the aforementioned Minnie Wilde, Lemon Twist, and RAG, but also consider local lines like Saffron Rare Threads (www.saffronrare threads.com), with its richly hued tailoring, and dramatic Cari Borja (www.cariborja.com), with contemporary materials and over-the-top styling. The romantic separates of Erica Tanov (p151) are another local favourite. Or swing by one of the boutiques that showcase Bay designers, such as MAC Modern Appealing Clothing (p151).

Bargain hunting

Those intent on sniffing out deals will keep an eye on the newspapers for weekend sample sales presented by such discounted fashion event producers as Billion Dollar Babes and Shecky's Girls Night Out, as well as holiday fashion fairs at venues like 111 Minpna Gallery (p83) and 12 Galaxies (p117). Also invaluable for cut-rate designer finds are markdown outlets such as Loehman's (p54), where label hounds will be stunned by the finds by Missoni, Prada, Dolce e Gabbana, and many other big-ticket names.

Speaking of malls, what better way to relax your weary bones than indulging in a little light shopping at just one locale? The Westfield San Francisco Centre at Market Street in Downtown is your one-stop spot for major retailers like Bloomingdale's and Nordstrom (p57), in addition to Adidas, Juicy Couture, Zara, H&M, Borders, J Crew, BCBG, Bebe, Abercrombie and Fitch, Oilily, Kenneth Cole, and Bennetton, among others. All the universal rules apply: be sure to swoop up bargains during the post-holiday sales.

Milk p26

WHAT'S BEST
Nightlife

In keeping with its funky
cosmopolitan spirit, San Francisco
offers a mindboggling array of
nightlife experiences, despite the
fact that most parties end when
the bar closes at 2am. Still, a lot
of craziness gets jammed into
the hours between 8pm and
closing time.

Four areas rule the scene: SoMa,
where 11th Street is brimming with
bars and clubs that serve every
taste; the Mission District, which
explodes with hipsters and arty-
types as soon as the sun goes down;
meanwhile, the Castro caters to
enthusiastically attired gays and
friends; and North Beach mixes
strip clubs, time-honoured Beat
poet watering-holes, and upscale
meat markets to dizzying effect.

To begin

Every good evening should start
with a preliminary fortifying drink.
For those seeking the fancier (and
higher-priced) end of the cocktail
spectrum, a tart kumquat
Caipirissima or smooth Melograno
Cosmo at the Americano (p62), with
its spectacular views of Downtown,
should do the trick. Also lovely
for those with deeper pockets:
the elegantly packed (usually
with model-types and the young
investment bankers who worship
them) Redwood Room (p67) at the
Clift Hotel, where the glowing golden
bar and deeply stained interior is the
epitome of California class.

For those of a less extravagant
bent, the appealingly ambient
Alembic (p127) in the Haight

offers a number of whistle-wetting whiskey drinks. Another favourite, if somewhat grittier, spot to catch a starter cocktail and some interesting local colour is the Transfer (p122), on the outer edge of the Castro, which plays host to a plethora of groovable DJs each night as well. (For a real taste of the underground scene, don't miss the Transfer's Frisco Disco nights every Saturday).

On the dancefloor

Then it's off to the dancefloor races. If you're after cutting-edge electro, techno, breaks, and hip-hop, you'd do no better than Mighty (p117) on the edge of the Mission, nationally acknowledged as one of the best places to spot up-and-coming DJ talent and the place to be to catch most major dance music tours (often playing surprise gigs). Mighty, alas, is a bit out of the way of the mainstream party circuit, but definitely worth the trip.

If your party plans include more than one stop you may want to hit up other four-on-the-floor hotspots Mezzanine (p83), which focuses on live shows and big names on the turntables; the brand spankin' new Temple (p85), hosting world-class superstar DJs in an immaculately white megaclub atmosphere, or the newly remodelled and lounge-a-licious 1015 Folsom (p83), a club that's been the centre of local DJ culture since the beginning of rave, and showcases quite a few trance blowouts. All three of these clubs stay open until 4am or later and are located relatively close together, the better to immerse you in a full nightlife experience.

Hip-hop takes centre stage at Milk (p132) in the Haight, a dive-y little club with an awesome sound system and very downtown-stylish patrons. The club functions as a proving ground for young local MCs and budding disc-droppers. Hip hop is also on the schedule at the 222 Club (p69), one of San Francisco's funkiest, along with house, techno and electro nights. Great for hip hop (and indie rock and punk) is the Independent (p135) in the up-and-coming Western Addition neighbourhood, a concert venue with lines around the block nightly.

Jazzy and uplifting house music has its shrines here as well, especially Pink (p117), well-appointed in the eponymous hue, which pumps bass-heavy tunes at the weekends for a crowd of urban sophisticates who aren't afraid to sweat through their designer wear. Ruby Skye (p157) in the Theater District, a huge player on the house scene, unfortunately mixes delectable guest-DJ lineups with a high-roller crowd more into VIP status and Cuban cigars than actual dancing (dress code is strictly enforced), but if you can brave the expensively perfumed crowd

Ruby Skye

a core of dedicated househeads usually greets you on the floor. And no rundown of the club scene would be complete without a hats-off to the grand-daddy of fabulous house venues, the End Up (p83) in SoMa, now more than 35 years old, still open all night long on weekends for wild partiers, and immortalised in such founding documents of San Franciscan bacchanalia as the *Tales of the City* series. If you hit one club while you're in town, this should be it, just to feel a part of history.

For more on San Francisco's legendary gay clubs and bars, see p44-46.

Different strokes

The city's constant influx of newcomers lends itself to plenty of alternative music and dance flavours. Out in Potrero Hill, Café Conomo (650 Indiana Street, www.cafecocomo.com) offers salsa dancing with jaw-dropping live bands, as well as lessons and DJs, while over in the East Bay, the Ashkenaz Music & Dance Community Center (p164) in Berkeley devotes itself to the cause of music and dance from around the world – from Balkan to Berber. If the tabla-driven tunes of South Asia are more your style, head to one of NonStop Bhangra's events (www.nonstopbhangra.com), or a party hosted by the more electronic-oriented crew Surya Dub (www.suryadub.com).

Less international, but still internationally renowned, DNA Lounge (p83) is a cavernous venue where San Francisco's highly influential mashup scene started, and has become a sort of in-city Burning Man, with burlesque acts, punkrock sideshows, circus-themed goth events, and wacky costumery of all kinds highlighted on its everchanging schedule.

SHORTLIST

Best newcomers
- 222 Club (p66)
- Mighty (p117)
- Temple (p32)

Best legendary San Francisco
- Stud (p83)
- Endup (p83)

Best drag shows
- Asia SF (p83)
- Cookie Dough Monster Show at Harvey's (p84)
- Hot Boxxx at Aunt Charlie's Lounge (p84)
- Trannyshack at the Stud (p84)

Best for big-name DJs
- 1015 Folsom Street (p83)
- Mezzanine (p83)
- Ruby Skye (57)
- Temple (p85)

Best for bands
- 12 Galaxies (p117)
- Annie's Social Club (p85)
- Hemlock (70)
- Hotel Utah (p85)
- Independent (p135)
- Make-Our Room (p118)

Best for hip hop
- Milk (p132)

Best for world music
- Ashkenaz Music & Dance Community Center (p164)

Best for jazz
- Biscuits & Blues (57)
- Boom Boom Room (p135)
- Elbo Room (p118)
- Jazz at Pearl's (p101)
- Rasselas Jazz (p136)

Best gay
- Club Eight (p46)
- Eagle Tavern (p46)
- Endup (p83)
- Harvey's (p121)
- Stud (p83)
- Transfer (p122)

Castro Theatre

Arts & Leisure

Off the NYC-LA industry axis, yet lively and provocative in the taboo-shattering and sophisticated tradition of Left Coast iconoclasm, the San Francisco arts scene abounds with compelling performances almost every night of the week, with world-class productions on their way to Broadway bumping up against homegrown experimentalists.

Theatre

Known for its forward-thinking commissions and outstanding actors, the Bay Area's theatrical scene has fostered such landmark works as Tony Kushner's *Angels in America* and more recent toasts like Stew and Heidi Rodewald's *Passing Strange* on its intimate stages.

Make no mistake: you can have your cake and eat it, too. Dazzling touring productions of hits straight off the Great White Way – outfitted with stars such as Kathleen Turner and Cherry Jones – are here, thanks to Best of Broadway (www.shnsf.com).

The elegant, jewel-like Geary Theater is home to the venerable American Conservatory Theater (p69), whose conservatory has nurtured such acting powerhouses as Denzel Washington and Annette Bening. The company's staging of contemporary classics by playwrights like David Mamet and Tom Stoppard have only consolidated the sterling reputation of the institution. Equally esteemed for its early championing of such luminaries as Sam Shepard is the Magic Theatre (p156), flung far across town on a windy point at Fort Mason. And just as acclaimed for its risk-taking commissioned works by Denis Johnson, Jessica Hagedorn, and Philip Kan Gotanda is the Mission District's tiny yet feisty Intersection for the Arts (p79) and its resident company Campo Santo. For a range of challenging dramatic and arts programming, glance at the schedule for the blue-box theatre at the Yerba Buena Center for the Arts (p118), which hosts such events as the Afro Solo Festival.

But your best chance to capture that elusive brilliancy, that lightning in a bottle that is true theatrical talent, lies amid the rich, raucous, edgy works and voices at the annual SF Fringe Festival (p36) at EXIT Theatre (p70) in September. And for a free sampling of Bay drama as well as dance and music, check out the Yerba Buena Gardens Festival (May to October), or see about the free SF Shakespeare Festival (p36), which produces one play, *en plein air*, each summer at the Presidio.

Film

San Francisco's true must-see cinemas are the magnificent grand-dame movie palaces, the finest of which is the 1922-built Castro Theatre (p124): sit back and behold the gilt ceiling while enjoying the sounds of the Mighty Wurlitzer organ before a repertory classic.

Movie buffs will also likely want to duck into the city's other repertory houses: the staunchly independent and documentary-championing Roxie and Little Roxie (p119) in the Mission, with an array of special programmes, horror flicks, campy curiosities, and cerebral meta-cinematic fare,

S H O R T L I S T

Best music festivals
- Fillmore Street Jazz Festival (p36)
- North Beach Jazz Festival (p36)
- San Francisco Blues Festival (p36)

Best film festivals
- Jewish Film Festival (p36)
- San Francisco International Film Festival (p35)
- San Francisco International LGBT Film Festival (p36)

Best theatre festivals
- San Francisco Fringe Festival (p36)
- San Francisco Shakespeare Festival (p36)

For classical grandeur
- War Memorial Opera House (p73)
- Louise M Davies Symphony Hall (p73)

For contemporary work
- EXIT Theatre (p70)
- Intersection for the Arts (p118)
- Yuerba Buena Center for the Arts Theater (p85)

SF's most famous show
- Beach Blanket Babylon (p101)

SF's best sport setting
- AT&T Stadium (p87)

Best movie houses
- Castro Theatre (p124)
- Roxie & LIttle Roxie (p119)
- Red Vic (p134)
- Yerba Buena Center for the Arts (p79)

Best dance groups
- San Francisco Ballet (p73)
- Smuin Ballet (p32)
- Alonzo King's Lines (p32)

For cheap tickets
- TIX Bay Area booth (p32)

Yerba Buena Center for the Arts

and the quirky Red Vic (p134) in the Haight-Ashbury, with its worn couches, wooden bowls of popcorn, and second-run films.

For those experimental films you simply won't see elsewhere, there is the madly brilliant, gritty Artists' Television Access (www.atasite.org). The San Francisco Cinematheque (www.sfcinematheque.org) also has screenings of experimental films at various venues, including the Yerba Buena Center for the Arts. Unpredictably vibrant rep programming also shines at the Yerba Buena Center's petite screening room.

Naturally, this city of festivals is also the spot to see a slew of fine, possibly never-to-be-distributed movies in one fell swoop. At 51 and counting as North America's oldest film festival, the San Francisco International Film Festival (p35) gathers more than 200 films, special events, and competitions each year. There are many more specialist festivals, including the San Francisco International LGBT Film Festival (p36), along with the Arab Film Festival, Jewish Film Festival, Festival Cine Latino, and

Berlin and Beyond, showcasing films from around the globe.

To see a crowd-pleasing flick absolutely free of charge, unfurl a blanket on the grass for Dolores Park Movie Night, beneath the stars each summer on the second Thursday of each month.

Classical music

Music lovers will discover some of the most progressive programming in the country, and virtuoso performances can be found at reasonable prices in spaces as different as the massive, modern Louise M Davies Symphony Hall (p73) and the cosy, historic St Patrick's Church overlooking Yerba Buena Gardens. Many larger ensembles sell tickets via subscription packages, and the most popular shows sell out, but tickets are often made available – even concerts deemed sell-outs usually offer a few seats on the evening of the performance.

Of the major companies, San Francisco Opera (p73), which found renown under the visionary helm of former general director Pamela Rosenberg, and San Francisco Symphony (p73), holding steady under the direction of Michael Tilson Thomas, are must-hears. The former's productions – including 2007's commissioned Philip Glass-Christopher Hampton opera, *Appomattox* – continue to entice music lovers, as will a new co-production of Wagner's *Ring*. San Francisco Symphony continues to pick up Grammys for its work, including a recent series of Mahler concerts that has had the classical music world trilling.

Also of note is San Francisco Performances, which brings such stars as Anne-Sophie Mutter and the Billy Childs Ensemble for some 200 concerts in diverse genres each year to various venues. And Yerba Buena Center for the Arts Theater (p85) stages excellent concerts by the internationally recognised SF ensemble, Kronos Quartet, and the San Francisco Contemporary Music Players.

Churches throughout the Bay Area play host to a variety of recitals and chamber concerts, often free of charge: St Patrick's, Grace Cathedral (p88) and St Mary's Cathedral (p136) are just three of many.

Dance

From ballet to classical Indian undulations to contemporary moves, dance in all its forms has found a home in San Francisco. The longest-running professional company of its kind in the states, San Francisco Ballet (p73) presented the first full-length production of *Coppelia*, *Swan Lake* and *Nutcracker* in this country, and continues to unfurl a mixture of traditional and new works in its home at the War Memorial Opera House (p73). Yerba Buena Center for the Arts' company Smuin Ballet (www.smuinballet.org) and Alonzo King's Lines (www.linesballet.org)

carry the art into the 21st century with contemporary pieces, and works by choreographers like Mark Morris and Alvin Ailey can be caught in action through UC Berkeley's Cal Performances. Also scan the calendars of Yerba Buena for visiting companies.

San Francisco also shines in modern dance. Look for pieces by imaginative, sure-footed, and edge-skating choreographers such as Joanna Haigood, David Gordon, Erika Shuch, Margaret Jenkins, Benjamin Levy and Sean Dorsey. ODC (www.odcdance.org) maintains its exquisite footing as an innovative modern dance epicentre, along with the thoughtful Joe Goode Performance Group (www.joegoode.org), based at the Yerba Buena Center.

For a full body experience of local dance, be sure to get a ticket to West Wave Dance Festival in July or the San Francisco Hip Hop DanceFest in November. Free looks at local companies and ethnic dance groups can be had at the Yerba Buena Gardens Festival (May-October).

What's on?

How do you decide what to see, or where to go? There are listings and reviews in the Sunday Datebook section of the *San Francisco Chronicle*, as well as those of the city's free weeklies, the *San Francisco Bay Guardian* and *SF Weekly* (all also available online). Or look to sites like www.sfarts.org and www.laughingsquid.org.

To avoid booking fees, it's best to book through a venue's own box office, or book online at its website. If you're willing to take a chance, the TIX Bay Area booth in Union Square (433 7827, www.tixbayarea.org) sees half-price tickets for many shows on the day of the performance.

Calendar

Bay to Breakers Foot Race p34

The following is the pick of annual events that take place in San Francisco. Further information and exact dates can be found nearer the time in the *Chronicle*'s Sunday 'Datebook' section, accessible online at www.sfgate/com. The *San Francisco Weekly* (www.sf weekly.com) and San *Francisco Bay Guardian* (www.sfbg.com), two weekly freesheets, also have information on events and festivals.

January

31 Dec **New Year's Eve**
Around the city
Crowds gather at Union Square or Ocean Beach to ring in the new year; a cavalcade of bands performs in tents along the Embarcadero.

Mon after 15 Jan **Martin Luther King Jr Birthday Celebration**
Around the city
www.norcalmlk.org
Parade celebrating MLK's birthday.

Jan **Noir City**
Palace of Fine Arts; Balboa Theatre
www.noircity.com
Two weeks of classic film noir, with talks and other special events.

Jan-Feb **Tet Festival**
Around Civic Center & Tenderloin
885 2743/www.vietccsf.org
A multicultural carnival.

February

Early Feb **San Francisco Tribal, Folk & Textile Arts Show**
Fort Mason Center
www.caskeylees.com
Folk and ethnic-art dealers sell work.

Feb **Noise Pop**
Various venues
www.noisepop.com
A week-long series of indie shows takes place during San Francisco's biggest rock festival.

Feb **Chinese New Year**
Market Street, at 2nd Street, & around Chinatown
www.chineseparade.com

Carnaval

Beauty pageants, drumming, martial arts competitions, food stalls, firework displays and a huge procession.

March

Sun before 17 Mar **St Patrick's Day Parade**
From 2nd & Market Streets to Civic Center

Mid Mar **San Francisco International Asian American Film Festival**
Various venues
863 0814/www.festival.asianamerican media.org.

April

Mar/Apr (date varies) **Sisters of Perpetual Indulgence Easter Celebrations**
Mission Dolores Park
www.thesisters.org
At Easter these 'gay male nuns' bestow sainthoods and preside over Easter Bonnet and Hunky Jesus contests.

1 Apr **St Stupid's Day Parade**
Transamerica Pyramid
www.saintstupid.com
A riotous costumed procession.

Apr **Cherry Blossom Festival**
Japan Center
www.nccbf.org

Mid Apr-early May **San Francisco International Film Festival**
Various venues
561 5000/www.sfiff.org
North America's longest-running film festival, and one of its best.

May

Ongoing San Francisco International Film Festival (see Apr)

Weekend before 5 May
Cinco de Mayo
Around the city & Mission Dolores Park
www.sfcincodemayo.com
A weekend of parades, fireworks and music, to celebrate General Zaragoza's defeat of the French army in 1862.

May-Oct **Yerba Buena Gardens Festival**
Yerba Buena Gardens
www.ybgf.org
Free music, theatre, dance and other cultural events.

3rd Sun in May **AIDS Candlelight Memorial March & Vigil**
Castro & Market Streets, Castro
www.aidscandlelightvigil.org

3rd Sun in May **Bay to Breakers Foot Race**
From Howard & Spear Streets, SoMa, to Ocean Beach
359 2800/www.baytobreakers.com

Race from the foot of Howard Street (Bay), a distance of about 7.5 miles to Ocean Beach (breakers).

Memorial Day weekend (last weekend in May) **Carnaval**
Harrison Street, between 16th & 23rd Streets, Mission
www.carnavalsf.com
A parade of skimpily costumed dancers gyrating to fizzing Latin music.

June

Ongoing Yerba Buena Gardens Festival (see May)

Early June **Union Street Festival**
Union Street, Cow Hollow
www.unionstreetfestival.com
A weekend-long street fair.

Early June **Haight Ashbury Street Fair** Haight Street, Haight-Ashbury
www.haightashburystreetfair.org

June **North Beach Festival**
Grant Avenue, Green Street, Stockton Street & Washington Square, North Beach
www.sfnorthbeach.org
San Francisco's oldest street party.

June-Aug **Stern Grove Festival**
Sigmund Stern Grove, 19th Avenue & Sloat Boulevard
www.sterngrove.org

All kinds of music, from rock to opera, are performed on Sundays from June to August in an idyllic amphitheatre. Admission is free.

21 June **Summer Solstice**
Around the city
Join San Francisco's pagans at a sunset drum circle in Justin Herman Plaza or join the Baker Beach bonfires.

Late June **San Francisco International LGBT Film Festival**
Various venues
703 8650/www.frameline.org
A crucial part of the month-long Gay Pride festivities.

Last Sun in June **San Francisco LGBT Pride Celebration Parade**
Market Street, between Embarcadero & 8th Street, Downtown
www.sfpride.org
A San Francisco institution. The parade is the culmination of a weekend of Pride, with a celebration at Civic Center on Saturday.

July

Ongoing Yerba Buena Gardens Festival (see May); Stern Grove Festival (see June)

4 July **Fourth of July Waterfront Festival**
Fisherman's Wharf

San Francisco LGBT Pride Celebration Parade

Live entertainment and food stalls here during the day; a spectacular fireworks display gets under way around 9pm.

Early July **Fillmore Street Jazz Festival**
Fillmore Street, between Jackson & Eddy Streets
www.fillmorejazzfestival.com
Two days of diverse sounds at the west coast's largest free jazz festival.

Mid July **Mission Creek Music & Arts Festival**
Various venues
www.mcmf.org
A four-day music festival concentrating on alternative rock, with a local focus and experimental edge.

Late July **North Beach Jazz Festival**
Various venues, North Beach
www.nbjazzfest.com
A five-day festival, with local musicians.

Late July-early Aug **Jewish Film Festival**
Various venues
621 0556/www.sfjff.org
The world's largest Jewish film festival, held over a two-week period.

Ghirardelli Square Chocolate Festival

August

Ongoing Yerba Buena Gardens Festival (see May); Jewish Film Festival (see July); Stern Grove Festival (see June)

Usually 1st Sun in Aug **San Francisco Marathon**
Around the city
1-800 958 6668/www.runsfm.com

September

Ongoing Yerba Buena Gardens Festival (see May)

Early Sept **Ghirardelli Square Chocolate Festival**
Ghirardelli Square
www.ghirardellisq.com
Proceeds go to a local charity.

Sept **San Francisco Fringe Festival**
Various venues
www.sffringe.org
Diverse and alternative performances over 10 days.

Sept **San Francisco Shakespeare Festival**
Main Post, Presidio
www.sfshakes.org
Three weeks of open-air performances.

Mid Sept-early Oct **MadCat Women's International Film Festival**
Various venues
436 9523/www.madcatfilmfestival.org
Three weeks of women's films.

Late Sept **San Francisco Blues Festival**
Great Meadow, Fort Mason
www.sfblues.com
The US's oldest blues festival.

Last Sun in Sept **Folsom Street Fair**
Folsom Street, SoMa
www.folsomstreetfair.org
The Queen Mother of all leather street fairs. Needless to say, this might not be suitable for the whole family.

October

Ongoing MadCat Women's International Film Festival (see Sept)

Gearing up

Critical Mass

You'd think that with all the seemingly insurmountable hills that dot San Francisco, leisurely bike rides would be out of the question. In keeping with its spirit of quaint contrarianism, however, residents have taken to bikes like fishes to water, streaming across the Golden Gate Bridge at weekends and to bars and clubs at night. (This may explain the muscular thighs and firm buttocks on display among much of the populace.) In fact, bike love has even spawned a particular kind of fashion here, with enthusiasts donning colorful balaclavas and ill-fitting second-hand clothes as they mount their 'fixies' – an exceedingly popular, home-engineered style of bicycle that rides in only one gear and has no brakes. Sounds dangerous? That's the kick.

Several major events bring bikers of all stripes together, most thrillingly **Critical Mass** (www.critical-mass.org), a massive, somewhat chaotic ride and party that takes over the streets every last Friday evening of the month. Similar Critical Mass rides now happen in cities throughout the world, but the event started here and it's a sight to behold.

Other bike events of note include **Healthy Sundays**, during which Golden Gate Park is mostly closed to car traffic; the **AIDS/LifeCycle** (www.aidslife cycle.org) in June, a gruelling yet charitable seven-day ride from San Francisco to Los Angeles that launches with several large celebrations, and the loony and astounding **Bike Rodeo**, put on several times a year by Cyclecide (www.cyclecide.com).

For more bike events and news, check out the San Francisco Bicycle Coalition's Web site (www.sfbike.org).

San Francisco Shakespeare Festival p36

Early Oct Castro Street Fair
Market & Castro Streets, Castro
www.castrostreetfair.org

Oct ArtSpan Open Studios
Various venues
861 9838/www.artspan.org
More than 900 artists' studios open up
to the public.

Oct Fleet Week
Fisherman's Wharf & Piers 30-32,
Embarcadero
www.military.com/fleetweek
The US Navy's Blue Angels tear up the
skies on Columbus Day weekend.

Oct Arab Film Festival
Various venues
564 1100/www.aff.org
An inclusive mix of features, documentaries and shorts.

**Oct-end Nov San Francisco
Jazz Festival**
Various venues
www.sfjazz.org
Big names in a terrific series of shows.

31 Oct Halloween San Francisco
Market Street & Castro Street,
Castro

November

Ongoing San Francisco Jazz
Festival (see Oct)

2 Nov Día de los Muertos
24th & Bryant Streets, Mission
www.dayofthedeadsf.org
Marchers celebrate the Mexican Day of
the Dead.

**Early Nov Film Arts Festival of
Independent Cinema**
Various venues
*552 8760/www.filmarts.org Venues
various theatres. Date .*
The essential festival for a real snapshot
of the work of NorCal independents.

Nov Miss Trannyshack Pageant
The Gift Center, 888 Brannan
Street, at 8th Street, SoMA
www.trannyshack.com
An array of gender-bending beauties
face off in a showdown for the coveted
Miss Trannyshack tiara.

Nov Festival ¡Cine Latino!
Various venues
www.latinofilmfestival.org
The best recent works from Central
and South America.

**Late Nov Holiday Lighting
Festivities**
Union Square, Downtown;
Ghirardelli Square, Fisherman's
Wharf
http://gosanfrancisco.about.com
The lights go on all over town as the
holidays approach, including at the
above locations.

Itineraries

Bay Bridge p86

The 49-Mile Scenic Drive

Dreamed up as a promotion for the 1939 Golden Gate International Exposition, the 49-Mile Scenic Drive was a novel way to show off the city and its amazing feats of modern engineering and design. Lots of people who drove the circuitous route when it debuted in 1938 had never seen what we now think of as 'the sights' of San Francisco – because many of them had just been built. The Golden Gate Bridge was spanking new, having opened to vehicular traffic on 28 May 1937, just six months after the Bay Bridge.

The drive was, and is, a great way to see the city. Beginning and ending in Civic Center, its labyrinthine, counterclockwise route goes through virtually every neighbourhood. There are some notable omissions, though, for 21st-century visitors: the gay Castro neighbourhood; the '60s hippie heartland of the Haight-Ashbury intersection, and the 24th Street hub in the Mission.

Simply driving the route without stopping takes around four hours, but because you'll probably want to stop along the way to check out the views, visit a museum or grab some lunch, the drive can easily occupy an entire day.

The drive today

Don't rely too much on following the famous seagull signs that mark the route; many of them have been appropriated by members of the public. Best to have a reliable map. You'll find useful maps of the route at these addresses: www.onlyinsan francisco.com/maps/49miledrive. asp; and http://tinyurl.com/3792oq.

The long & winding road

The drive officially begins at
Larkin and McAllister Streets,
just across from City Hall. Judging
from the first few blocks, you may
wonder just how scenic this drive
actually is, as you pass the strip
clubs and dive bars of Little Saigon.
It gets better. Keep an eye out for
the first of approximately 72
turns on the drive: left on Geary
Boulevard towards Japantown.

Driving along Geary Street,
you will first pass the impressive,
sculptural form of the **Cathedral
of St Mary of the Assumption**
(p136), then head down the hill
into Japantown, home to the **Japan
Center** (p136) – a collection of
Japanese businesses – and **Peace
Plaza**. After a 14-block shot
down Post Street, the next major
landmark is hard to miss: **Union
Square** (p50).

Next stop is **Chinatown Gate**
(p92), the southern entrance to
San Francisco's Chinatown. A gift
from Taiwan in 1970, the green-
tiled portal is made to a traditional

design, complete with a quotation
from Confucius that urges passers-
by to work for the common good.

The steep climb up California
Street lands you on top of **Nob
Hill**, once the home of the city's
wealthy 'nobs' and now the perch
for the luxurious Fairmont, Mark
Hopkins and Huntington Hotels.
The beautiful, gothic **Grace
Cathedral** (p89) is also here.

Turning right on Washington
Street, you'll soon see the narrow-
gauge tracks of the cable car
system and note that they turn
into the garage of the **Cable Car
Museum** (p88) at the corner of
Mason Street, where you can view
the cable-winding machinery that
actually powers the cars.

Snaking back through Chinatown,
you'll pass **Portsmouth Square**
at the corner of Kearny and Clay
Streets. It was here that Captain
John B Montgomery first hoisted
the US flag after capturing the city
from Mexico on 9 July 1846. It was
here, too, that it was announced
that gold had been discovered,
prompting Gold Rush hysteria.

The copper sheathed **Columbus
Tower** at the corner of Columbus
Avenue and Kearny Street is owned
by Francis Ford Coppola and
houses his Zoetrope Studios, and
his restaurant, Café Zoetrope.

A bit further up Columbus
Avenue stands the still-beating
heart of the Beat movement, **City
Lights Bookstore** (p100), run –
as it has always been – by 88-year-
old poet Lawrence Ferlinghetti.
Step across Jack Kerouac Alley to
Vesuvio (p100), which welcomes
mad poets and tourists in equal
measure, much as it did when
Kerouac and crew drank here
in the 1950s.

The priapic **Coit Tower**
(p96) offers panoramic views
of the Marina and Angel Island
– but the vistas aren't the tower's

only attraction. Wonderful murals grace its circular vestibule, a series of socialist-realist images so subversive that the tower's opening was delayed so they could be 'corrected'. But look carefully and you can still find volumes of Marx among the books on mural's painted shelves.

Then it's on to **Fisherman's Wharf**. One of the most popular tourist draws in the city, it's the bane of locals, who rarely stray into its warren of souvenir shops and attractions.

Past **Fort Mason** (p153), Marina Green Drive offers excellent views of the Golden Gate Bridge and Alcatraz along with the curious **Wave Organ** just across the inlet. Part artwork, part musical instrument, the mostly underwater structure is made up of pipes and benches from San Francisco's dismantled cemeteries; the tubes make eerie music with the ebb and flow of the Bay.

Further along, the dome of the **Palace of Fine Arts** (p154) looms in the distance. The stunning neo-classical structure is supported by a curved colonnade and flanked by a pond alive with ducks, swans and waterlilies: this picturesque spot is a popular location for wedding photos and picnics.

Entering the large green space of the **Presidio**, the **Letterman Digital Arts Center** on your right is home to *Star Wars* creator George Lucas's Industrial Light and Magic studios, responsible for digital post-production and special effects. It's also home to the Yoda Fountain, featuring the diminutive Jedi Master, now one of the Presidio's top attractions.

In the heart of the Presidio, the **San Francisco National Cemetery** (p157) is the only cemetery within San Francisco city limits and the last resting place of more than 450 'Buffalo Soldiers,' African-American servicemen from the segregation era, among others. For a quick detour, follow the signs to **Fort Point** (p158) about a mile further one, down a steep ramp that takes you to a gem featured in Alfred Hitchock's *Vertigo*. The fort, completed in 1861, was meant to repel sea invasion, and the Golden Gate Bridge is directly above it. Back up on the route you can see the top of the iconic **Golden Gate Bridge** (p158) at the viewing area, where parking is available for those who'd like to walk the bridge.

Presidio p156

Further up the coast the beautiful **California Palace of the Legion of Honor** (p159), at Lincoln Park, is sister to the striking, modern de Young Museum in Golden Gate Park.

As the drive begins to wind down towards the Pacific, the freshly remodelled **Cliff House** (p159) and the remains of the **Sutro Baths**, once a public waterpark filled by the sea, are worth a look before you hit the virtual dragstrip that is the Great Highway, the long stretch of road that runs alongside **Ocean Beach**.

The drive then heads all the way out to the entrance of **Fort Funston**, a famed launch point for hangliders, then around the placid **Lake Merced,** its southern tip at the very outer reaches of the city. A long straight stretch up Sunset Boulevard brings you to **Golden Gate Park**. Driving through the park, the road to the **Japanese Tea Garden** (p141) also marks the entrance to the concourse that is home to the **de Young Museum** (p142) and the **California Academy of Sciences** (p145).

Leaving Golden Gate Park on Stanyan Street, you'll pass (though not travel down) **Haight Street**, the epicentre of '60s Flower Power.

The next landmark is the massive antenna of **Sutro Tower** at the top of Twin Peaks, where you'll find spectacular views of the Bay Area on a clear day.

As you head back downhill on the Mission District's Dolores Street you'll pass **Mission Dolores** (p107), the 18th-century church that is the birthplace of modern-day San Francisco, founded by a tiny band of Spanish missionaries and soldiers.

After the long jaunt down the palm-lined Dolores Street, the official route takes you left at Cesar Chavez Street, a main thoroughfare

with zero personality other than its name, on to major highway 280 to the King Street exit. A much more interesting route (which will lead you to King Street, as well) is to turn left at 24th Street for a true taste of the Mexican, South and Central American melting pot of the **Mission District**. Packed with shops, bakeries and excellent mom-and-pop restaurants, **24th Street** is great place to grab a Mission burrito and admire the district's famous murals.

Back on the route, drive by the Willie Mays statue at **AT&T Park** (p87), the home of the San Francisco Giants baseball team. Next, wheel along the **Embarcadero**, the road that hugs the shores of San Francisco Bay. Passing under the mighty **Bay Bridge**, past the culinary wonders of the **Ferry Building** (p60), keep a close eye out for the next turn coming up on your left, Washington Street, which shoots you into the only place in San Francisco you're likely to see someone wearing a tie: the **Financial District**. Crossing Market Street, you're in the home stretch as you turn on to Howard Street and pass near the **San Francisco Museum of Modern Art** (p75), **Yerba Buena Center for the Arts** (p86), the sprawling convention complex of the Moscone Center and the vast entertainment complex of the Metreon.

Hopping back across Market Street, you emerge back in front of **City Hall** and the fascinating **Asian Art Museum of San Francisco** (p70). You've now completed a circuit that few San Franciscans can claim to have driven all in one go. For a worthy souvenir of your efforts, head into the City Hall gift shop, where you can buy a copy of that by now very familiar sign with the seagull motif.

ITINERARIES

The Castro

One Gay Day

Whatever your orientation, you're in the gay mecca now – so you may as well do as the locals do. Everything you need to know about queer events and resources can be found at San Francisco's fabulous centrally located **GLBT Community Centre** (1800 Market Street, at Octavia Boulevard, 865 5555, www.sfcenter.org). Meanwhile, follow our suggestions below for a great gay day out.

Brunch

No one is anyone without a good brunch. On sunny early afternoons any day of the week, a sizeable crowd can be found on the huge patio at **Café Flore** (2298 Market Street, 621 8579, www.cafe flore.com) in the Castro, enjoying gourmet egg dishes, large cocktails, and spirited conversation. Also popular on weekdays is **Caffe Luna Piena** (558 Castro Street, 621 2566), where the shaded back

garden and Italian-influenced menu is perfect for those days when dark sunglasses and heartier fare is required. At weekends, **Lime** (2247 Market Street, between Noe and Sanchez Streets, 621 5256, www.lime-sf.com), a smart space with white and purple futuristic design elements, attracts a well-dressed retinue of young brunchers in search of old-school soul tunes and high-end mixed drinks – the Bloody Marys here will knock your socks off.

Shop

After suitable fortification, it's time to hit the shops. If you want to avoid the megastore crunch of Union Square, the boutique-heavy, gay-friendly enclave of Hayes Valley offers everything from one-of-a-kind fashions to artisanal truffles. **RAG – Resident's Apparel Gallery** (541 Octavia Street, between Grove & Ivy

ITINERARIES

Café Flore

Streets) and **Seventh Heart**
(1592 Market Street, at Page
Street) feature the best in cutting-
edge San Francisco clothing.
Alabaster (p139) is renowned
for inventive home decor creations.
And **Bibliohead** (334 Gough
Street, at Hayes Street), one of the
funkiest little bookstores in the
city, is proudly dyke-owned and
gets delightfully cruisy for both
men and women in the evenings.

If you wish to browse more
than the merchandise, may we
recommend heading over to the
Castro to **Cliff's Variety** (479
Castro Street, at 18th Street)? A
cavernous hardware store and San
Francisco treasure, this is where
you're sure to find the brawniest of
all genders checking out the latest
in home improvement gadgets (and
each other). Better yet, grab a cup
of java at the ever-hopping **Peet's
Coffee & Tea** over on Market
Street (no.2257, between Noe &
Sanchez Streets) and watch from
the window as the parade of well-
toned eligibles prances by. Now
that's what we call shopping!

Visit

Besides standing awestruck beneath
the giant rainbow flag flapping free
over the Castro, there are three more
must-dos for queer folks visiting
San Francisco for the first time.
The **GLBT Historical Society**
(box p81) operates a museum
and archive containing the largest
collection of gay-related ephemera
in the world. Among its fascinating
and thought-provoking artifacts are
the sewing machine that stitched
the first rainbow flag and the bullet-
riddled suit jacket worn by gay
rights pioneer Harvey Milk on the
night he was assassinated. Another
essential stop is the **National
AIDS Memorial Grove**
(www.aidsmemorial.org) in Golden
Gate Park, a beautiful cedar-shaded
area commemorating the many
people lost to the epidemic.

Relax

It usually rains in San Francisco
from December to March, and
summers are notoriously frigid.
But there are occasional bright

spots, and the months of August, September and October can feel downright Californian. It's at these times that gay men and women shed their layers and flock to the beach. **Castro Beach**, also known as Dolores Beach, isn't a beach at all – it's a grassy exposed shelf high atop Dolores Park, miles away from any substantial body of water but packed with barely clothed sunbathers when the weather is good. If you're looking to shed your entire outfit, and maybe join in a game of naked volleyball, the insanely popular, clothing-optional and cruisy **Baker Beach** on the city's west side should do nicely.

Dine

Now you're sunned, refreshed, and freshly dressed. And hungry. Dive into hearty portions of traditional, spicy Mexican food at the gay-owned **Regalito** in the Mission (3481 18th Street, at Valencia Street, 503 0650, www.regalitosf.com) or dine on the best of San Francisco's organic dishes at the Castro's swanky **Frisée** (p121). **Barracuda** (2251 Market Street, between Noe & Sanchez Streets, 558 8567, www.barracudasushi.com), also in the Castro, may be the gayest restaurant of the moment, serving inventive Japanese-influenced creations and inventive cocktails beneath diva-broadcasting video screens.

Go out

On to cocktails and dancing. At first glance, the gay club scene in San Francisco can feel rather fragmented. The young and mainstream flood Castro bars like the **Bar on Castro** (p120) and **Badlands** (p120), dancing to chart-topping pop and hip-hop while sniffing at each other's designer colognes, upscale labels, and spiky hairstyles. Bears and their admirers flock to **Lone Star Saloon** (Harrison Street, between 9th & 10th Streets), where onscreen sports and mugs of beer are the order of the day. Sexy leather types hang out at **Powerhouse** (p80), cruising to hard techno and video porn. Shirtless circuit revellers adore the many, many all-night affairs of **Gus Presents** (www.guspresents.com). Hip lesbians adore DJ Nuxx and her **Cockblock** parties (www.cockblocksf.com), while alternaqueers into underground dance music follow the boys of Honey Soundsystem (www.honeysoundsystem.com) to various, usually quite legal, party destinations.

But there are some venues that cater to all types, with something nearly every night of the week for different tastes. **Club Eight** (1151 Folsom Street, between 7th & 8th Streets, 431 1151, www.eightsf.com) in SoMa hosts wild Asian hi-nrg, queer punk, gay Middle Eastern, and HIV-positive-centred events. The straight-friendly **Transfer** (p122), near the Castro, features fashion shows, heavy metal and hip-hop shows, breakdance tournaments, and drag spectaculars, as does the decades-old **Stud** (p83) in SoMa.

The two nightlife must-sees, however, for those seeking a taste of the great diversity of the San Francisco gay scene are the **Eagle Tavern** in SoMa (398 12th Street, at Harrison Street), a grungy gay leather-biker bar that pumps an ear-opening array of rock tunes (especially during the alarmingly packed Sunday afternoon beer busts) and the legendary **EndUp** (p83), a 35-year-old institution whose dancefloors are crowded from Friday evening to Monday morning with ecstatic house and techno groovers. What you do after hitting those is up to you and your new acquaintants.

Cable car

Get Around Town

San Francisco is like a life-size Disneyland – all those precipitously steep hills, neighbourhoods with names like Little Italy and Chinatown that seem straight out of a theme-park brochure, and modes of public transport that could double as thrill rides. The best part is that for a few dollars, you can tour the city from one end to the other – and even venture across the Bay – without ever having to sit in traffic behind the wheel of a car.

Start out at Powell and Market streets at the terminus for the Powell-Hyde or Powell-Mason **cable car** lines. Invented in 1873 by Scotsman Andrew Hallidie, the little cars that 'climb halfway to the stars' were an ingenious solution to scaling San Francisco's formidable slopes. They work via a motorless underground cable-grip system – essentially the cars are pulled up the hills by a cable that is continuously wound and unwound around enormous wheels. Catch one going up Nob Hill, and, for extra thrills, hang off the running boards, Doris Day-style, until you reach Washington and Mason streets. Here, hop down for a pitstop at the Cable Car Museum (p88), where you can see Hallidie's original 1873 trolley, as well as the powerful turbines and gears that keep the cars humming along at a steady 9.5mph. Then get back on and hang tight for the rollercoaster descent into Fisherman's Wharf.

From there, flag down one of the city's intrepid **bicycle rickshaw** drivers for a slow ramble down

Jefferson Street, soaking up the steam of the crab pots and carnival atmosphere of the Wharf. Or, if that's too slow for you, rent a **GoCar** (Hyde and Beach Streets, www.gocartours.com), a bright-yellow mini-electric car with a built-in talking GPS tour guide. In addition to helping you navigate the city's notorious one-way streets, the car offers a narrated tour of sights around San Francisco.

Afterwards, walk down a couple of blocks to Pier 39, where you can catch a **Blue & Gold ferry** to Sausalito and Tiburon, two charming harbour villages just beyond the Golden Gate Bridge (either route takes you past Alcatraz Island and Angel Island, and gives you a bird's eye view of the San Francisco skyline). Sit on the deck at Sam's Anchor Café (27 Main Street, Tiburon, www.samscafe.com) or at Horizons in Sausalito (558 Bridgeway, www.horizonssausalito.com) and

sip a cool cocktail as you watch sailboats race across the Bay. At Sausalito harbour, the elaborately tricked-out houseboats docked at the end of Gate 5 and Gate 6 roads provide a snapshot of how this picturesque seaside community has changed over the years. Once the arty crashpads of hippies, the houseboats were considered a blight by rich hill dwellers back in the '60s. Nowadays, those same homeowners would have to pay up to a million dollars for the privilege of living on the water.

Take the return ferry back to Fisherman's Wharf and walk over to Jefferson or Beach Street to catch a **vintage streetcar** to downtown. The historic F-line is a fleet of lovingly restored streetcars that hail from all around the world – Hamburg to Blackpool, Milan to Philly. Each car still bears the markings and design details of its native city and for $1.50, you can ride one up to the top of Market Street, getting a city tour and a rolling lesson in public-transport history in the process.

If you happen to be in town on the last Friday of the month, you may want to take the streetcar back to Justin Herman Plaza on the Embarcadero, where you can join the hundreds of cyclists known as **Critical Mass** (box p35) on their monthly joy ride. The hootin' hollerin' jaunt starts out at the plaza at 5.30pm and tours around town with no specific route or destination in mind. The idea is to both celebrate and encourage cycling, as well as to assert cyclists' rights on the road.

But if you don't have the stamina to keep up with the crowd, no worries – you can load your bike on the front of any **Muni bus** (racks hold two bikes at a time) and cruise back to your hotel in time for happy hour.

San Francisco
by Area

Union Square

Downtown

SAN FRANCISCO BY AREA

San Francisco's Downtown area may be the hub that saves the city from being seen simply as a series of villages. Its cultural attractions and stellar shopping give the city a cosmopolitanism that exceeds its modest size. Luckily, Downtown's compactness means it's a breeze to navigate on foot. And if you want to climb its daunting hills, there are always the famous cable cars.

Union Square & around

Union Square's name dates back to its use in 1861 as a pro-Union rallying point on the eve of the Civil War. In 1941, the square was rebuilt according to a somewhat severe design by Timothy Pflueger,

and in 1997 a competition was held to create a new Union Square. After much wrangling, April Phillips and Michael Fotheringham's winning design was unveiled in 2002. Conceived to encourage use by shoppers and lunchtime throngs, the new layout altered the character of the square and its surroundings overnight, with a more open design and plenty of benches.

The stretch of Powell Street that links Union Square to Market Street is among the city's busiest thoroughfares. Watching the cable cars clatter past, only to realise that the cables are still humming under your feet, is a quintessential San Francisco experience. At the foot of Powell, where it joins Market Street, huge queues of tourists hang around and wait to catch a cable car at

**50 Time Out** Shortlist | San Francisco

the roundabout where conductors manually rotate the cars on a giant turntable for the return journey back up the hill.

Sights & museums

San Francisco Museum of Craft & Design

550 Sutter Street, between Powell & Mason Streets (773 0303/www.sf mcd.org). Bus 2, 3, 4, 76/cable car Powell-Mason & Powell-Hyde. **Open** 10am-5pm Tue, Wed, Fri, Sat; 10am-7pm Thur; noon-5pm Sun. **Admission** Suggested donation $3; $2 discounts. **Map** p51 B1 ❶
This modest, three-room museum highlights how contemporary craft and design can enrich everyday life. Exhibitions have included contemporary studio furniture from Tanzania and the United States, and the confluence of art and wine label design.

Eating & drinking

Café Claude

7 Claude Lane, off Sutter Street, between Kearny Street & Grant Avenue (392 3505/www.cafeclaude.com). BART & Metro to Montgomery/bus 2, 3, 4, 9X, 30, 38, 45, 76 & Market Street routes/cable car Powell-Hyde or Powell-Mason. **Open** 11.30am-4.30pm, 5.30-10.30pm Mon-Sat; 5.30-10.30pm Sun. **$$**. **French**. **Map** p51 C1 ❷
Le Barbizon café was bought in Paris and shipped over to San Francisco one piece at a time. The result is set in an alleyway and resplendent with French style and attitude – it's as close to a true French café as can be found in America. Typical dishes include salad niçoise and steak tartare.

Café de la Presse

352 Grant Avenue, at Bush Street (398 2680/www.cafedelapresse.com). BART & Metro to Montgomery/bus 2, 3, 4, 9X,

© Copyright Time Out Group 2008

Union Square, Tenderloin & Civic Center

*30, 38, 45, 76 & Market Street routes/
cable car Powell-Hyde or Powell-Mason.*
Open 7.30-10am, 11.30am-2.30pm, 5.30-
9.30pm Mon-Thur; 7.30-10am, 11.30am-
2.30pm, 5.30-10pm Fri; 8am-4pm,
5.30-10pm Sat; 8am-4pm, 5.30-9.30pm
Sun. **$$$. French.** Map p51 C1 ❸
Since its transformation into a fully
fledged bistro, this bustling spot has
become one of the most reliable in the
downtown area. The classic French-
inspired fare and café-style choices are
always winners. It also stocks a bevy
of foreign newspapers and magazines
for the news hungry.

Colibrí Mexican Bistro

*438 Geary Street, between Taylor &
Mason Streets (440 2737/www.colibri
mexicanbistro.com). BART & Metro
to Powell/bus 2, 3, 4, 9X, 30, 38, 45,
76 & Market Street routes/cable car
Powell-Hyde or Powell-Mason.* **Open**
11.30am-10pm Mon-Thur; 11.30am-
11pm Fri; 10am-11pm Sat; 10am-10pm
Sun. **$$. Mexican.** Map p51 B1 ❹
In the heart of Theatre District, this
unpretentious tucked-away restaurant
serves delicious and atypical Mexican
fare. Dishes are presented tapas-style,
with unfamiliar regional flavours:
tamarind-sautéed shrimp served with
corn cakes, for example, and a fire-
roasted *chile relleno*.

Fifth Floor

*Hotel Palomar, 12 4th Street, at
Market Street (348 1555/www.fifth
floorrestaurant.com). BART & Metro
to Powell/bus 9X, 27, 30, 45 & Market
Street routes/cable car Powell-Hyde or
Powell-Mason.* **Open** 5.30-10pm Mon-
Thur; 5.30-11pm Fri, Sat. **$$$$.**
French. Map p51 C2 ❺
One of the best places in the city to find
a five-star French experience. The dining room is reliably sophisticated and
stylish, and the daily changing menu is
among the city's best. Preparations are
unfussy, and service is top-notch. The
wine list is among the best in the region.

Masa's

*648 Bush Street, between Stockton &
Powell Streets (989 7154www.masas
restaurant.com). Bus 2, 3, 4, 9X, 30,*
*38, 45, 76/cable car Powell-Hyde or
Powell-Mason.* **Open** 5.30-9.30pm Tue-
Sat. **$$$$. French.** Map p51 C1 ❻
Masa's was the first notable restaurant
to combine SF haute cuisine with a
French dining aesthetic. The kitchen
has seen many talented chefs, but each
has maintained the high level of care
taken by his predecessor, ensuring the
Masa's experience remains one worth
having (and paying for).

Michael Mina

*Westin-St Francis Hotel, 335 Powell
Street, at Geary Street (397 9222/
www.michaelmina.net). BART & Metro
to Powell/bus 2, 3, 4, 9X, 30, 38, 45,
76 & Market Street routes/cable car
Powell-Hyde or Powell-Mason.* **Open**
5.30-10pm Mon-Sat; 5.30-9.30pm Sun.
$$$$. International. Map p51 C1 ❼
This spare-no-expense room introduced Union Square to famed chef
Mina, who micromanaged much of
the restaurant much like he does his
artistic food. Meals are offered in a
three-course menu, each with three
preparations of a theme, or as a seven-
course tasting menu.

Scala's Bistro

*Sir Francis Drake Hotel, 432 Powell
Street, between Post & Sutter Streets
(395 8555/www.scalasbistro. com).
BART & Metro to Powell/bus 2, 3, 4,
9X, 30, 38, 45, 76 & Market Street
routes/cable car Powell-Hyde or Powell-
Mason.* **Open** 8am-midnight daily.
$$$. Italian. Map p51 C1 ❽
Recently refurbished to fine effect, this
bustling bistro serves robust, reason-
ably priced Cal-Mediterranean food.
Reliable choices range from the daily
risotto to fresh-made pasta. Meal-size
salads are a hit during lunch. The wine
list is well chosen from nearby regions,
with occasional surprises from beyond
the borders.

Tunnel Top

*601 Bush Street, at Stockton Street
(986 8900/www.tunneltop.com).
Bus 2, 3, 4, 30, 45, 76/cable car
Powell-Hyde or Powell-Mason.* **Open**
5pm-2am Mon-Sat. No credit cards.
Bar. Map p51 C1 ❾

The two-storey Tunnel Top is perched above the Stockton Tunnel, and looks a little shabby from the outside. Inside, however, the decor is urban-decay cool; films are projected against rust-coloured walls, while a DJ soundtracks the conversation. Just outside is the spot where Sam Spade surveys the scene of his partner's murder at the beginning of *The Maltese Falcon*.

Shopping

Anthropologie

880 Market Street, between Powell & Stockton Streets (434 2210/ www.anthropologie.com). BART & Metro to Powell/bus 2, 3, 4, 14, 15,30, 45 & Market Street routes/cable car Powell-Hyde or Powell-Mason. **Open** 10am-8pm Mon-Sat; 11am-7pm Sun. **Map** p51 C2 ⑩

Indulge your desire for beaded cardigans, patterned and floral A-line skirts and romantic, swingy jackets, plus home furnishings, decadent scented candles, cute pyjamas and coquettish lingerie. The sale racks are at the back.

NEW Barneys New York

77 O'Farrell Street, at Stockton Street, Union Square & Around (268 3500/ www.barneys.com). BART & Metro to Powell/bus 2, 3, 4, 15, 30, 38, 45, 76 & Market Street routes/cable car Powell-Hyde or Powell-Mason. **Open** 10am-7pm Mon-Wed, Fri, Sat; 10am-8pm Thur; 11am-6pm Sun. **Map** p51 C1 ⑪

Barneys has proved a hit among San Francisco followers of fashion with its spare modernist decor and laid-back style of selling.

Bloomingdale's

Westfield San Francisco Centre, 845 Market Street, between 4th & 5th Streets (856 5300/www.bloomingdales. com). BART & Metro to Powell/bus 27, 30, 45 & Market Street routes/cable car Powell-Hyde or Powell-Mason. **Open** 9am-9pm Mon-Sat; 10am-7pm Sun. **Map** p51 C2 ⑫

Filling the retail gap between Macy's and Neiman Marcus, the Little Brown Bag's temple to luxe wares has finally touched down in San Francisco.

Coach

190 Post Street, at Grant Avenue (392 1772/www.coach.com). BART & Metro to Powell/bus 2, 3, 4, 15, 30, 38, 45, 76 & Market Street routes/ cable car Powell-Hyde or Powell-Mason. **Open** 10am-8pm Mon-Sat; 11am-6pm Sun. **Map** p51 C1 ⑬

High-quality leather or suede totes, satchels and accessories are Coach's stock in trade. The returns policy is incredible: staff will hand you a new bag if but a single stitch comes out.

De Vera

29 Maiden Lane, between Grant Avenue & Kearny Street (788 0828/ www. deveraobjects.com). BART & Metro to Powell/bus 2, 3, 4, 15, 30, 38, 45, 76 & Market Street routes/cable car Powell-Hyde or Powell-Mason. **Open** 10am-6pm Tue-Sat. **Map** 51 C1 ⑭

Federico de Vera's covetable jewellery – yellow tourmaline, carnelian, rose-cut diamond – ranges from intricate beadwork to clean-lined intaglios. Don't miss the stunning collection of objets.

Diana Slavin

3 Claude Lane, between Sutter & Bush Streets (677 9939/www.diana slavin.com). BART & Metro to Montgomery/bus 2, 3, 4, 15, 30, 38, 45, 76/cable car Powell-Hyde or Powell-Mason. **Open** 11am-6pm Tue-Fri; noon-5pm Sat. **Map** p51 C1 ⑮

Slavin displays her trademark fashions here: menswear-inspired clothing in rich, subtle colours and lush fabrics. Vintage Vuarnet shades and Vera Wang shoes complete the look.

Diesel

101 Post Street, at Kearny Street (982 7077/www.diesel.com). BART & Metro to Montgomery/bus 2, 3, 4, 15, 30, 38, 45, 76/cable car Powell-Hyde or Powell-Mason. **Open** 10am-9pm Mon-Fri; 10am-7pm Sat; noon-6pm Sun. **Map** p51 C1 ⑯

Not just a zillion styles of jeans, retro sneakers and edgy separates, spread over three floors, but also the StyleLab line for those extra-experimental types who covet jeans made out of astronaut suits.

Forever 21

7 Powell Street, at Market Street (984 0380/www.forever21.com). BART & Metro to Powell/bus 2, 3, 4, 15, 30, 38, 45, 76 & Market Street routes/cable car Powell-Hyde or Powell-Mason. **Open** 9.30am-9pm Mon-Sat; 10am-7pm Sun. **Map** p51 C2 ⑰

Juniors will go knock-off crazy for this rock-bottom low-priced mecca of flirty dresses, skimpy club-kid gear and skinny jeans. Larger sizes will have to content themselves with the glitzy jewellery, fun shoes, hip hats and adorable bags.

Fresh

301 Sutter Street, at Grant Avenue (248 0210/www.fresh.com). BART & Metro to Montgomery/bus 2, 3, 4, 15, 30, 38, 45, 76/cable car Powell-Hyde or Powell-Mason. **Open** 10am-7pm Mon-Wed, Sat; 10am-8pm Thur; 10am-6pm Sun. **Map** p51 C1 ⑱

Ensconced in a Victorian corner spot, Fresh purveys its own inimitable soaps, perfumes, lotions, shower gels and make-up.

Gump's

135 Post Street, between Grant Avenue & Kearny Street (984 9439/www.gumps.com). BART & Metro to Montgomery/bus 2, 3, 4, 15, 30, 38, 45, 76 & Market Street routes/cable car Powell-Hyde or Powell-Mason. **Open** 10am-6pm Mon-Sat; noon-5pm Sun. **Map** p51 C1 ⑲

Established in 1861, Gump's is the place where moneyed San Franciscans buy wedding presents, china and jewellery. It's a thoroughly elegant shopping experience for those who think a silver service for less than 12 is simply out of the question.

Kate Spade

227 Grant Avenue, between Post & Sutter Streets (216 0880/www.katespade.com). BART & Metro to Powell/bus 2, 3, 4, 15, 30, 38, 45, 76/cable car Powell-Hyde or Powell-Mason. **Open** 10am-6pm Mon-Sat; noon-5pm Sun. **Map** p51 C1 ⑳

Once a neatly sewn label on a simple black nylon handbag, Kate Spade is now a full-blown lifestyle, selling luggage, shoes, fragrances and jewellery. The bags, of course, remain exemplary.

Loehmann's

222 Sutter Street, between Grant Avenue & Kearny Street (982 3215/www.loehmanns.com). BART & Metro to Montgomery/bus 2, 3, 4, 15, 30, 38, 45, 76/cable car Powell-Hyde or Powell-Mason. **Open** 9am-8pm Mon-Fri; 9.30am-8pm Sat; 11am-7pm Sun. **Map** p51 C1 ㉑

Communal dressing rooms, eh? Don't be put off: the prices make Loehmann's worth a look. Designer clothes (Prada, Marc by Marc Jacobs, Diane von Furstenberg, Michael Kors, Moschino) hang from the rafters; you can get more than 50% off activewear.

Macy's

170 O'Farrell Street, between Powell & Stockton Streets (397 3333/www.macys.com). BART & Metro to Powell/bus 2, 3, 4, 15, 30, 38, 45, 76 & Market Street routes/cable car Powell-Hyde or Powell-Mason. **Open** 10am-9pm Mon-Sat; 11am-7pm Sun. **Map** p51 C1 ㉒

The definitive department store: what Macy's lacks in grace, it more than makes up for in discounts.

Marc Jacobs

125 Maiden Lane, between Stockton Street & Grant Avenue (362 6500/www.marcjacobs.com). BART & Metro to Powell/bus 2, 3, 4, 15, 30, 38, 45, 76 & Market Street routes/cable car Powell-Hyde or Powell-Mason. **Open** 10am-7pm Mon-Sat; noon-6pm Sun. **Map** p51 C1 ㉓

Terminally cool Marc Jacobs keeps lines fresh and just affordable enough for the under-30s. The bags sit on glowing shelves drawing you in with their utilitarian glamour.

Metier

355 Sutter Street, between Stockton Street & Grant Avenue (989 5395/www.metiersf.com). BART & Metro to Powell/bus 2, 3, 4, 15, 30, 38, 45, 76/cable car Powell-Hyde or Powell-Mason. **Open** 10am-6pm Mon-Sat. **Map** p51 C1 ㉔

The magic tent

A feast of food, fools, and fantasy, Teatro Zinzanni's *Love Chaos & Dinner*, currently enjoying a long-running hit on the Embarcadero, draws inspiration from European circus traditions, cabaret and brash American comedy.

Zinzanni's beautiful antique tent now sits permanently pitched at Pier 29. One of only eight such *spiegeltents* (huge mirrored tents, originally from Belgium) in existence, the eye-catching circular pavilion engulfs the visitor in a dreamy embrace of rich French velvet, hand-carved wood, stained glass and sparkling mirrors. Guests first enter a bar and boutique area whose intoxicating atmosphere is suffused with old-fashioned decadence and a giddy sense of anticipation.

They then take their seats in the intimate main dining area, where hors d'oeuvres and champagne await, to the accompaniment of a live band and a sensuous and extravagant floor show. Food is good and carefully timed: courses are smoothly integrated with the acts unfurling in close proximity to the diners (some of whom inevitably get coaxed into joining in). Performers include contortionists, equilibrists (hand-balancers), flying and static trapeze artists, mesmerising aerial dancers, incredible juggling acts, and of course a 'staff' of hilarious buffoons led by characters such as Madame Zinzanni, the Chef, and the haughty Maitre D'Hotel.

Such is Zinzanni's reputation that it is able to draw world-class performers from the US and abroad – and not just stars of the circus world. Among the luminaries recently heading up the astounding cast of regulars have been actor-comedian Geoff Hoyle, recording artist Duffy Bishop, folk legend Joan Baez, and actress-chanteuse Sally Kellerman. *http://4382668/love.zinzanni.org.*

Saks Fifth Avenue

Metier is Serious Fashion. From slouchy sophistication care of Cathy Waterman, the glamorous detailing of Vena Cava and the bohemian chic of Mayle, the 'hot mom' set at last has a place to call home.

Murik

73 Geary Street, at Grant Avenue (395 9200/www.murikwebstore.com). BART & Metro to Powell/bus 2, 3, 4, 15, 30, 38, 45, 76 & Market routes/cable car Powell-Hyde or Powell-Mason. **Open** 10am-6pm daily. **Map** p51 C1 ㉕
Sweet, affordable togs by European makers such as Joha, Juttum, Filou & Friends and Micro Bulle, using whimsical motifs and tasteful, muted colours.

Neiman Marcus

150 Stockton Street, between Geary & O'Farrell Streets (362 3900/www. neimanmarcus.com). BART & Metro to Powell/bus 2, 3, 4, 15, 30, 38, 45, 76 & Market Street routes/cable car Powell-Hyde or Powell-Mason. **Open** 10am-7pm Mon-Wed, Fri, Sat; 10am-8pm Thur; noon-6pm Sun. **Map** p51 C1 ㉖
Neiman Marcus was revered by old San Francisco society back in the day – when labels said 'Exclusively for Neiman Marcus'. Today, luxury of the mink-covered coat-hanger variety can still be yours, along with designer and diffusion labels.

Nordstrom

Westfield San Francisco Centre, 865 Market Street, at 5th Street (243 8500/ www.nordstrom.com). BART & Metro to Powell/bus 27, 30, 45 & Market Street routes/cable car Powell-Hyde or Powell-Mason. **Open** 9.30am-9pm Mon-Sat; 10am-7pm Sun. **Map** p51 C2 ㉗
Bourgeois old Nordstrom has something for everyone – there's even a spa on the top floor. The vast women's section features a majestic shoe section.

Saks Fifth Avenue

*384 Post Street, at Powell Street
(986 4300/www.saksfifthavenue.com).
BART & Metro to Powell/bus 2, 3, 4,
30, 45, 76 & Market Street routes/
cable car Powell-Hyde or Powell-Mason.*
Open 10am-7pm Mon-Wed, Fri, Sat;
10am-8pm Thur; 11am-6pm Sun.
Map p51 C1 ㉘

This branch of the upmarket store is
less claustrophobic than most. The
second floor offers designers such as
Marc Jacobs, Moschino and Gucci, but
several storeys up you'll find less pricey,
but just as trendy, labels such as
Temperley London, Tory Burch and
Diane von Furstenberg.

Sephora

*33 Powell Street, at Market Street
(362 9360/www.sephora.com). BART
& Metro to Powell/bus 27, 30, 31,
45 & Market Street routes/cable car
Powell-Hyde or Powell-Mason.* **Open**
10am-9pm Mon-Sat; 11am-7pm Sun.
Map p51 C2 ㉙

Sephora's USP is its interactive floor
plan: customers can touch, smell and
try on most of the premier perfumes
and make-up brands without enduring
the hard sell.

Urban Outfitters

*80 Powell Street, at Ellis Street
(989 1515/www.urbanoutfitters.com).
BART & Metro to Powell/bus 2, 3,
4, 15, 30, 38, 45, 76 & Market
Street routes/cable car Powell-Hyde
or Powell-Mason.* **Open** 9.30am-
9.30pm Mon-Sat; 10.30am-9pm Sun.
Map p51 C2 ㉚

Sturdy Ben Sherman trousers,
adorable Free People cardigans, old-
school T-shirts, funky jewellery and
tons of jeans at seriously affordable
prices. Urban Outfitters is great for
those just out of college – or those who
wish they were.

Arts & leisure

Biscuits & Blues

*401 Mason Street, at Geary Street
(292 2583/www.biscuitsandblues.com).
Bus 2, 3, 4, 27, 38, 76/cable car
Powell-Hyde or Powell-Mason.*

Open 6pm-midnight Tue-Sun. *Shows*
8pm and/or 10pm. **Admission** $10-
$15. **Map** p51 B1 ㉛

This subterranean nightclub and
restaurant is a pretty basic affair,
and it can get fairly stuffy when the
place is crowded. However, it's still
the best spot in town to catch mainstream blues, played for genuinely
excited crowds. The American food
has a Southern accent.

Ruby Skye

*420 Mason Street, between Geary &
Post Streets (693 0777/www.ruby
skye.com). BART & Metro to Powell/
bus 2, 3, 4, 38, 76 & Market Street
routes/cable car Powell-Hyde or Powell-
Mason.* **Open** 9pm-2am Thur; 9pm-
3am Fri; 8pm-4am Sat. **Admission**
$10-$30. **Map** p51 B1 ㉜

Converted from an elegant 1890s theatre, Ruby Skye has retained a good
many ornate Victorian touches, while
gaining thoroughly modern sound
and lighting systems. With its huge
dancefloor and endless parade of sur-
gically enhanced women, it can feel as
if it's been imported straight from LA.
Not surprisingly, it's a second home
for rave-circuit big names like Sasha
and Digweed.

Vessel

*85 Campton Place, off Stockton Street,
between Sutter & Post Streets (433
8585/www.vesselsf.com). Bart & Metro
to Montgomery/bus 2, 3, 4, 38, 76 &
Market Street routes/cable car Powell-
Hyde or Powell-Mason.* **Open** 5pm-
midnight Wed, Thur; 5pm-2am Fri;
9pm-2am Sat. **Admission** free-$20.
Map p51 C1 ㉝

A blast from the city's ostentatious
dotcom past – a person could easily
spend upwards of $1,000 here on
fancy champagne service. Still, cruising through this incredibly well-
appointed bar early in the evening
can be fun (you're guaranteed a long
wait in line and the often disapprov-
ing scrutiny of the bouncers if you
arrive after 10pm), if only to revel in
the screeching decadence of San
Francisco's monied class.

The Financial District

Bounded by Market, Kearny and Jackson Streets, plus the Embarcadero to the east, the Financial District has been the business and banking hub of San Francisco, and the West at large, since the Gold Rush of the mid 19th century.

Its northern edge is overlooked by the Transamerica Pyramid. South from the Transamerica, the area's history as the financial heart of the American West reveals itself further in its architecture. Perhaps the most striking building is the **Bank of America Center**, now officially known as **555 California Street**, which towers over the Financial District. The skyscraper is 75 feet shorter than the Transamerica, but feels more massive thanks to its larger girth and carnelian granite zigzag frame.

Sights & museums

Pacific Coast Stock Exchange

155 Sansome Street, at Pine Street (421 9939/tours 202 9700 ext 72). Bus 1, 10, 12, 15, 41/cable car California. **Open** tours by appointment. **Admission** $5 donation. **Map** p65 A4 ③④
The Exchange was modernised in 1928 by architect Timothy Pflueger, who believed art should be an integral part of architecture. He commissioned sculptor Ralph Stackpole to create the two granite statues outside, which represent Agriculture and Industry, while above the entrance is a figure called Progress of Man with arms outstretched. The building's main attraction is Diego Rivera's 1930 mural *Allegory of California*. Tours can be arranged by appointment through the City Club, (www.cityclubsf.com), a members-only club, on the tenth floor.

Pacific Heritage Museum

608 Commercial Street, at Montgomery Street (399 1124/www.ibankunited. com/phm). Bus 1, 10, 12, 15, 41/cable car California. **Open** 10am-4pm Tue-Sat. **Admission** free. **Map** p65 A4 ③⑤
Once the city's mint, this building now houses a Bank of Canton as well as a museum. Emphasising San Francisco's connections with the Pacific Rim, the museum features changing exhibits of contemporary artists from countries such as China, Taiwan, Japan and Thailand.

Transamerica Pyramid

600 Montgomery Street, between Washington & Clay Streets. Bus 1, 10, 12, 15, 41/cable car California. **Map** p65 A4 ③⑥
The Transamerica provoked public outrage when William Pereira's design was unveiled. However, since its completion in 1972, the 853-foot building has become an iconic spike that defines the city's skyline. The pyramid sits on giant rollers that allow it to rock safely in the event of an earthquake. Sadly, the only people who get to access the vertiginous observation deck are those who work in the building.

Wells Fargo History Museum

420 Montgomery Street, at California Street (396 2619/www.wellsfargo history.com/museums/museum_sf.htm). Bus 1, 10, 30, 41/cable car California. **Open** 9am-5pm Mon-Fri. **Admission** free. **Map** p65 A4 ③⑦
Wells Fargo is California's oldest bank, and this collection of Gold Rush memorabilia gives a good history of banking in California. You'll find gold nuggets, an old telegraph machine and a Concord stagecoach, built in 1867, plus historical photos.

Eating & drinking

Aqua

252 California Street, between Battery & Front Streets (956 9662/www. aqua-sf.com). BART & Metro to Embarcadero/bus 1, 10, 12, 15,

Bank of America Center

41 & Market Street routes/cable car California. **Open** 11.30am-2.30pm, 5.30-10.30pm Mon-Fri; 5.30-11pm Sat; 5.30-9.30pm Sun. **$$$. Fish. Map** p65 B4 ⊛

The seasonal menu for this sleek and handsomely appointed space includes local and imported fish, prepared with brilliant flourishes. The wine list is award-winning, the service exemplary.

Bix

56 Gold Street, between Montgomery & Sansome Streets (433 6300/www. bixrestaurant.com). Bus 9X, 10, 12, 20, 41. **Open** *Bar* 4.30-10pm Mon-Thur; 11.30am-midnight Fri, 5.30pm-midnight Sat; 5.30-10pm Sun. **Bar. Map** pA3 ⊛

The secretive locale and supper-club menu of Bix, named for owner Doug 'Bix' Biederbeck ('very vaguely relat-ed' to 1920s and '30s jazz cornet legend Bix Beiderbecke), evoke the opulence of the Jazz Age.

Bubble Lounge

714 Montgomery Street, between Washington & Jackson Streets (4344204/www.sanfrancisco.bubble lounge.com). Bus 1, 9X, 10, 12, 20, 41. **Open** 5.30pm-1am Tue-Thur; 5pm-2am Fri; 6.30pm-2am Sat. **Bar. Map** p65 A3 ⊛

After the stock market closes, stockbro-kers and short-skirted executives tickle their noses with an incredible selection of sparkling wines and champagnes at this upscale hangout. The booze is paired with fine pâté, salads and caviar.

Jeanty at Jack's

615 Sacramento Street, at Montgomery Street (693 0941/www.jeantyat jacks.com). BART & Metro to Montgomery/bus 1, 9X, 10, 12, 41/cable car California. **Open** 11.30am-10.30pm Mon-Fri; 5-10.30pm Sat, Sun. **$$$. French. Map** p65 A4 ⊛

The 'Jack's' of the name is a brasserie that opened in 1864; the 'Jeanty' is chef Philippe, who has consolidated his rep-utation over the last decade at his excellent bistro in the Napa Valley's Yountville. The two have combined to create one of the city's better and more authentic French restaurants.

Kokkari Estiatorio

200 Jackson Street, at Front Street (981 0983/www.kokkari.com). BART & Metro to Embarcdero/bus 1, 10, 12, 20, 41. **Open** 11.30am-10pm Mon-Thur; 11.30am-11pm Fri; 5-11pm Sat. **$$$. Greek. Map** p65 B3 ⊛

Kokkari serves what it describes as 'Hellenic cuisine'. It's quite outstand-ing, although highly priced, and unlike what most people think of when it comes to Greek food. Grilled lamb chops, pan-roasted fish and traditional dishes like moussaka are the main-course highlights.

NEW Perbacco

230 Califoria Street, between Front & Battery Streets (955 0663/www. perbaccosf.com). **Open** 11.30am-10pm

Mon-Thur; 530-10pm Sat. **$$$**.
Italian. Map p65 B4
Perbacco serves upscale, power-lunch
and business-dinner Cal-Italian cuisine
in a brightly lit dining room and lower-
ceilinged loft. Suited types prefer the
beef short ribs and hangar steak, while
less-hearty appetites opt for local
petrale sole or seared tuna.

Plouf

*40 Belden Place, between Bush
& Pine Streets (986 6491/www.
plouf sf.com). BART & Metro to
Montgomery/bus 2, 3, 4, 9X,
30, 38, 45, 76 & Market Street
routes/cable car Powell-Hyde or
Powell-Mason.* **Open** *11.30am-3pm,
5.30-10pm Mon-Thur; 11am-3pm,
5.30-11pm Fri; 5.30-11pm Sat.* **$$$**.
French. Map p65 A4
This charming, always-packed restaurant is named after the French word for
'splash'. No dining experience here is
complete without a bucket of steamed
mussels, but the ever-changing array
of fish is also excellent.

Sam's Grill

*374 Bush Street, between Montgomery
& Kearny Streets (421 0594). Bus 15,
45, 76.* **Open** *11am-9pm Mon-Fri.*
$$$. American. Map p65 A4
Sam's has been satisfying San
Franciscan appetites for over 140
years and holds fast to history, with a
friendly atmosphere and charming
dining room panelled in dark wood
and punctuated by white tablecloths.
The American menu is largely driven
by seafood, but it's worth opting for
such local specialities as the wonder-
ful Hangtown Fry.

NEW Waterbar

*399 The Embarcadero, between Folsom
& Harrison Streets (284 9922/www.
waterbarsf.com).* **Open** *11.30am-2pm,
5.30-10pm daily.* **$$$$. Seafood**.
Map p65 C5
The Bay views may be priceless, but
the food will set you back at the
Waterbar and neighbouring Eric
Roadhouse (369 Embarcadero, 369
9955, www.epicroasthousesf.com), the

SAN FRANCISCO BY AREA

Ferry Building

fantastical brainchildren of über-restaurateur Pat Kuleto. Epic offers bold, New Orleans-inspired steakhouse far. Next door, at Waterbar, the theme is sustainable seafood, from oysters to whole fish, including those swimming in pillar aquariums throughout the dining room

Shopping

Stacey's

581 Market Street, between 1st & 2nd Streets (1-800 926 6511/421 4687/ www.staceys.com). BART & Metro to Montgomery/bus 2, 3, 4, 31 & Market Street routes. **Open** 9.30am-7pm Mon-Fri; 11am-6.30pm Sat. **Map** p65 B5 ⑰
The city's oldest and largest independent bookshop, Stacey's offers an impressive selection of signed books, makes excellent staff recommendations, and co-sponsors lectures (from the likes of Gore Vidal) with the Commonwealth Club.

The Embarcadero

For decades, San Franciscans old enough to recall the majesty of the original Embarcadero became misty-eyed for the old days when it was a palm-lined thoroughfare – as opposed to a double-decker freeway. Then came the devastating 1989 Loma Prieta earthquake, which felled the Embarcadero's ill-considered upper deck, returning it to its former glory. Today, refurbished antique streetcars from around the world ply the ribbon of road that unfurls along the Bay.

At the foot of Market Street stands the centrepiece of the Embarcadero: the beautifully restored **Ferry Building**, which divides even-numbered piers (to the south) from odd (to the north). The building now bustles with the unmatched Ferry Plaza Farmers' Market.

Sights & museums

Rincon Center

*101 Spear Street, at Mission Street
(243 0473). BART & Metro to
Embarcadero/bus 1, 12, 20, 30, 41
& Market Street routes.* **Open** 24hrs
daily. **Admission** free. **Map** p65 C4 ㊾
The lobby (facing Mission Street) of this
art deco post office cum residential and
office tower has an intriguing mural.
Painted in 1941 by Russian Social
Realist painter Anton Refregier, it was
controversial at the time not only
because it was the most expensive of
the WPA mural projects, but also
because it included dark moments from
California's past. The central atrium has
an all-water sculpture by Doug Hollis.

Eating & drinking

Americano

*Hotel Vitale, 8 Mission Street, at the
Embarcadero (278 3777/www.
americanorestaurant.com). BART
& Metro to Embarcadero/ streetcar F/
bus 2, 14, 12, 20, 21, 31, 41, 71 &
Market Street routes.* **Open** 6.30-
10.30am, 11.30am-2.30pm, 5.30-10pm
Mon-Thur; 6.30-10.30am, 11.30am-
2.30pm, 5.30-11pm Fri; 7.30am-3pm,
5.30-11pm Sat; 7.30am-3pm, 5.30-10pm
Sun. **$$$**. **American**. **Map** p65 C4 ㊾
This sleek, understatedly elegant
restaurant offers seasonally fresh,
Italian-inspired food, cooked and served
with Californian flair. Chef Paul
Arenstam frequently employs seasonal
ingredients sourced from the Ferry
Plaza Farmers' Market across the street.

Boulevard

*1 Mission Street, at Steuart Street (543
6084/www.boulevardrestaurant.com).
BART & Metro to Embarcadero/
streetcar F/bus 2, 14, 12, 20, 21, 31,
41, 71 & Market Street routes.* **Open**
11.30am-2pm, 5.30-10pm Mon-Thur;
11.30am-2pm, 5.30-10.30pm Fri; 5.30-
10.30pm Sat; 5.30-10pm Sun. **$$$$**.
American. **Map** p65 C4 ㊿

The Embarcadero

Since 1993, this classic-looking restaurant has been one of San Francisco's most consistently reliable. Always busy, it attracts diners with waterfront views and hearty food. Self-taught chef Nancy Oakes specialises in elaborate New American dishes.

Café de Stijl

1 Union Street, at Front Street (291 0808/www.destijl.com). Streetcar F/bus 10. **Open** 6.30am-5pm Mon-Fri. **$**.
International. Map p65 B3 ⑤

A small but lively café with sleek decor, pleasant ambience and a wideranging menu. Middle Eastern dishes are a speciality, as are Tuscan-style roast chicken and bowl-sized lattes.

Chaya Brasserie

132 the Embarcadero, at Mission Street (777 8688/www.thechaya.com). BART & Metro to Embarcadero/ streetcar F/bus 2, 14, 12, 20, 21, 31, 41, 71 & Market Street routes. **Open** 11.30am-2.30pm, 5.30-10pm Mon-Wed; 11.30am-2.30pm, 5.30-10.30pm Thur, Fri; 5.30-10.30pm Sat; 5-9.30pm Sun. **$$$**. **American**. Map p65 C4 ⑤

A southern California transplant, this large and bustling restaurant offers an extensive menu of Japanese-meets-French specialities and sweeping Bay views to enjoy it by. The toughest decision is deciding which country to lean towards when ordering – the sushi is excellent, but the grilled meat specialities are also always tempting.

Fog City Diner

1300 Battery Street, at Greenwich Street (982 2000/www.fogcitydiner. com). Streetcar F to Lombard & Embarcadero/bus 10. **Open** 11.30am-10pm Mon-Thur; 11.30am-11pm Fri; 10.30am-11pm Sat; 10.30am-10pm Sun. **$$**. **American**. Map p65 A2 ⑤

From outside, this looks like a modern update of a classic 1950s diner. Inside, the decor is swankier, and the menu lurches from burgers and steaks to crab cakes and grilled salmon. Prices are higher than they should be, but you can still eat well here.

Frisson

244 Jackson Street, between Battery & Front Streets (956 3004/www.frisson sf.com). Streetcar F/bus 1, 10, 12, 20, 41. **Open** 5.30-10pm Mon-Thur; 5.30-11pm Fri, Sat. **$$$**. **American**.
Map p65 B3 ⑤

Be prepared to people-watch and to be watched by people: this is a social showcase, from its high-design modern decor to the playful interpretations of French-Californian cuisine. There is a tendency to overdo things, but staples such as slow-cooked chicken are outstanding.

Globe Restaurant

290 Pacific Avenue, at Battery Street (391 4132/www.globerestaurant.com). Bus 1, 10, 12, 41. **Open** 11.30am-3pm, 6pm-1am Mon-Fri; 6pm-1am Sat; 6pm-midnight Sun. **$$$**. **American**.
Map p65 B3 ⑤

A popular hangout for off-duty chefs, this dining room has an exposed-brick look that imparts an urban, New York feel. The menu offers such standards

SAN FRANCISCO BY AREA

as wood-oven pizzas, braised short ribs and grilled salmon, prepared with fresh ingredients and without complications.

Imperial Tea Court

27 Ferry Market Place, Ferry Building, at the Embarcadero (544 9830/www. imperialtea.com). BART & Metro to Embarcadero/streetcar F/ bus 2, 14, 12, 20, 21, 31, 41, 71 & Market Street routes. **Open** 10am-6pm daily. **Tea shop.** Map p65 C4 ⑤⑥

This serene tea house, an offshoot of the original Chinatown shop, offers a vast array of teas, served in the traditional Chinese *gaiwan* (covered cup), and drunk to the accompaniment of birds chirping in cages. Don't expect serious food, although traditional nibbles are served.

Market Bar

1 Ferry Building, at the Embarcadero (434 1100/ www.marketbar.com). BART & Metro to Embarcadero/ streetcar F/bus 2, 14, 12, 20, 21, 31, 41, 71 & Market Street routes. **Open** 11.30am-10pm Mon-Fri; 9am-10pm Sat, Sun. **$$$. American.** Map p65 C4 ⑤⑦

This casual brasserie at the waterfront features hearty California cuisine and some Italian fare. It's known for excellent seafood: soul-warming bouillabaisse and *cioppino*.

Ozumo

161 Steuart Street, at Mission Street (882 1333/ www.ozumo.com). BART & Metro to Embarcadero/ streetcar F/bus 2, 14, 12, 20, 21, 31, 41, 71 & Market Street routes. **Open** 11.30am-2pm, 5.30-10pm Mon-Wed; 11.30am-2pm, 5.30-10.30pm Thur; 11.30am-2.30pm, 5.30-11pm Fri; 5.30-11pm Sat; 5.30-10pm Sun. **$$$. Japanese.** Map p65 C4 ⑤⑧

Some 6,000sq ft of design panache swaddles an equally chic crowd at this contemporary Japanese restaurant. The front dining room holds a bar and lounge serving an exhaustive menu of sakés and rare teas. Amble past the robata grill – the meat, fish and vegetables from the robata menu are the real attractions – and you'll come to an enormous main dining room, with a sushi bar and Bay Bridge views.

Slanted Door

1 Ferry Building, at the Embarcadero (861 8032/www.slanteddoor.com). BART & Metro to Embarcadero/ streetcar F/bus 2, 14, 12, 20, 21, 31, 41, 71 & Market Street routes. **Open** 11am-2.30pm, 5.30-10pm Mon-Thur, Sun; 11am-2.30pm, 5.30-10.30pm Fri, Sat. **$$$. Vietnamese.** Map p65 C4 ⑤⑨

The sleek lines and Bay views of Charles Phan's popular restaurant are alluring, but the attraction remains Phan's incredible, inventive Vietnamese-inspired food. There isn't a bad choice on the menu, although the shaking beef, the spicy short ribs and the shrimp and crab spring rolls continue to stand out.

Taylor's Refresher

1 Ferry Building, at the Embarcadero (1-866 328 3663/www.taylors refresher.com). BART & Metro to Embarcadero/streetcar F/bus 2, 14, 12, 20, 21, 31, 41, 71 & Market Street routes. **Open** 10.30am-10pm daily. **$$. American.** Map p65 C4 ⑥⓪

Over 50 years after the original opened its drive-thru window in the Napa Valley, the second branch of Taylor's Refresher set up shop in the Ferry Building. The decor is rather more modern than at the original, and the menu a little posher in parts, but the basics – burgers, fries, malts and shakes – remain peerless.

Yank Sing

Rincon Center, 101 Spear Street, at Mission Street (781 1111/www. yanksing.com). BART & Metro to Montgomery/bus 2, 3, 4, 31 & Market Street routes. **Open** 11am-3pm Mon-Fri; 10am-4pm Sat, Sun. **$$. Chinese.** Map p65 C4 ⑥①

The quality of Yank Sing's food explains how it manages to thrive in the corner of a massive office complex. Non-English-speaking waitresses roll out an endless array of steaming dumplings; a loyal, on-the-go business crowd snaps them up with speed.

Financial District & Embarcadero

A   **B**   **C**

0   500 m
0   500 yds

© Copyright Time Out Group 2008

Cruise Ship Terminal

Ferries to Alcatraz

San Francisco Bay

TELEGRAPH HILL

Coit Tower

FILBERT STREET

Macchiarini Steps

BATTERY STREET

SANSOME STREET

BROADWAY

Jackson Square

Chinese Culture Center

Transamerica Pyramid

Golden Gateway Center

CLAY ST

Justin Herman Plaza

Ferry Building

Portsmouth Square

Embarcadero Center

COMMERCIAL ST

Bank of California

Cable Car

Wells Fargo History Museum

Merchant's Exchange

PINE STREET

Rincon Center

STUART STREET

Bank of America

KEARNY ST

Pacific Coast Stock Exchange

MARKET STREET

BART Embarcadero

Muni Metro Folsom

Muni Metro BART Embarcadero

Crocker Galleria

SUTTER STREET

Muni Metro BART Montgomery

Transbay Terminal & Greyhound Bus Depot

BEALE STREET

FREMONT STREET

SPEAR STREET

HOWARD STREET

FOLSOM STREET

Cartoon Art Museum

Center for the Arts

Contemporary Jewish Museum

SEMOMA

SOMA

Ferries to North Bay

THE EMBARCADERO

1 Sights & museums
1 Eating & drinking
1 Shopping
1 Nightlife
1 Arts & leisure

Shopping

Ferry Plaza Farmers' Market

Ferry Building, Embarcadero, at Market Street. BART & Metro to Montgomery/bus 1, 9, 14, 31 & Market Street routes (291 3276/www.ferry building marketplace.com). **Open** *Farmers' Market* 10am-2pm Tue; 8am-2pm Sat. *Ferry Building Marketplace* 10am-6pm Mon-Fri; 9am-6pm Sat; 11am-5pm Sun. **Map** p65 C4 ⑫

Since the restored Ferry Building reopened in 2002, the Ferry Plaza farmers' market has become a sightseeing attraction in its own right. White tents spill out into the open air; shoppers graze from stalls of aged goat's cheese, freshly baked bread slathered in flavoured olive oil, pasta and gourmet sausages. There's lots of bustle, especially on a Saturday. Non-market days are a good time to check out the excellent food shops and restaurants inside the building. Note that hours for individual shops and restaurants may vary.

The Tenderloin

The Tenderloin is a far cry from the retail mecca of Union Square a few blocks to the east – this is a district that has always lived on the wild side. However, its gritty reputation shouldn't put people off visiting the local theatres, staying in one of the stylish hotels or checking out the myriad terrific bars. Depending on where you're planning to walk (Geary Street and points north are usually safe; streets south of it can get a bit sketchy), it may be best to hail a cab at night.

Sights & museums

St Boniface Catholic Church

133 Golden Gate Avenue, at Leavenworth Street (863 7515). BART & Metro to Civic Center/bus 19, 31 & Market Street routes. **Open** hours vary. **Map** p51 B2 ⑬

St Boniface's Romanesque interior, restored in the 1980s, has some impeccable stencilling and a beautifully gilded apse topped by a four-storey cupola. Outside Mass times, the church is gated, so ring the buzzer to get in. Be sure to get there before 1.30pm during the week, when the church closes for cleaning until the next morning.

Eating & drinking

Asia de Cuba

Clift Hotel, 495 Geary Street, at Taylor Street (929 2300/www.chinagrill management.com/adecSF). BART & Metro to Powell/bus 2, 3, 4, 27, 38, 76/ cable car Powell-Hyde or Powell-Mason. **Open** 7am-2.30pm, 5.30-10.30pm Mon-Wed, Sun; 7am-2.30pm, 5.30-11.30pm Thur-Sat. **$$$$. Asian. Map** p51 B1 ⑭

Popular with business travellers with unlimited expense accounts, this swishy Starck-designed room at the Clift is worth popping in to just to see what all the fuss is about. The intensely flavoured dishes on the Chino-Latino menu are good for groups, with many designed to be shared.

Aunt Charlie's Lounge

133 Turk Street, at Taylor Street, Tenderloin (441 2922/www.aunt charlieslounge.com). BART & Metro to Powell/streetcar F/bus 27, 30, 45 & Market Street routes/cable car Powell-Hyde or Powell-Mason. **Open** noon-midnight Mon, Wed; noon-2am Tue, Thur, Fri; 10am-2am Sat; 10am-midnight Sun. No credit cards. **Bar. Map** p51 B2 ⑮

Sports nights, stiff drinks, old-fashioned drag shows and lip-synching on weekends, plus a long-standing Tenderloin location all combine to make this a popular spot with gay attendees.

Cortez Restaurant & Bar

550 Geary Street, between Taylor & Jones Streets (292 6360/www.cortez restaurant.com). BART & Metro to Powell/bus 2, 3, 4, 27, 38, 76/cable car Powell-Hyde or Powell-Mason. **Open** 5.30-10.30pm daily. **$$$. International. Map** p51 B1 ⑯

This stylish restaurant seems an anomaly, with its location on an unseemly stretch of Geary Street. The room is modern and energetic, filled with well-dressed patrons eager to experience the assortment of small plates, which range from the Far East to the American West. Wash down the maze of tasties with a house cocktail.

Dottie's True Blue Café

522 Jones Street, at O'Farrell Street (885 2767). BART & Metro to Powell/bus 2, 3, 4, 27, 38, 76/cable car Powell-Hyde or Powell-Mason. **Open** 7.30am-3pm Mon, Wed-Sun. **$**. **Café**. **Map** p51 B1 ❻❼

Be prepared to wait a little to be seated for your breakfast: maybe *huevos rancheros*, perhaps pancakes, possibly a funky omelette or huge scramble of cheese and veg. It's worth the wait as it may well be one of the best breakfasts you've ever tasted. A quintessential piece of West Coast Americana.

Edinburgh Castle

950 Geary Street, between Larkin & Polk Streets (885 4074/www.castle news.com). Bus 2, 3, 4, 19, 38, 47. **Open** 5pm-2am daily. **Bar**. **Map** p51 A1 ❻❽

Once through the humble entranceway of what appears to be a small, dark dive, the adventurous are rewarded with a raffish, capacious booze hall with 30ft vaulted ceilings. Upstairs is a small cultural venue, playing host to local bands, DJ nights, literary readings and even the odd play. Downstairs, the jukebox cranks favourite obscurities while patrons order fish and chips and settle in with the other unpretentious patrons. The drinks highlight is the vast and affordable range of single malt whiskies.

NEW Fish & Farm

339 Taylor Street, at Ellis Street (474 3474/www. fishandfarmsf.com). BART & Metro to Powell/bus 2, 3, 4, 27, 31, 38, 76/cable car Powell-Hyde or Powell-Mason. **Open** 5-10pm Tue, Wed, Sun; 5-11pm Thur-Sat. **$$$**. **American**. **Map** p51 B2 ❻❾

A chic, intimate restaurant that endeavours to source items on its menu from no more than 100 miles away. Dishes are simple, tasty and elegantly plated, and include many familiar American favourites (seafood chowder, pork chops, pasta), along with more unusual choices such as sablefish.

Millennium

Hotel California, 580 Geary Street, at Jones Street (345 3900/www. millenniumrestaurant.com). BART & Metro to Powell/bus 2, 3, 4, 27, 38, 76/cable car Powell-Hyde or Powell-Mason. **Open** 5.30-9.30pm Mon-Thur, Sun; 5.30-10pm Fri, Sat. **$$$**. **International**. **Map** p51 B1 ❼⓿

Casual, elegant Millennium is still setting the pace when it comes to vegetarian and vegan cooking in San Francisco, doing things with vegetables that you'd never dream possible. The food, both the carte and the $65 tasting menu, changes frequently; it's accompanied by one of the best all-organic wine lists in the US.

Redwood Room

Clift Hotel, 495 Geary Street, at Taylor Street (929 2372/www.clifthotel.com). BART & metro to Powell/bus 2, 3, 4, 27, 38, 76/cable car Powell-Hyde or Powell-Mason. **Open** 5pm-2am Mon-Thur, Sun; 4pm-2am Fri, Sat. **Bar**. **Map** p51 B1 ❼❶

No time was wasted in adding a bar to the Clift after the repeal of Prohibition in 1933, and the magnificent result has been a fixture for high-end cocktailing ever since. Although the decor shifted from art deco to postmodern under Schrager, the bar is neither tacky nor too flamboyant, its towering walls still panelled in redwood. A DJ spins four nights a week.

Shalimar

532 Jones Street, at O'Farrell Street (928 0333/www.shalimarsf.com). BART & Metro to Powell/bus 2, 3, 4, 27, 38, 76/cable car Powell-Hyde or Powell-Mason. **Open** noon-3pm, 5-11.30pm daily. **$**. No credit cards. **Indian**. **Map** p51 B1 ❼❷

Hyphy hits and misses

There may be a passing linguistic resemblance, but the blinged-out party animals of the Bay Area hyphy movement couldn't be more different from the hippies who danced on these same streets almost half a century ago.

Okay, so there are similarities – the rabid anti-authoritarianism and semi-theatrical dress code (although even the hippies might have baulked at the hyphy kids' mega-long sports jerseys and Elton John-style 'stunna shades'). But where the hippies strived to expand consciousness, advocates of hyphy (pronounced 'high-fee') take pride in 'going dumb' or 'getting stupid', and have patented countless acts of pointless flamboyance – 'thizzing', for example, a formless dance employed after consuming all the bud, booze and ecstasy on the premises, or 'ghostriding the whip', which involves getting out of cars and walking alongside them as they roll driverless down the street.

There's something self-consciously faddish about hyphy – the insensible muddle of its gruff mumbling; its cartoon basslines and comically uptempo beats – and it has more than its fair share of detractors as a result. In 2006 the Bay Area's resident musical deity DJ Shadow secured a dismal reception for his third studio album, *The Outsider*, by using it to showcase the talents of various local hyphy prodigals – including Turf Talk, The Animaniaks and Keak Da Sneak. It was a far from sound investment on Shadow's part, with media interest in the hyphy movement already beginning to wane thanks to airplay blacklisting by west coast kingmakers KMEL and a general weariness of the vandalism, violence and general stupidity associated with its illegal street parties or 'sideshows'. Nor is it getting easier to 'pop your collar' locally: following the closure of original hyphy hub Mingles, in Oakland, the onus passed across Jack London Square to Zazoo's, which subsequently had its own Saturday club shut down after a shooting in February 2008. The best way to check out the Bay Area's stars is to keep tabs on tour dates via their Myspace sites, although their records do get aired at local hip hop nights in clubs like **Milk** (p132) and **Duplex** (1525 Mission Street, between 11th and Lafayette Streets, 355 1525, www.duplexsf.com), or at Sucker Punch, a free Monday night hip hop extravaganza at the **Transfer** (p122).

DJ Shadow

Perhaps the best Indian and Pakistan cuisine in this grubby corner of the Tenderloin. The dishes here are fairly spicy, turned out at speed and at predictably keen prices.

Shopping

Kayo Books
814 Post Street, between Hyde & Leavenworth Streets (749 0554/ www.kayobooks.com). Bus 2, 3, 4, 19, 38, 47. **Open** 11am-6pm Thur-Sat. **Map** p51 B1 ⓱
This emporium of pulp delivers the goods for those who like their mysteries hard-boiled, their juveniles delinquent and their porn quaintly smutty. Specialities include vintage paperbacks and dime-store novels from the 1940s to the '70s, and exploitation ephemera of all levels of debasement.

Nightlife

NEW 222 Club
222 Hyde Street, at Turk Street (440 0222/www.222club.net). BART & Metro to Civic Center/bus 5, 16, 19, 31 & Market Street routes. **Open** 6pm-2am Tue-Sat. **Admission** varies. **Map** p51 B2 ⓴
One of the funkiest little clubs in San Francisco, the 222 Club hosts hip hop, house, techno and electro nights, alongside a smattering of experimental live performances, in a hipper-than-hip yet eminently friendly atmosphere. This is the place to scope out the upper crust of the city's underground as they munch away on gourmet pizzas or sip cocktails.

Bambuddha Lounge
Phoenix Hotel, 601 Eddy Street, at Larkin Street (885 5088/www. bambuddhalounge.com). Bus 19, 31, 38. **Open** 5.30-10pm Wed, Thur; 5.30pm-2am Fri, Sat. **Admission** $10 Fri, Sat from 10pm. **Map** p51 A2 ⓯
Gentle lighting complements the numerous conversation-promoting nooks and the bamboo daybeds alongside the cabaña-style pool in this sleek nouveau South-east Asian hangout.

The glittering bar and roaring fireplace area are inviting spots in which a see-and-be-seen crowd sits back and enjoys DJs spinning acid jazz, funky disco and other downtempo sounds. Club nights are Friday and Saturday.

Deco Lounge
510 Larkin Street, at Turk Street, Tenderloin (346 2025/www.deco sf.com). Bus 19, 31, 38. **Open** 10am-2am Wed, Thur, Sun; 10am-4am Fri, Sat. No credit cards. **Bay Map** p51 A2 ⓰
Laid out like a spacious 1940s piano bar, complete with plush decor and classic movie posters, Deco somewhat incongruously hosts some of the wildest gay parties in the Tenderloin. Wet jockstrap contests, offbeat drag shows and techno-driven bear parties can be found here on many weekend nights.

Suite One8one
181 Eddy Street, at Taylor Street (345 9900/www.suiteone8one.com). BART & Metro to Powell/bus 27, 31, 38 & Market Street routes. **Open** 9pm-4am Thur-Sat. **Admission** $20. **Map** p51 B2 ⓱
The ultra-swank Suite One8one is one of SF's hottest spots, but it's not for everyone. Some cologne-soaked folks are suckers for a $20 cover, and that's potentially the appeal. Past the rather surly doormen, three floors boast a series of plush rooms and VIP areas. However, the pedestrian music, not to mention the rather snooty crowd, can leave one feeling a bit empty.

Arts & leisure

American Conservatory Theater
Geary Theater, 415 Geary Street, between Mason & Taylor Streets, Tenderloin (information 834 3200/box office 749 2228/www.act-sfbay.org). Bus 2, 3, 4, 27, 38/cable car Powell-Hyde or Powell-Mason. **Tickets** $12-$80. **Map** p51 B1 ⓱
Since opening in 1967, the ACT has been staging modern classics and new works by the likes of David Mamet,

earning it a solid reputation. It is also known for its fine conservatory, whose alumni include Annette Bening and Denzel Washington. In addition to ACT shows, the exquisite Geary Theater usually hosts one or two touring productions per season.

EXIT Theatre

156 Eddy Street, between Mason & Taylor Streets (673 3847/tickets 1-800 838 3006/www.theexit.org). BART & Metro to Powell/bus 27, 30, 45 & Market Street routes/cable car Powell-Hyde or Powell-Mason. **Tickets** *$10-$20.* **Map** p51 B2 ⑦⑨
This three-stage set-up offers eclectic, provocative shows, from new one-acts to work by well-known authors. The Exit also hosts the annual San Francisco Fringe Festival every autumn, the largest in the US. The main location has the added attraction of a refreshment lounge; a fourth stage (Exit on Taylor) lies just around the corner at 277 Taylor Street.

Grand at the Regency Center

1300 Van Ness Avenue, at Sutter Street (673 5716). Bus 2, 3, 4, 19, 38, 47, 49, 76. **Box office** *Ticketmaster only.* **Tickets** *prices vary.* **Map** p51 A1 ⑧⓪
Formerly a Masonic temple, a dance studio, a Polish arts foundation and a movie theatre, this gorgeous Beaux Arts-style ballroom, with its horse-shoe-shaped balcony, hardwood floors and teardrop chandeliers, now stages everything from opera to rock and jazz gigs to dance events. The building incorporates the legendary Avalon Ballroom, which once hosted shows by Janis Joplin and Country Joe & the Fish.

Hemlock Tavern

1131 Polk Street, at Post Street (923 0923/www.hemlocktavern.com). Bus 2, 3, 4, 19, 38, 47, 49, 76. **Open** *4pm-2am daily.* **Shows** *9.30pm daily.* **Admission** *free-$10. No credit cards.* **Map** p51 A1 ⑧①
Out front, the Hemlock looks like a capacious, matey watering hole, a

lively mix of young tastemakers, art snobs and yuppies playing pool, yapping at the central bar or puffing in the open-air smoking 'room'. At the back, however, an intimate live room plays host to some of the more edgy and intelligent musical programming in the city. The roster is built around hipster-friendly artists such as Deerhoof and Wolf Eyes.

Civic Center

South-west of the Tenderloin and north of Market Street, San Francisco's Civic Center is a complex of imposing government buildings and immense performance halls centred on the Civic Center Plaza, an expansive and well-tended lawn. By day, it's populated by an extreme spread of locals, from smartly turned-out officials and dignitaries from the buildings to the homeless folk who hang around outside them. At night, the worker bees are replaced by culture vultures, here to take in a concert, ballet, lecture or opera.

Facing the plaza, and dominating the area, is the stunning Beaux Arts **City Hall**. Across the four lanes of traffic on Van Ness Avenue is a trio of grand edifices: the **Louise M Davies Symphony Hall**; the **War Memorial Opera House**, and the **Veterans' Memorial Building**, a venerable workhorse that is home to offices, performance theatres and even galleries. It is a little-known part of San Francisco history that the UN charter was drafted and signed by 51 nations in what is now the Herbst Theatre here in 1945.

Sights & museums

Asian Art Museum

200 Larkin Street, at Fulton Street (581 3500/www.asianart.org). BART & Metro to Civic Center/streetcar F/

bus 5, 19, 21, 47, 49 & Market Street routes. **Open** 10am-5pm Tue, Wed, Fri-Sun; 10am-9pm Thur. **Admission** $12; $7-$8 reductions. **Map** p51 B2 ㉜

This popular museum has one of the world's most comprehensive collections of Asian art, with exhibits spanning 6,000 years of Asian history and with more than 15,000 objects on display. The outdoor café is a great place to enjoy American- and Asian-inspired dishes on sunny days, and the gift shop is well stocked with high-quality stationery, decorative items and a handsome selection of coffee-table books. The museum once resided in Golden Gate Park, but in 2003 it reopened in this building, former home of the San Francisco Public Library, extensively and beautifully redesigned by Gae Aulenti.

City Hall

1 Dr Carlton B Goodlett Place (Polk Street), between McAllister & Grove Streets (554 4933/tours 554 6023).

BART & Metro to Civic Center/streetcar F/bus 19, 21, 47, 49 & Market Street routes. **Open** 8am-8pm daily. **Tours** 10am, noon, 2pm Mon-Fri. **Admission** free. **Map** p51 A3 ㉝

Built in 1915 to designs by Arthur Brown and John Bakewell, City Hall is the epitome of the Beaux Arts style visible across the whole Civic Center. The building has lots of ornamental ironwork, elaborate plasterwork and a dome – modelled on the one at St Peter's in Rome – that is higher than the one on the nation's Capitol. The central rotunda, with its sweeping staircase, is a magnificent space and the dome overlooks a five-storey colonnade, limestone and granite masonry, regal lighting and majestic marble floors.

Today, the building houses the legislative and executive branches of both the San Francisco city government and the county government. Free tours

Asian Art Museum

SAN FRANCISCO BY AREA

offering behind the scenes views of the Board of Supervisors' chambers (panelled in hand-carved Manchurian oak) are available Monday to Friday at 10am, noon and 2pm.

NEW Museum of Performance & Design

4th floor, Veterans' Memorial Building, 401 Van Ness Avenue, at McAllister Street (255 4800/www.sfpalm.org). BART & Metro to Civic Center/bus 21, 47, 49 & Market Street routes. **Open** noon-5pm Tue-Sat. **Admission** free. **Map** p51 A2 ㉞

The former San Francisco Performing Arts Library & Museum reopened in March 2008 as the Museum of Performance and Design. Exhibitions at this enjoyable museum relate to every one of the performing arts, from puppet shows to operas, but the principal attraction for scholars is the prodigious amount of resource material: thousands of books on design, fashion, music, theatre, opera and other art forms. From 18 March until 20 August 2008 the featured exhibition is Art & Artifice: 75 Years of Design at San Francisco Ballet.

San Francisco Main Library

100 Larkin Street, between Grove & Fulton Streets (library 557 4400/ history room 557 4567/www.sfpl.org). BART & Metro to Civic Center/bus 5, 21, 47, 49 & Market Street routes. Library 10am-6pm Mon, Sat; 9am-8pm Tue-Thur; noon-6pm Fri; noon-5pm Sun. History room 10am-6pm Tue-Thur, Sat; noon-6pm Fri; noon-5pm Sun. Tours 2.30pm Wed, Fri. **Admission** free; 3mth visitor's card $10. **Map** p51 B3 ㉟

Built in 1996 by the architectural firm Pei Cobb Freed & Partners, San Francisco's public library is a beautifully designed. On the top floor, the San Francisco History Room hosts changing exhibitions, a large photo archive and knowledgeable, friendly staff. Readings by big-name and up and coming authors are held here on a regular basis.

Eating & drinking

Indigo

687 McAllister Street, at Gough Street (673 9353/www.indigorestaurant.com). Bus 5, 21, 47, 49. **Open** 5-11pm Tue-Sun. **$$. American. Map** p51 A3 ㊱

The key to Indigo's success is good food, well priced and served in an edgy, chic environment that defies modishness. The lounge-like setting features a long, open kitchen, from which emerges a broad mix of inventive New American dishes. The three-course evening special prix fixe (5-7pm) is one of the best deals in town at just $34.

Jardinière

300 Grove Street, at Franklin Street (861 5555/www.jardiniere.com). BART & Metro to Civic Center Metro to Van Ness/bus 5, 21, 47, 49 & Market Street routes. **Open** from 5pm (last reservation 10pm) Mon, Sun; from 5pm (last reservation 10.30pm) Tue-Sat. **$$$. French. Map** p51 A3 ㊲

This beautiful, whimsically shaped (meant to resemble an overturned champagne glass) restaurant is one of the best high-dollar special-occasion eateries around. Chef Traci Des Jardins continues to seek out the best and most environmentally friendly local ingredients. Starters can be a meal in themselves, but save room for the stellar mains.

Saigon Sandwich Café

560 Larkin Street, between Turk & Eddy Streets (474 5698). BART & Metro to Civic Center/bus 5, 19, 31 & Market Street routes. **Open** 6am-6pm Mon-Sat; 7.30am-5pm Sun. **$. No credit cards. Café. Map** pA2 ㊳

Still the Civic Center's best unsung spot, this tiny, dingy room is typically jammed with foodies and federal workers who file in for huge sandwiches at rock-bottom prices. The bare-bones menu is made up almost entirely of Vietnamese *banh mi* sandwiches, which are prepared with such ingredients as roast pork with a chilli sauce.

Zuni Café

1658 Market Street, between Franklin & Gough Streets (552 2522/www.zuni cafe.com). Metro to Van Ness/ streetcar F/bus 6, 7, 26, 47, 49 71. **Open** 11.30am-midnight Tue-Sat; 11am-11pm Sun. **$$$**. **American**. **Map** p51 A3 ⑥⑨
After more than 25 years, Zuni has developed a cult following on a par with Berkeley's Chez Panisse. Chef Judy Rodgers's Cal-Ital food manages to be both memorable and transparently simple. The art-filled setting, comprising four separate dining rooms, can be quite a scene before and after cultural events in the vicinity, but the sourdough bread and oysters on an iced platter, the roast chicken for two and the wood-fired pizzettas are attractions in themselves.

Arts & leisure

San Francisco Ballet

War Memorial Opera House, 301 Van Ness Avenue, between Grove & McAllister Streets (information 861 5600/tickets 865 2000/www.sf ballet.org). BART & Metro to Civic Center/bus 21, 47, 49 & Market Street routes. **Tickets** $12-$135. **Map** p51 A3 ⑨⓪
Founded in 1933, the San Francisco Ballet is the longest-running professional ballet company in the US. The company is based in the War Memorial Opera House, and its annual season (February to May) is typically an even blend of traditional pieces and new works.

San Francisco Opera

War Memorial Opera House, 301 Van Ness Avenue, at Grove Street (864 3330/www. sfopera.com). BART & Metro to Civic Center, Metro to Van Ness/bus 21, 47, 49 & Market Street routes. **Box office** 10am-5pm Mon; 10am-6pm Tue-Sat. **Tickets** $25-$235. **Map** p51 A3 ⑨①
In 2008 the San Francisco Opera, under general director David Gockley, plans to present Stewart Wallace and local novelist Amy Tan's *The Bonesetter's Daughter*, along with a new co-produc-

tion (with Washington National Opera) of Wagner's Ring Cycle, beginning with *Das Rheingold* in 2008 and culminating with the entire cycle in the 2010-11 season. The fall season runs early September to December; the summer season runs May to July.

The SF Opera is based in the War Memorial Opera House, a grand Beaux Arts building designed by City Hall architect Arthur Brown Jr and built in 1932 as a memorial to the soldiers who fought in World War I. The 3,176-seat auditorium is modelled on European opera houses, with a vaulted ceiling, a huge art deco metal chandelier and a marble foyer. An $84-million revamp in 1997 not only restored the elegant building, but installed up-to-date electronics and stage gear.

San Francisco Symphony

Louise M Davies Symphony Hall, 201 Van Ness Avenue, at Hayes Street (864 6000/www.sfsymphony.org). BART & Metro to Civic Center, Metro to Van Ness/bus 21, 47, 49 & Market Street routes. **Box office** 10am-6pm Mon-Fri; noon-6pm Sat; 2hrs before concert Sun. **Tickets** $20-$125. **Map** p51 A3 ⑨②
Under the dynamic direction of Michael Tilson Thomas, the San Francisco Symphony is internationally recognised for its innovative work, winning several Grammy awards in the process. The symphony's series of Mahler concerts has garnered the ensemble particular acclaim.

The Symphony is based at the Louise M Davies Symphony Hall. Commonly known as the Davies, the striking, multi-tiered, curved-glass edifice has flawless acoustics and clear sightlines. There isn't a bad seat in the house, and that includes the 40 in the centre terrace section behind the orchestra that sell for just $20 and go on sale two hours before most performances (call for details). In addition to SF Symphony concerts, look out for events in the Great Performers series, which imports world-renowned soloists, conductors and ensembles for one-nighters.

SAN FRANCISCO BY AREA

Yerba Buena Gardens

SoMa & South Beach

For much of the 20th century, the streets south of Market Street and east of 10th Street were an industrial wasteland, filled with warehouses and sweatshops. The 1990s dotcom boom brought rapid regeneration: warehouses were converted into expensive loft apartments, bars opened to serve the new locals, and the neighbourhood of SoMa ('South of Market', a nod to SoHo in New York City) took off.

The dotcom boom burst in a hurry, and 2002 to 2006 were lean years for the neighbourhood as San Francisco's property market fell into a slump. But recently money and ideas have begun to flow into the area once again.

Yerba Buena Gardens & around

Bounded by Mission, 3rd, Folsom and 4th Streets, the Yerba Buena Gardens complex was renovated as part of a city-funded project in the 1980s and '90s. Attractions and businesses are housed in a purpose-built series of structures that is half above ground and half below it. The Esplanade within the Gardens is an urban park with sculpture walks, shady trees and the Revelations waterfall, constructed in 1993 in memory of Martin Luther King Jr. Today, the area has become a hub for the city's museums (box p81).

Sights & museums

California Historical Society

678 Mission Street, between 3rd & New Montgomery Streets (357 1848/ www.calhist.org). BART & Metro to Montgomery/bus 9, 9X, 10, 14, 30, 45, 71. **Open** noon-4.30pm Wed-Sat. **Admission** $3; $1 reductions. **Map** p77 D2 ❶

The state's official historical group has focused its efforts on assembling this impressive collection of Californiana. The vaults hold half a million photographs and thousands of books, magazines and paintings, as well as an extensive Gold Rush collection; selections are presented as changing displays on the state's history.

Cartoon Art Museum

655 Mission Street, between 3rd & New Montgomery Streets (227 8666/ www.cartoonart.org). BART & Metro to Montgomery/bus 9, 10, 14, 30, 45, 71. **Open** 11am-5pm Tue-Sun. **Admission** $6; $4 reductions; $2 6-12s. **Map** p77 D2 ❷

The camera that was used to create the first animation for television graces the lobby of this museum. Boasting over 5,000 pieces of cartoon and animation art, as well as a research library, this is the only museum in the western US dedicated to the form. The bookstore contains a large and eclectic selection of books, 'zines, periodicals and coffee-table tomes.

ⓝⓔⓦ Contemporary Jewish Museum

736 Mission Street, between 3rd & 4th Streets (655 7800/www.thecjm.org). BART & Metro to Montgomery/bus 9, 9X, 10, 14, 30, 45, 71. **Open** 11am-5.30pm Mon, Tue, Fri-Sun; 1-8.30pm Thur. **Admission** $8; $6 reductions. **Map** p77 D2 ❸

Open on its new Yerba Buena Gardens site since June 2008, the Contemporary Jewish Museum is devoted to linking the art of the Jewish community with the community at large. Its new home, in a Willis Polk power substation that dates from 1907, has been in the planning stage for the better part of a decade. Architect Daniel Libeskind is responsible for the museum's black box design. Its opening exhibition, In the Beginning: Artists Respond to Genesis, runs until 4 January 2009 and explores the range of artistic interpretations of the creation story through the centuries.

Museum of the African Diaspora

685 Mission Street, at 3rd Street (358 7200/www. moadsf.org). BART & Metro to Montgomery/bus 9, 9X, 10, 14, 30, 45, 71. **Open** 11am-6pm Wed-Sat; noon-5pm Sun. **Admission** $10; $5 reductions; free under-12s. **Map** p77 D2 ❹

The Museum of the African Diaspora (MoAD) is the world's first museum dedicated to exploring the impact of the diaspora of African peoples across the globe. Rotating exhibitions highlight art and culture. Until 28 September 2008 the museum is hosting Double Exposure: African Americans Before and Behind the Camera. This is followed by works from the Hewitt collection of African American art (15 October 2008-11 January 2009).

San Francisco Museum of Modern Art (SFMOMA)

151 3rd Street, between Mission & Howard Streets (357 4000/www.sf moma.org). BART & Metro to Montgomery/bus 9, 9X, 10, 14, 30, 45, 71. **Open** *Memorial Day-Labor Day* 10am-5.45pm Mon, Tue, Fri-Sun; 10am-8.45pm Thur. *Labor Day-Memorial Day* 11am-5.45pm Mon, Tue, Fri-Sun; 11am-8.45pm Thur. **Admission** $12.50; $7-$8 reductions; free under-12s. Half price 6-8.45pm Thur; free 1st Tue of mth. **Map** p77 D2 ❺

Swiss architect Mario Botta's redbrick building, with its huge, circular skylight, is as dramatic from the outside as within. Don't miss the spectacular catwalk beneath the skylight. Accessible from the top-floor galleries, it offers a stunning view of the striped marble below.

SoMa & South Beach

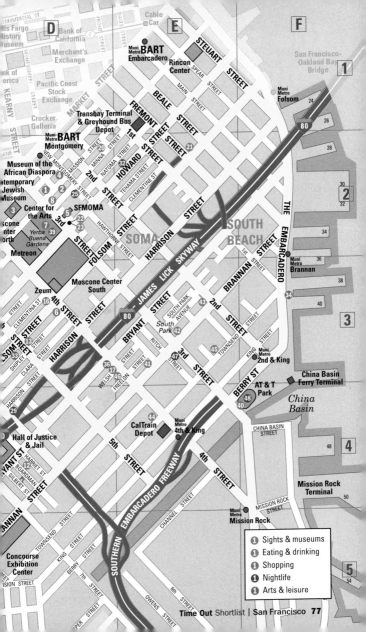

COMMERCIAL STREET

Wells Fargo History Museum

Bank of California

Merchant's Exchange

Pacific Coast Stock Exchange

Crocker Galleria

Bank of America

Cable Car

D

E

F

San Francisco-Oakland Bay Bridge

Muni Metro **BART** Embarcadero

STEUART STREET

Rincon Center

BEALE STREET

SPEAR STREET

MAIN STREET

Muni Metro Folsom

1

24

26

28

Transbay Terminal & Greyhound Bus Depot

FREMONT STREET

1st STREET

Muni Metro **BART** Montgomery

20

21

Museum of the African Diaspora

Contemporary Jewish Museum

MISSION STREET

NEW MONTGOMERY STREET

2nd STREET

MINNA STREET

NATOMA STREET

32

HOWARD STREET

TEHAMA STREET

CLEMENTINE ST

4

1

2

25

8

5

SFMOMA

3rd STREET

22

23

HAWTHORNE STREET

HARRISON STREET

SOUTH BEACH

THE EMBARCADERO

Muni Metro Brannan

30

32

34

36

2

Center for the Arts

7

Moscone Center North

39

SOMA

JAMES LICK SKYWAY

1st STREET

BRANNAN STREET

Yerba Buena Gardens

Metreon

FOLSOM STREET

38

40

34

Zeum

CLEMENTINA ST

16

6

4th STREET

Moscone Center South

80

BRYANT STREET

43

2nd STREET

TOWNSEND STREET

45

Muni Metro 2nd & King

3

HARRISON STREET

13

SHIPLEY ST

CLARA ST

South Park

SOUTH PARK AVENUE

42

RITCH ST

3rd STREET

41

King STREET

China Basin Ferry Terminal

China Basin

36

17

46

WELSH ST

FREELON ST

41

BERRY ST

48

AT & T Park

40

29

Hall of Justice & Jail

44

CalTrain Depot

Muni Metro 4th & King

CHINA BASIN STREET

48

4

BRYANT ST

HARRIET ST

BOARDMAN PL

GILBERT ST

12

5th STREET

4th STREET

Mission Rock Terminal

50

BRANNAN STREET

SOUTHERN EMBARCADERO FREEWAY

CHANNEL STREET

MISSION ROCK STREET

Muni Metro Mission Rock

Concourse Exhibition Center

TOWNSEND STREET

KING STREET

BERRY STREET

7th STREET

6th STREET

OWENS STREET

MISSION STREET

5

54

1 Sights & museums

1 Eating & drinking

1 Shopping

1 Nightlife

1 Arts & leisure

The four floors of galleries that rise above the stark black-marble reception area house a solid permanent collection, with some 15,000 paintings, sculptures and works on paper, as well as thousands of photographs and a range of works related to the media arts. However, the special exhibits are the real draw. Ongoing exhibitions include Picturing Modernity: the Photography Collection, and Matisse and Beyond, with works by Alberto Giacometti, Vija Celmins, Jim Hodges, Robert Rauschenberg, Piet Mondrian, Georgia O'Keeffe, Diego Rivera, and Andy Warhol.

Society of California Pioneers Seymour Pioneer Museum

300 4th Street, at Folsom Street (957 1849/www.californiapioneers.org). BART & Metro to Montgomery/bus 9X, 12, 27, 30, 45. **Open** 10am-4pm Wed-Fri, 1st Sat of mth. Library by appointment. **Admission** $5; $2.50 reductions. **Map** p77 D3 ❻
Operated by descendants of the state's first settlers, this small museum has occasional intriguing displays on California's past, alongside 10,000 books, 50,000 prints and all kinds of other ephemera, such as 19th-century paintings, sculpture and furniture.

Yerba Buena Center for the Arts

701 Mission Street, at 3rd Street (978 2787/www.ybca.org). BART & Metro to Montgomery/ bus 9, 9X, 10, 14, 30, 45, 71. **Open** noon-5pm Tue, Wed, Fri-Sun; noon-8pm Thur. **Admission** $7; $5 reductions. Free 1st Tue of mth. **Map** p77 D2 ❼
Yerba Buena Center stands opposite SFMOMA and is somewhat in its shadow, yet it seems unintimidated, tugging at the modern art scene's shirt-tails with a scrappy itinerary and great attitude. Housed in Fumihiko Maki's futuristic-looking building, it contains four changing galleries and a 96-seat theatre (p85). The focus here is on the contemporary and the challenging (installation and video art, outsider art).

Eating & drinking

Ame

St Regis Hotel, 689 Mission Street, at 3rd Street (284 4040/www.ame restaurant.com). BART & Metro to Montgomery/bus 9, 9X, 10, 12, 14, 30, 45, 76. **Open** 5.30-10pm daily. **$$$**.
International. **Map** p77 D2 ❽
Hiro Sone and Lissa Doumani have brought their Japonesque sensibilities to this stylish dining room in the St Regis Hotel. The menu emphasises raw – sashimi, crudo, tartare, carpaccio – and southern France: grilled duck with a ragout of wild mushrooms, with a confit of giblets and bok choy, say.

Bossa Nova

139 8th Street, at Minna Street (558 8004/www.bossanovasf.com). BART & Metro to Civic Center/bus 12, 14, 19, 26, 27, 47. **Open** 5.30pm-midnight Tue-Sat. Bar until 2am. **$$$**.
International. **Map** p76 B4 ❾
Although its off the beaten track and lacks a sign, locals have found their way to this hip, eclectically appointed and quite tasty bit of Rio in the city. It's popular for its bossa nova as well as for its refreshing take on Brazilian food.

Brainwash

1122 Folsom Street, between 7th & 8th Streets (861 3663/www.brain wash.com). BART & Metro to Civic Center/bus 12, 14, 19, 27, 47. **Open** *Café* 8am-9pm daily. *Laundromat* 7am-11pm Mon-Thur, Sun; 7am-midnight Fri, Sat. **$**. **Bar/café**. **Map** p76 C4 ❿
Part laundromat, part bar/café and part performance space, this popular spot remains a premier singles hangout. People bring along their washing and a wandering eye as they peruse the array of potential mates and the menu of soups, salads and burgers. On most evenings, there's live music, poetry readings or improv comedy.

Butter

354 11th Street, between Folsom & Harrison Streets (863 5964/www. smoothasbutter.com). Bus 9, 12, 27, 47. **Open** 6pm-2am Wed-Sun. **Bar**.
Map p76 B5 ⓫

Butter combines chill-room vibe (complete with DJ) with trailer-trash kitsch and food. After several years on the scene, it still packs people in, and its magic formula repast of a corn dog, Twinkie and can of Pabst Blue Ribbon may just prove to be the elixir of life.

Catalyst Cocktails

312 Harriet Street, between Bryant & Brannan Streets (621 1722/www. catalystcocktails.com). Bus 9X, 12, 19, 27, 47. **Open** 4-11pm Tue-Thur; 4pm-2am Fri, Sat. **Bar**. **Map** p77 D4 ⓬

Sipping cocktails beneath the spires of Catalyst's art deco bar is a bit like making a toast under a miniature Statue of Liberty. The daunting four-page cocktail menus include the wildly named Ukrainian Quaalude, Black Dahlia and Hairy Cherry.

Le Charm

315 5th Street, at Folsom Street (546 6128/www. lecharm.com). BART & Metro to Powell/bus 9X, 12, 27, 30, 45, 76. **Open** 11.30am-2pm, 5.30-9.30pm Tue-Thur; 11.30am-2pm, 5.30-10pm Fri; 5.30-10pm Sat; 5-8.30pm Sun. **$$$**. **French**. **Map** p77 D3 ⓭

One of the few places in town where you can enjoy eating your way through an authentic French bistro menu without having to make a massive cash outlay. Alongside an excellent standard carte, Le Charm has a three-course prix fixe menu ($30) that includes main courses such as pan-roasted calf's liver and steak-frites.

City Beer Store

1168 Folsom Street, between 7th & 8th Streets (503 1033/www.citybeer store.com). Bus 9X, 12, 19, 27, 47. **Open** noon-9pm, Tue-Sat; noon-6pm Sun. **Bar**. **Map** p76 C4 ⓮

This modest storefront operation consists of four tables and floor-to-ceiling refrigerators packed with over 300 kinds of bottled beers and six on draught. Grab a beer from the cooler, order a small plate of regional cheeses and salametto and banter with the other beer-o-philes.

Hole in the Wall

289 8th Street, between Howard & Folsom Streets (431 4695/www.holein thewallsaloon.com). Bus 12, 19, 27, 47. **Open** noon-2am daily. No credit cards. **Bar**. **Map** p76 C4 ⓯

This SoMa institution is a magnet for the biker crowd, although gay locals and tourists love it too. There's a lovely pool table, video games, pinball, rock 'n' roll oldies on repeat and a bewildering array of gay memorabilia covering the walls and ceiling.

LuLu

816 Folsom Street, between 4th & 5th Streets (495 5775/www.restaurant lulu.com). BART & Metro to Powell/bus 9X, 12, 27, 30, 45, 76. **Open** 11.30am-10pm Mon-Thur, Sun; 11.30am-11pm Fri, Sat. **$$$$**. **Italian**. **Map** p77 D3 ⓰

LuLu majors in rustic, Italian-influenced cuisine, with dishes from the wood-fired oven, rotisserie and grill. Many come on large platters, designed for sharing. LuLu's wine bar next door offers a more intimate alternative.

NEW Orson

508 Fourth Street, at Bryant Street (777 1058/www.orsonsf.com). Bus 9X, 30, 45, 47, 76. **Open** *Restaurant* 6-10pm Mon; 6-11pm Tue-Sat. *Bar* 5-10pm Mon; 5pm-midnight Tue, Wed; 5pm-2am Thur-Sat. **$$$**. **American**. **Map** p77 D3 ⓱

Monied business people and local winemakers alike flock to this industrial Euro-chic space to have their palates wowed. Famed for her Citizen Cake restaurant (p138) and creative desserts, chef Elizabeth Falkner is now whipping up tantalising tastes like spicy pork buns and a chooclate/olive oil/sea salt pizza, with handcrafted cocktails to match.

Powerhouse

1347 Folsom Street, between 9th & 10th Streets (552 8689/www.power house-sf.com). Bus 12, 19, 27, 47. **Open** 4pm-2am daily. No credit cards. **Bar**. **Map** p76 C4 ⓲

White-hot and cruisey as hell, Powerhouse is one of the city's most

New Yerba Buena

For anyone who's lived in San Francisco long enough, the transformation of the Yerba Buena district has been nothing short of a miracle. Thirty years ago, the area mouldered in the rubble of abandoned industry. But the construction of the Moscone Convention Center in 1981 and its annex in 1992 sparked a sea change. Following on its heels in 1995 came the bold Mario Botta-designed **Museum of Modern Art** (p75). Shortly after that, the adjacent square block was made over into the **Yerba Buena Center for the Arts** (p79) – part museum and performing arts complex, part park, and part indoor/outdoor shopping and dining mecca. YBCA is connected via an elevated bridge to the Rooftop at Yerba Buena Gardens, which features an array of children's attractions.

Museum of Modern Art

Now a series of smaller museums and cultural outlets are transforming the district even further. In 2005, the **Museum of the African Diaspora** (p75) opened in the luxe St Regis Museum Tower. And in June 2008, famed New York architect Daniel Libeskind will unveil his über-modern **Contemporary Jewish Museum** (p75), a striking blue-steel cube that emerges from a 1907, brick Willis Polk-designed power substation. The Libeskind museum flanks the historic façade of the 1851 St Patrick's Church, and lies opposite the newly relocated **Museum of Craft and Folk Art** (51 Yerba Buena Lane, 227-4888, amocfa.org) on a pedestrian walkway that a few years ago was a grungy alley populated by indigents.

Then there's the **Cartoon Art Museum** on Mission Street (p75), housing some 5,000 pieces of cartoon and animation art. Next door, the **GLBT Historical Society** (657 Mission Street, 777.5455, www.glbthistory.com) collects, preserves, and interprets the history of gay, lesbian, bisexual and transgendered people and mounts exhibitions on history and culture. Across the street, the **California Historical Society** (p75) offers an impressive assemblage of photographs, books, magazines, and paintings on early California, along with a bookshop.

Art galleries, wine bars, restaurants, hip hotels, and a multiplex cinema fill out the eight-block area, which is fast becoming the locus of the city's vibrant arts scene.
Between Market, Folsom, 2nd & 4th streets, www.ybca.org & www.yerbabuena.org.

popular gay bars. Entertainment includes buzz-cut nights, underwear or bare-chest parties, wrestling, leather nights and S&M lessons.

Public

1489 Folsom Street, at 11th Street (552 3065/www.thepublicsf.com). Bus 9, 12, 27, 47. **Open** 6-9.30pm Tue-Thur; 6-10.30pm Fri, Sat. **$$$.**
American. **Map** p76 B5 ⑲
A deft mix of fine-dining sophistication and nightclub energy, Public is built into a historic brick building. American-Italian comfort food is the theme: highlights might include braised duck leg with pappardelle, or pan-roasted ribeye with a balsamic glaze. The stylish bars continue buzzing long after the kitchen closes.

NEW Salt House

545 Mission Street, between 1st & 2nd Streets (543 8900/www.salthouse sf.com). BART & Metro to Montgomery/bus 9, 9X, 10, 12, 14, 30, 45, 76. **Open** 11.30am-11pm Mon-Thur; 11.30am-midnight Fri; 5.30pm-midnight Sat; 5-10pm Sun. **$$$.** **American**. **Map** p77 D2 ⑳
One of the most vibrant new additions to the SF dining scene, built into a loft-style space in a small brick building, the restaurant always looks great, especially at night, when soft glowing light illuminates the noisy crowd as they enjoy the inventive contemporary American cuisine.

Town Hall Restaurant

342 Howard Street, at Fremont Street (908 3900/www.townhallsf.com). BART & Metro to Embarcadero/bus 1, 10, 14, 21, 41, 76. **Open** 11.30am-2.30pm, 5.30-10pm Mon-Thur; 11.30am-2.30pm, 5.30-11pm Fri; 5.30-11pm Sat; 5.30-10pm Sun. **$$$. American**. **Map** p77 E2 ㉑
This little slice of New England, a collaboration between Mitchell and Steven Rosenthal, and legendary front-of-house man Doug Washington, is a great-looking restaurant. The frequently changing menu recalls American classics, often with southern inspiration; high-

lights might include sautéed dayboat scallops or Chimay-seasoned short ribs. The bar is known for its speciality cocktails, including an excellent sazerac.

W Hotel

181 3rd Street, at Howard Street (817 7836/www.starwoodhotels.com). BART & Metro to Montgomery/bus 9X, 12, 30, 45, 76 and Market Street routes. **Open** 7pm-2am Tue-Sat. **Bar**. **Map** p77 D2 ㉒
The two bars at this fashionable hotel (p176) are filled with beautiful people. The first bar is a circular affair in the lobby, while the main room lies behind a beaded curtain above. Some may find the atmosphere a bit competitive, but the scene shifts nightly and banquettes upstairs encourage an intimate vibe.

XYZ

W Hotel, 181 3rd Street, at Howard Street 817 7836/www.xyz-sf.com). BART & Metro to Montgomery/bus 9X, 12, 30, 45, 76. **Open** 6.30-10.30am, 11.30am-2.30pm, 6-10.30pm Mon-Thur; 6.30-10.30am, 11.30am-2.30pm, 6-11pm Fri; 6.30am-2.30pm, 6-11pm Sat; 6.30am-2.30pm, 6-10.30pm Sun. **$$$$.**
American. **Map** p77 D2 ㉓
Adjacent to the lobby of the W, XYZ holds fast to its austere decor and sophisticated clientele. Although a long parage of chefs has worked here, the kitchen has been re-energised recently with a tempting choice of modern Californian fare with Provençal touches.

Nightlife

6ix

60 6th Street, at Jessie Street (863 1221/www.clubsix1.com). BART & Metro to Powell/bus 14, 26 & Market Street routes. **Open** 9pm-2am Tue-Sat. **Admission** $5-$20. **Map** p76 C3 ㉔
Behind the doors of this venue, located on one of the city's grubbiest blocks, you'll find a chill-out room above and bar with a dancefloor below. DJs spin house, dub, dancehall and whatever else may be filling floors at a particular moment. The upstairs space features paintings and photography.

111 Minna

111 Minna Street, between 2nd & New Montgomery Streets (974 1719/www. 111minnagallery.com). BART & Metro to Montgomery/bus 9, 9X, 10, 12, 14, 15, 30, 45, 76 & Market Street routes. **Open** *Gallery* noon-5pm Tue-Fri. *Bar* 5-10pm Wed; 5pm-2am Thur-Sat. **Admission** $3-$15. **Map** p77 D2 ②⑤

An art gallery by day but a truly happening dance club by night, 111 Minna draws an unusual hybrid clientele – serious rave yuppies – but is popular with all kinds of dance-music freaks thanks to a music policy that travels from garage to Afrobeat, stopping at all stations in between.

1015 Folsom

1015 Folsom Street, at 6th Street (431 7444/www. 1015.com). Bus 12, 14X, 27. **Open** 10pm-7am Fri, Sat; other nights vary. **Admission** free-$20. No credit cards. **Map** p76 C4 ②⑥

A meat-and-potatoes dance club, 1015 is always a safe bet. The three rooms each have their own vibe. You'll find the same suburban crowd of pick-up artists and bimbos as in any big club, but they don't overwhelm the place.

Asia SF

201 9th Street, at Howard Street (255 2742/www.asiasf.com). BART & Metro to Civic Center/ streetcar F/bus 12, 14, 19, 26, 47. **Open** *Restaurant* 6.30-10pm Tue, Wed; 6-10.30pm Thur, Sun; 7-11pm Fri; 5-11.15pm Sat. *Club* 7pm-3am Fri, Sat. **$$**. **Map** p76 B4 ②⑦

A restaurant, lounge and club all in one. And those lovely ladies who serve you? They're not. Not women, that is, nor drag queens. The sexy creatures who bring the food and dance seductively atop the long red bar are 'gender illusionists'. The food is inventive Cal-Asian, with small plates and shareable portions. Reservations essential.

DNA Lounge

375 11th Street, between Folson & Harrison Streets (626 1409/www.dna lounge.com). Bus 9, 12, 27, 47. **Open** 9pm-2am Tue-Thur; 9pm-4am Fri, Sat. **Admission** $5-$20. No credit cards. **Map** p76 B5 ②⑧

Goth kids flock to SoMa for all manner of musical fetishes and countercultural indulgences. But none of their nights is complete without a stop in at the DNA Lounge. This long-time fixture now hosts DJ nights and concerts by the likes of Laibach. However, the wonderful stage set-up has turned even hip hop acts on to this gem of a nightspot.

Endup

401 6th Street, at Harrison Street (646 0999/www.theendup.com). Bus 12, 27, 47. **Open** 10pm-4am Thur; 10pm-6am Fri; 6am-1pm, 10pm-4am Sat; 6am-4am Sun. **Admission** free-$20. No credit cards. **Map** p77 D4 ②⑨

A gay fixture since 1973, the Endup boasts all-night house and techno madness on the weekends, plus a Saturday morning club from 6am and the legendary T-Dance from 6am on Sundays, which sees drag queens and straight ravers revelling together.

Mezzanine

444 Jessie Street, at 6th Street (820 9669/www.mezzaninesf.com). BART & Metro to Powell/bus 14, 26 & Market Street routes. **Open** 10pm-2am Fri; 10pm-7am Sat; other nights vary. **Admission** free-$30. No credit cards. **Map** p76 C3 ③⓪

This 900-capacity club and art gallery has two long bars bordering the ample dancefloor and lofty space upstairs. Local DJs and even some live acts hold court on the weekends, while touring techno acts such as Richie Hawtin and Miss Kittin make it their sole stop in SF.

Stud

399 9th Street, at Harrison Street (252 7883/www.studsf.com). Bus 12, 19, 27, 47. **Open** from 5pm daily, closing varies. **Admission** free-$15. No credit cards. **Map** p76 C4 ③①

Now more than 40 years old, the Stud still has dancing every night of the week. The crowd is mainly gay and male, but the club prides itself on being 'omnisexual'. Wondrous Heklina hosts the best drag in town on Tuesdays at Trannyshack; other nights range from queer punk and '80s disco to house.

Life's a drag

Asia SF p83

There are plenty of eyebrow-raising gender benders around San Francisco by day – be on the lookout, especially, for surprise afternoon appearances by the Sisters of Perpetual Indulgence (www.thesisters.org), a 30-year-old organisation whose members dress in nuns' habits and raise money for AIDS awareness.

It's after dark, however, that bars and clubs around the city come alive with a long and storied tradition of feminine illusion, one that stretches back to the 1930s, when the legendary Finocchio's in North Beach became the first official drag bar in the United States.

Drag went mainstream in the 1970s, when the clownish and trippy Cockettes performance troupe mixed cross-dressing with hippie antics and became world-famous, mostly for their disastrous onstage meltdowns.

The dizzy ghosts of the Cockettes still linger over the current scene. Drag in San Francisco is different: messy, confrontational, and hilarious. Queens here are more apt to spit fake blood while lip-synching to Black Sabbath than induce polite applause with tasteful Judy Garland interpretations. Ground Zero for hair-raising performances is **Trannyshack** (www.trannyshack.com), a Tuesday night weekly at the Stud (p83), where prickly godmother Heklina rules over a court of misshapen musical misfits. Heklina's offspring Anna Conda hosts a thrilling – and free – Friday night weekly at the very divey **Cinch Saloon** (1723 Polk Street, 776 4162, www.the cinch.com), with a heavy focus on trash, dazzle, and pratfalls. Another wild child of Heklina, Cookie Dough, plays mistress at the **Cookie Dough Monster Show** (www.cookievision.com), her biweekly star-studded train wreck at Harvey's bar and restaurant (p121) in the Castro.

For a peek at San Francisco drag as it was in its old-school glory days, catch sequin-drenched weekend performances by the grande dames of **Hot Boxxx** at Tenderloin watering hole Aunt Charlie's Lounge (p66), or the many, many boozy glamour blitzes at **Marlena's** (488 Hayes Street, Hayes Valley, 864 6672, www.marlenas barsf.com). Marlena's is even owned by a drag queen, so how can you go wrong?

On Saturdays there are Nude Dude drinks specials and big dick contests.

NEW Temple

540 Howard Street, between 1st & 2nd Streets (978 9942/www.templesf.com). BART & Metro to Montgomery/bus 10, 14, 76 & Market Street routes. **Open** 10pm-4am Fri, Sat; other nights vary. **Map** p77 E2 ❷

This three-storey behemoth, featuring an in-house Thai restaurant and several VIP enclaves, opened in 2007 to great acclaim. Temple's after-hours music programming includes some of the hottest house, techno and hip hop acts performing in a superclub environment.

Arts & leisure

Annie's Social Club

917 Folsom Street, at 5th Street (974 1585/ www.anniessocialclub.com). Bus 9X, 12, 27, 30, 45, 76. **Open** 4pm-2am Mon-Fri; varies Sat, Sun. Show times vary. **Admission** free-$15. No credit cards. **Map** p76 D4 ❸

Annie's Social Club proudly maintains its dive-joint roots. However, it's looking a little smarter these days, and runs a wider spectrum of entertainments: everything from metal to singer-songwriter shows, Britpop nights and punk rock karaoke.

Bike Hut

Pier 40, Embarcadero, at 1st Street (543 4335/www.thebikehut.com). Metro to Brannan/bus 10. **Open** (unless raining) 10am-6pm daily. **Rates** (incl lock & helmet) $5/hr or $20/day. **Map** p77 F3 ❹

This excellent little enterprise, staffed by volunteers, rents and repairs bicycles from a location just south of the Bay Bridge.

Fat City

314 11th Street, at Folsom Street (www.myspace.com/fatcitysf). Bus 9, 12, 27, 47. **Open/shows** times vary. **Admission** free-$15. No credit cards. **Map** p76 B5 ❺

The venue hosts everything from international DJ nights to live metal, rock and comedy. Its new owners wisely retained the exposed red-brick walls and hardwood floors of the sizeable main room.

Hotel Utah

500 4th Street, at Bryant Street (546 6300/www.thehotelutahsaloon.com). Bus 9X, 30, 45, 47, 76. **Open** 11.30am-2am Mon-Fri; 6pm-2am Sat, Sun. **Shows** usually 9pm daily. **Admission** $6-$10. **Map** p77 D3 ❻

The down-and-dirty days of the Barbary Coast are ingrained in the timbers of this 1908 watering hole. Now gaining a fresh lease of life, the Utah is both a characterful bar and a cosy music room.

Ninth Street Independent Film Center

145 Ninth Street, between Mission & Howard Streets (no phone/www.ninth street.org). Bus 14, 19. **Tickets** vary. No credit cards. **Map** p76 B4 ❼

Eight arts organisations banded together to bring the work of independent filmmakers to the public, resulting in this state-of-the-art facility.

Slim's

333 11th Street, between Folsom & Harrison Streets (255 0333/www.slims-sf.com). Bus 9, 12, 27, 47. **Box office** 10.30am-6pm Mon-Fri. **Tickets** $8-$35. **Map** p76 B5 ❽

It may be well known, but the 550-capacity Slim's isn't particularly comfortable: most patrons have to stand, sightlines are compromised by pillars and it can get pretty steamy. The schedule is mostly filled with rock bands, with a few hip hop acts, reggae groups and rootsy singer/songwriters.

Yerba Buena Center for the Arts Theater

701 Mission Street, at 3rd Street (978 2787/ www.ybca.org). BART & Metro to Montgomery/bus 9, 9X, 10, 14, 30, 45, 71, 76. **Box office** noon-5pm Tue, Wed, Fri-Sun; noon-8pm Thur. **Tickets** $20-$100. **Map** p77 D2 ❾

This 757-seat auditorium plays host to some of the most exciting contemporary music and dance companies in the country. Designed by modernist architect

James Stewart Polshek, the exterior of the cube-shaped theatre is covered in aluminium panels that catch the light.

South Beach & South Park

South Beach had been neglected for decades until a tornado of dotcommers arrived in the 1990s. The madness of multimedia gulch has pretty much mellowed, but some remnants of the revival remain. The area is also dominated by the **AT&T Stadium**, home of the San Francisco Giants, and by the **Bay Bridge**, linking San Francisco to the East Bay.

Eating & drinking

Acme Chop House

24 Willie Mays Plaza, corner of King & 3rd Streets (644 0240/www.acmechop house.com). Metro to 2nd & King/bus 9X, 10, 30, 45, 47. **Open** 11am-2.30pm, 5.30-10pm Tue-Fri; 5.30-10pm Sat, Sun. **$$$$. American. Map** p77 F4 ④

A commitment to sustainability and organically raised meat sets Acme apart from most steakhouses. Needless to say, it gets crowded on game days.

Bacar

448 Brannan Street, between 3rd & 4th Streets (904 4100/www.bacar sf.com). Metro to 4th & King/bus 9X, 10, 30, 45, 47, 76. **Open** 5.30-10pm Mon-Thur, Sun; 5.30-11pm Fri, Sat. **$$$. American. Map** p77 E3 ④

The 'wine wall' is the most eye-catching aspect of this converted warehouse, but these days the food is also worth talking about. Wood-fired pizzas are the best bet, although the mesquite-grilled meat, seared diver scallops and the smoked sturgeon are also highlights.

Coco 500

500 Brannan Street, at 4th Street (543 2222/www.coco500.com). Metro to 4th & King. **Open** 11.30am-10pm Mon-Thur; 11.30am-11pm Fri; 5.30-11pm Sat. **$$. Mediterranean. Map** p77 E3 ④

This SoMa restaurant is a reinvention of sorts for its proprietor, Loretta Keller, whose penchant for Parisian hospitality has given way to a small plate style. Med-influenced dishes prepared with organic, today-fresh ingredients range from light pizzas from a wood-fired oven to beef-cheek mole and whole fish with fennel saffron sauce. Seafood, steaks and poultry are also cooked *a la plancha*.

Jack Falstaff

598 2nd Street, at Brannan Street (836 9239/www. plumpjack.com). Metro to 2nd & King/bus 9X, 10, 12, 30, 45, 76. **Open** 11.30am-2pm, 5.30-10pm Mon-Thur; 11.30am-2pm, 5.30-11pm Fri; 5.30-11pm Sat; 5.30-10pm Sun. Also open for lunch on Giants game days Sat, Sun. **$$$. American. Map** p77 E3 ④

This smart restaurant has an urban appeal that doesn't forsake comfort or hospitality. The often-changing menu features reassuring dishes, prepared with organic touches and a slow-food approach. Highlights include pan-roasted Liberty Farms duck and prosciutto-wrapped clay-pot baked monkfish.

South Food & Wine Bar

330 Townsend Street, at 4th Street (974 5599/www.southfwb.com). Metro to 4th & King/bus 9X, 10, 30, 45, 47, 76. **Open** 11.30am-3pm, 5.30-11pm Mon-Fri; 10am-3pm, 5.30-11pm Sat; 10am-3pm Sun. **$$$. International. Map** p77 E4 ④

San Francisco's first dining import from Australia is an intimate 50-seat dazzler with an international vibe and a chef (Luke Mangan) with a reputation for inventiveness and simplicity. Most dishes are imbued with Asian influence: the likes of marinated pork belly with scallops and tamarind dressing, and fish and chips with wasabi mayo.

Tres Agaves

130 Townsend Street, between 2nd & 3rd Streets, (227 0500/www.tres agaves.com). Metro to 2nd & King/ bus 9X, 10, 12, 30, 45, 76. **Open** 11.30am-10pm Mon-Wed; 11.30am-11pm Thur, Fri; 10am-11pm Sat; 10am-10pm Sun. **$$$. Mexican. Map** p77 E3 ④

Catalyst Cocktails p80

SAN FRANCISCO BY AREA

The Tres Agaves is a homage to the Mexican state of Jalisco, home to the town of Tequila. The cavernous brick and timber space houses ample bar space to serve a huge variety of artisan, pure-agave tequilas, while the display kitchen turns out gourmet regional Mexican cuisine around the clock.

Zuppa

564 4th Street, between Bryant & Brannan Streets (777 5900/www. zuppa-sf.com). Metro to 4th & King/ bus 9X, 10, 30, 45, 47, 76. **Open** 11.30am-2.30pm, 5.30-10pm Mon-Thur; 11.30am-2.30pm, 5.30-11pm Fri; 5.30-11pm Sat; 5.30-9pm Sun. **$$$. Italian.** **Map** p77 E3 ㊻

Despite the long banquettes and the post-work young professionals and adventurous Mission hipsters who sit in them, it's the rustic, fresh-made southern Italian cuisine that really steals the show at Zuppa, especially the house-cured meats and seasonal dishes that use ingredients from the rooftop garden. The wine list is all-Italian.

Nightlife

330 Ritch

330 Ritch Street, between Brannan & Townsend Streets (541 9574). Metro N to 2nd & King/bus 9X, 10, 30, 45, 47, 76. **Open** 5pm-2am Wed-Fri; 10pm-2am Sat, Sun. **Admission** free-$10. **Map** p77 E3 ㊼

A spacious yet intimate spot. Sounds include hip hop and classic soul. Popscene, on Thursdays, is a Britpop night that often features touring bands.

Arts & leisure

AT&T Park

24 Willie Mays Plaza, at 3rd & King Streets (972 2000/www.sfgiants.com). Metro to 2nd & King/bus 9X, 10, 30, 45. **Open** Box office 8.30am-5.30pm Mon-Fri; 2hrs before game Sat, Sun. **Tickets** $10-$110. **Map** p77 F4 ㊽

Home of the San Francisco Giants baseball team. Old-fashioned design and Bay views combine to create one of the most beautiful sports stadia in the country.

Chinatown Gate p92

Nob Hill & Chinatown

Nob Hill & Polk Gulch

Overlooking the Tenderloin
and Union Square, the Nob Hill
neighbourhood was named after
the wealthy nabobs – as they
were known – who built their
mansions on the steep hill after
the cable car started making the
ascent in the 1870s.

At the base of Nob Hill's western
slopes, the stretch of Polk Street
between Geary and Washington
Streets comprises a small
neighbourhood known as Polk
Gulch. Once the city's gay mecca,
the area fell on hard times in the
1970s and gained an unsavoury
reputation. Today, the ambience
has mellowed, with shops and
restaurants crowding every block.

Sights & museums

Cable Car Museum

*1201 Mason Street, at Washington
Street (474 1887/www.cablecar
museum.org). Bus 1, 9, 12, 30,
45/cable car Powell-Hyde or Powell-
Mason.* **Open** *Oct-Mar* 10am-5pm
daily. *Apr-Sept* 10am-6pm daily.
Admission free. **Map** pp89 B2 ➊
Find out how the cars work, and view
the cable-winding machinery that actually powers them. You'll also learn about
emergency procedures and the work-
manship that goes into each car. Vintage
cable cars, associated artefacts and
dozens of old photos complete matters.

Grace Cathedral

*1100 California Street, at Taylor Street
(749 6300/www.gracecathedral.org).
Bus 1, 2, 3, 4, 27/cable car California.*

Open 7am-6pm Mon-Fri, Sun; 8am-6pm
Sat. *Tours* 1-3pm Mon-Fri; 11.30am-
1.30pm Sat; 12.30-2pm Sun. **Admission**
donation requested. **Map** p82 B2 **2**
Begun in 1928, this Episcopalian cathedral was once a private mansion. The
façade is modelled on Paris's Notre
Dame, and other features include a fine
rose window and gilded bronze portals
made from casts of the Doors of
Paradise in Florence's Baptistery.
Murals depict the founding of the
United Nations and the burning of
Grace's predecesso. Two massive
labyrinths, based on the 13th-century
example at Chartres, allow visitors to
wander in a contemplative manner.

Eating & drinking

Cinch
*1723 Polk Street, between Clay &
Washington Streets, Polk Gulch (776
4162/www.thecinch.com). Bus 1, 12,*
19, 27, 47, 49, 76/cable car California.
Open 6am-2am daily. No credit cards.
Bar. **Map** p89 A2 **3**
A double-shot of old-school San
Francisco gay bar, circa 1979. With an
ostensible Western theme, this comfortably ramshackle haunt harks back
to the days when this stretch of Polk
Street was a more rough-and-tumble
area. A tiered smoking patio out back
is perfect for slurred conversation.

Le Colonial
*20 Cosmo Place, between Jones &
Taylor Streets (931 3600/www.le
colonialsf.com). Bus 2, 3, 4, 27, 38, 76.*
Open 4.30-10pm Mon-Wed, Sun; 4.30-
11pm Thur-Sat. **Bar**. **Map** p89 B3 **4**
Designed to approximate Vietnam in
its colonial era, this elegant hideaway
has a sizeable dining room, while the
stylish upstairs lounge serves tropical
drinks, exotic teas and a menu high-
lighting Vietnamese fusion cuisine.

© Copyright Time Out Group 2008

Dining Room

Ritz-Carlton Hotel, 600 Stockton Street, at California Street (773 6198/www. ritzcarlton.com). Bus 1, 15, 30, 45/cable car California. **Open** 6-9pm Tue-Thur; 5.30-9.30pm Fri, Sat. **$$$$. French.** **Map** p89 B2 **⑤**

The Dining Room has a global reputation and a waitstaff-to-diner ratio of almost 1:1. It's opulent without being over the top, although it can feel a little serious. The modern French menu is inventive and artfully executed by chef Ron Siegel, as are the famous seasonal speciality menus, such as the annual white truffle festival.

Fleur de Lys

777 Sutter Street, between Jones & Taylor Streets (673 7779/www.fleurde lyssf.com). Bus 2, 3, 4, 27, 38, 76. **Open** 6-9.30pm Mon-Thur; 5.30-10.30pm Fri; 5-10.30pm Sat. **$$$$. French.** **Map** p89 B3 **⑥**

A fine dining experience so memorable it's been duplicated in Las Vegas. Chef Hubert Keller's cuisine is deserving of a wider audience because of his vast repertoire: his menu is lush, even exorbitant. It all plays out like a symphony, a feast for the eyes as much as the palate.

Hidden Vine

1/2 Cosmo Place, at Taylor & Post Streets (674 3567/www.thehidden vine.com). Bus 2, 3, 4, 27, 38, 76. **Open** 5pm-midnight Tue-Thur; 5pm-2am Fri, Sat. **Bar.** **Map** p89 B3 **⑦**

Hidden is the operative word for this extremely cosy, husband-and-wife-owned wine bar that offers over 30 wines by the glass and 100 by the bottle. The thoughtfully conceived menu features numerous flights, allowing wine lovers to explore various varietals and regions. Cheese, crackers and charcuterie to complement the wine.

Red Room

827 Sutter Street, between Jones & Leavenworth Streets (346 7666). Bus 2, 3, 4, 27, 38, 76. **Open** 7pm-2am Tue-Thur, Sat; 5pm-2am Fri. No credit cards. **Bar.** **Map** p89 A3 **⑧**

Enough to inspire a craving in any vampire, this slick hotel bar is blood red: the walls, the tables, the semicircular bar, even one of the many speciality martinis. It's wildly popular but tiny – an uncomfortable combination at weekends. Best to come during the week.

Swan Oyster Depot

1517 Polk Street, between California & Sacramento Streets (673 1101). Bus 1, 19, 47, 49, 76/cable car California. **Open** 8am-5.30pm Mon-Sat. **$$$.** No credit cards. **Fish & seafood.** **Map** p89 A2 **⑨**

Don't miss this Polk Gulch institution: half fish market, half counter-service hole in the wall, it has been delighting locals since 1912. The best time to visit is between November and June, when the local Dungeness crab is in season. But at any time of year, the selections are straight-from-the-water fresh. Specialities include clam chowder and an obscenely large variety of oysters. You can buy shellfish to take away.

Tonga Room & Hurricane Bar

Fairmont, 950 Mason Street, between California & Sacramento Streets (772 5278/www.fairmont.com). Bus 1/cable car California, Powell-Hyde or Powell-Mason. **Open** 5pm-midnight Mon-Thur, Sun; 5pm-1am Fri, Sat. **Bar.** **Map** p89 B2 **⑩**

Despite the all-you-can-eat happy-hour dim sum, the sarong-clad waitresses and the enormous, exotic cocktails, the real attraction at this long-lived tiki bar is the spectacle of house musicians performing off-key covers of cheesy pop songs while afloat on a raft on the indoor 'lagoon'. There's even a thunderstorm every 20 minutes, with rain.

Top of the Mark

Inter-Continental Hotel Mark Hopkins, 1 Nob Hill, at California & Mason Streets (392 3434/www.topofthemark. com). Bus 1/cable car California, Powell-Hyde or Powell-Mason. **Open** 5pm-midnight Mon-Thur, Sun; 4pm-1am Fri, Sat. **Admission** $10 after 8pm Fri, Sat. **Bar.** **Map** p89 B2 **⑪**

Neatly named for its location at the summit of the InterContinental Mark Hopkins Hotel, Top of the Mark offers spectacular panoramic views. It's worth a quick visit to check them out and sip a cocktail from the extensive martini menu, but arrive early to avoid the cover charge and the dress code.

Arts & leisure

Red Devil Lounge

1695 Polk Street, at Clay Street, Polk Gulch (921 1695/www.reddevil lounge.com). Bus 1, 19, 27, 47, 49, 76. **Open** usually 8pm-2am daily. **Shows** usually 9pm daily. **Admission** $3-$30. **Map** p89 A2 ⑫

A venue done out with Gothic touches, the Red Devil has recently ramped up its music offerings, which sit alongside club nights in a fairly busy calendar. The line-ups aren't often cutting edge, but the venue has staged crowd-pulling acts like the Misfits and KRS-One.

SF Playhouse

533 Sutter Street, between Powell & Mason Streets, Nob Hill (677 9596/ www.sfplayhouse.org). Bus 2, 3, 4, 9X, 27, 38, 76/cable car Powell-Hyde or Powell-Mason. **Tickets** $20-$38. **Map** p89 B3 ⑬

A modest-sized repertory house known for its sophistication, the Playhouse consistently attracts prime local talent for its mix of revivals and edgy pre-mières. There's also an end-of-season musical, but you are likely to do well with anything on the programme.

Chinatown

The 1849 Gold Rush drew shiploads of Cantonese to California. The excitement didn't last, but many immigrants stayed. The Chinatown that grew up in San Francisco soon developed a reputation for vice, with cheap hookers, well-stocked opium dens and all-hours gambling. The crowded streets and dark alleys of Chinatown – bordered today by Bush Street to the south, Broadway to the north, and Powell and Kearny Streets from west to east – still evoke an earlier era. Some 10,000 Chinese still live in in the area.

Today, Chinatown feels like two distinct neighbourhoods. Along **Grant Avenue**, one of the two main north–south drags, store owners target tourists with plastic Buddhas and bright fabrics; conversely, little English is spoken at the ornate temples and food stalls on and near **Stockton Street**.

Sights & Museums

Bank of Canton

743 Washington Street, Portsmouth Square. Bus 1, 9, 12, 30, 45/cable car Powell-Hyde or Powell-Mason. **Map** p89 C2 ⑭

One of the most photographed spots in Chinatown. The pagoda-like structure was built in 1909 as the Chinese American Telephone Exchange; for

Grace Cathedral p89

Red Blossom Tea Company

four decades, multilingual operators routed calls throughout Chinatown by memory alone, since there was no area phone directory.

Chinatown Gate

Grant Avenue & Bush Street. Bus 1, 9, 12, 30, 45/cable car Powell-Hyde or Powell-Mason. **Map** p89 C2 ⑮
The dragon-topped Chinatown Gate heralds the southern entrance to Chinatown. A gift from Taiwan in 1970, the green-tiled portal is made to a traditional design, with a quotation from Confucius that urges passers-by to work for the common good.

Chinese American National Museum & Learning Center

965 Clay Street, between Stockton & Powell Streets (391 1188/www.chsa. org). Bus 1, 9, 12, 30, 45/cable car Powell-Hyde or Powell-Mason. **Open** noon-5pm Tue-Fri; noon-4pm Sat. **Admission** $3; $2 reductions; $1 6-17s; free 1st Thur of mth. **Map** p89 B2 ⑯
This long-established facility is now housed in the historic Chinese YWCA building, designed by renowned local architect Julia Morgan and completed

in 1932. Its mission is the promotion of an understanding of Chinese American history. Displays follow California's Chinese population from the frontier years to the Gold Rush, through the building of the railroads and the Barbary Coast opium dens.

Kong Chow Temple

855 Stockton Street, between Sacramento & Clay Streets (788 1339). Bus 9X, 12, 20, 30, 41, 45/cable car Powell-Mason. **Open** 9am-4pm Mon-Sat. **Map** p89 C2 ⑰
One of the oldest religious structures in San Francisco, the Kong Chow Temple, established in 1857, moved to its present home on the fourth floor of the Chinatown Post Office in 1977. Divination sticks, red satin banners and flowers flank a fabulous altar from which a statue of the god Kuan Ti has a keen view of the Bay.

Old St Mary's Cathedral

660 California Street, at Grant Avenue (288 3800/www.oldsaintmarys.org). Bus 1, 9X, 30, 45/cable car California. **Open** 7am-4.30pm Mon-Fri; 10am-6pm Sat; 7.30am-3pm Sun. **Admission** free. **Map** p89 C2 ⑱

Much early missionary work, and the city's first English lessons for Chinese immigrants, took place under this 19th-century building's foreboding clock tower: 'Son, observe the time and fly from evil', it warns. Lunchtime concerts are staged in the cathedral's dainty yet glorious interior.

Eating & drinking

Alfred's Steakhouse
659 Merchant Street, between Kearny & Montgomery Streets (781 7058/ www.alfredssteakhouse.com). Bus 1, 9X, 10, 12, 20, 30, 41, 45. **Open** 5-9pm Mon, Sat, Sun; 11.30am-9pm Tue-Thur; 11.30am-10pm Fri. **$$$.** **American**. Map p89 C1 ⑲
With decades of experience as one of the city's best steakhouses, Alfred's feels like a bit of San Francisco gone by, but it continues to prove itself worthy of a fiercely loyal fanbase. The bar, which mixes superlative martinis, stocks more than 100 single malts.

Li Po
916 Grant Avenue, at Washington Street (982 0072). Bus 1, 9X, 12, 20, 30, 41, 45. **Open** 2pm-2am daily. No credit cards. **Bar**. Map p89 C1 ⑳
A fun spot for a pick-me-up when you're done with the junk shops on Grant Avenue. Li Po is basically a dive, but the cave façade and giant, tattered Chinese lantern inside set it nicely apart from its neighbours. It'll take you back to Barbary Coast-era San Francisco with no risk of being shanghaied by anything except the potent cocktails.

Mr Bing's
201 Columbus Avenue, at Pacific Avenue (362 1545). Bus 9X, 12, 20, 30, 41, 45. **Open** noon-2am daily. No credit cards. **Bar**. Map p89 C1 ㉑
This shambles of a bar doesn't look like much from the outside, and looks like even less once you're inside. But is a prince among dives, frequented by a mix of idling Chinese, haggard old North Beach bums and those who are simply desperate for a drink.

R&G Lounge
631 Kearny Street, between Clay & Sacramento Streets (982 7877/www. rnglounge.com). Bus 1, 9X, 10, 12, 20, 30, 41, 45. **Open** 11am-9.30pm daily. **$$**. **Chinese**. Map p89 C2 ㉒
Always busy and often chaotic, R&G Lounge has two levels for dining, neither of them much to look at. The Hong Kong-style food is authentic, emphasising seafood that's taken mainly from the in-house tanks. People come from miles around for the deep-fried salt and pepper crab and barbecue pork.

Yuet Lee
1300 Stockton Street, at Broadway (982 6020). Bus 9X, 12, 20, 30, 41, 45/cable car Powell-Mason. **Open** 11am-3am Mon, Wed-Sun. **$$**. **Chinese**. Map p89 B1 ㉓
Terrific seafood and late hours attract folk to this tiny, bright-green eaterie. Roasted squab with fresh coriander and lemon, sautéed clams with black bean sauce, and 'eight precious noodle soup', made with eight kinds of meat, are all worth trying. Lighting is glaring and service matter-of-fact.

Shopping

Red Blossom Tea Company
831 Grant Avenue, between Washington & Clay Streets (395 0868/www.red blossomtea.com). Bus 1, 9, 15/cable car California. **Open** 10am-6.30pm Mon-Sat; 10am-6pm Sun. Map p89 C2 ㉔
Red Blossom has been in the tea business for more than two decades, and it shows. There's a selection of more than 100 teas, and you can get advice on the art of proper brewing.

Sam Bo Trading Co
38 Waverley Place, between Sacramento & Clay Streets (397 2998). Bus 1, 12, 15, 30, 41, 45/cable car Powell-Hyde or Powell-Mason. **Open** 9.30am-6pm daily. Map p89 C2 ㉕
A tiny shop selling Buddhist and Taoist religious items: ceremonial candles, incense and intriguing paper goods that are to be burned in honour of ancestors or to request a favour of the gods.

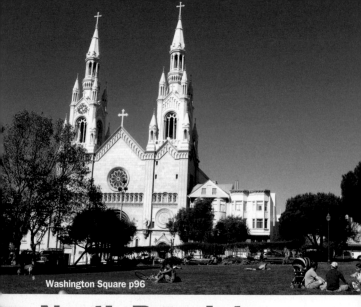
Washington Square p96

North Beach to Fisherman's Wharf

Among San Francisco's many notable neighbourhoods, North Beach is one of the best known, a popular destination for tourists, beloved by locals and an integral part of the Old Barbary Coast. Home to the legendary City Lights bookstore and a variety of cafés, the area is deeply bound to the Beat movement of the 1950s.

To the north of North Beach is an area looked upon by locals with something approaching despair. Once a genuine fishing port, Fisherman's Wharf is now a dreary tourist trap. And looking down on all this tomfoolery are the residents of Russian Hill, one of the city's richest neighbourhoods and also, it stands to reason, among its nicest.

North Beach

Much of North Beach's history and many of its treasures lie along **Columbus Avenue**, and especially close to the three-way junction of Columbus, Broadway and Grant Avenue that represents North Beach's beating heart. Even after the Beat Generation had come and gone, the area maintained its reputation for individualism and artistic endeavour. In the early '60s, nightclubs such as the Purple Onion and the Hungry i showcased an array of boundary-pushing comedians such as Woody Allen and Lenny Bruce.

The area of Broadway between Columbus Avenue and Montgomery

North Beach & Around

A **B** **C**

Ferries to
North Bay

1

Pier
39

Cruise Ship
Terminal

Ferries
Alcat

45 31

47 Fisherman's 32
Wharf

43 41

35

33

28

2

Hyde Street
Pier 29

Aquatic
Park

34 THE EMBARCADERO

JEFFERSON STREET

THE EMBARCADERO

National
Maritime
Museum

The Cannery

The Anchorage

BEACH STREET

30

35

Cable
Car

NORTH POINT STREET

STOCKTON STREET

FISHERMAN'S

33

37
36 PH

WHARF

Cable
Car

BAY STREET

TELEGRAPH
HILL

Ghirardelli
Square

BAY STREET

San Francisco
Art Institute

COLUMBUS

FRANCISCO STREET

Russian
Hill Park

38

24

CHESTNUT STREET

North
Beach
Playground

Coit
Tower

1

LOMBARD STREET

AVE

PM

NORTH

8

Lombard
Street

GREENWICH STREET

BEACH

21

STOCKTON STREET

GRANT AVENUE

RUSSIAN
HILL

LEAVENWORTH STREET

JONES STREET

TAYLOR STREET

FILBERT STREET

Washington
Square

10

9

14
22
23

KEARNY ST

MONTGOMERY ST

101

POLK STREET

LARKIN STREET

HYDE STREET

UNION STREET

MASON STREET

POWELL STREET

1 2
25

9 3

17

COLUMBUS

4

27 5

RHODE ISLAND

Macchia
Steps

3

GREEN STREET

Ina Coolbrith
Park

VALLEJO STREET

12

15 26
19 18 13

Jacks
Squa

40
39

42 PH

BROADWAY

20

16

KEROUAC ALLEY

AVE

41

VAN NESS AVENUE

BROADWAY

PACIFIC AVENUE

PH

CHINATOWN

Chinese
Culture
Center

JACKSON STREET

Cable Car
Museum

PM

WAVERLY PLACE

Portsmouth
Square

POLK
GULCH

CLAY STREET

NOB
HILL

PH

SACRAMENTO STREET

Old St Mary's
Cathedral

Bank
Amer

Haas-
Lilienthal
House

Huntington
Park

C

CALIFORNIA STREET

Grace
Cathedral

PINE STREET

MASON STREET

Chinatown
Gateway

Cable
Car

St Francis
Memorial Hospital

AUSTIN

BUSH STREET

LARKIN STREET

LEAVENWORTH ST

SUTTER STREET

MASON ST

POST

KEARNY ST

GRANT AVE

LANE

0   500 m
0   500 yds

' Copyright Time Out Group 2008

1 Sights & museums
1 Eating & drinking
1 Shopping
1 Nightlife
1 Arts & leisure

Street is lined with nighclubs with strippers and sexy floorshows.

Heading north along Columbus is **Washington Square**, a lovely patch of greenery overlooked by the white stucco Romanesque Church of St Peter and St Paul.

Sights & museums

Coit Tower

Peak of Telegraph Hill, at the end of Telegraph Hill Boulevard (362 0808). Bus 39. **Open** 10am-5pm daily. **Admission** Elevator $4.50. No credit cards. **Map** p95 C3 ❶

This 210ft concrete turret, built by City Hall architect Arthur Brown in 1933, was a gift to the city from the eccentric Lillie Hitchcock Coit. The spectacular views from the top aren't the tower's only attraction. Under the supervision of Diego Rivera, some wonderful murals were created here. See box.

Eating & drinking

Caffe Puccini

411 Columbus Avenue, at Vallejo Street (989 7033). Bus 9X, 12, 20, 30, 41, 45/cable car Powell-Mason. **Open** 6am-11.30pm Mon-Fri, Sun; 6am-12.30am Sat. **$**. No credit cards. **Café**. **Map** p95 C3 ❷

Like the composer after whom the café is named, friendly owner Graziano Lucchese is from Lucca in northern Italy. His welcoming café serves vast sandwiches stuffed with salami, prosciutto and mortadella.

Caffe Roma

526 Columbus Avenue, at Union Street (296 7942/www.cafferoma.com). Bus 9X, 12, 20, 30, 39, 41, 45/cable car Powell-Mason. **Open** 6am-7pm Mon-Thur; 6am-8pm Fri; 6.30am-11pm Sat; 7am-8pm Sun. **Café**. **Map** p95 C3 ❸

Some say it's the strongest coffee in the city – it's certainly the most coveted, roasted on the premises by three generations of the Azzollini family. A range of *gelati* is also served in the large, airy space.

Caffe Trieste

601 Vallejo Street, at Grant Avenue (982 2605/ www.caffetrieste.com). Bus 9X, 12, 20, 30, 39, 41, 45. **Open** 6.30am-11pm Mon-Thur, Sun; 6.30am-midnight Fri, Sat. **$**. No credit cards. **Café**. **Map** p95 C3 ❹

One of the city's great cafés, a former hangout for Kerouac and Ginsberg, and where Coppola is said to have written the screenplay for *The Godfather*. The dark walls are plastered with photos of opera singers and famous regulars. There are muffins, pastries and sandwiches to eat, and the lattes are legendary, as are the Saturday afternoon opera sessions.

House

1230 Grant Avenue, at Columbus Avenue & Vallejo Street (986 8612/www.thehse.com). Bus 9X, 12, 20, 30, 39, 41, 45. **Open** 11.30am-2.30pm, 5.30-10pm Mon-Thur; 11.30am-2.30pm, 5.30-11pm Fri; 11.30am-2.30pm, 5-11pm Sat; 5-10pm Sun. **$$**. **Asian**. **Map** p95 C3 ❺

This no-frills (though often extremely noisy) Chinese fusion dining room works wonders with fresh, seasonal produce and East-meets-West preparations. The menu changes often, resisting trends while remaining decidedly sophisticated.

Iluna Basque

701 Union Street, at Powell Street (402 0011/ www.ilunabasque.com). Bus 9X, 12, 20, 30, 39, 41, 45/cable car Powell-Mason. **Open** 5.30-10.30pm Mon-Thur, Sun; 5.30-11.30pm Fri, Sat. **$$**. **International**. **Map** p95 B3 ❻

With views of Washington Square and Coit Tower, this lively restaurant has become a fast favourite among locals, as much for its fun atmosphere as for its memorable Basque-influenced tapas.

Impala

501 Broadway, at Kearny Street (982 5299/www.impalasf.com). Bus 9X, 10, 12, 20, 30, 41, 45. **Open** 5.30-11pm Tue-Sat. **$$$**. **Mexican**. **Map** p95 C3 ❼

This chic restaurant aims to raise Mexican cuisine to a higher level and,

Art and activism

Recent times have seen a revival of interest in the Mexican artist **Diego Rivera**. San Francisco is home to three of his murals – all now accessible to the public free of charge. He was also involved in the creation of other murals in the city, notably at Coit Tower.

Rivera was at the peak of his powers when he created his San Francisco projects. They are some of his most significant surviving works, an expression of his radical sympathies and those of the era.

Rivera's first mural in America, *The Allegory of California* (1931), is located at the **City Club of San Francisco** (55 Sansome Street, 10th floor, 362 2480, www.city clubsf.com). It may seem ironic that Rivera, a committed Marxist, should create a 'public'-style work for a private gentlemen's club. But Rivera trod lightly with his first US work. Little of its content is controversial and his trademark razor wit was notably muted.

His next mural was at the then California School of Fine Arts, now the **San Francisco Art Institute** (800 Chestnut Street, between Jones & Leavenworth Streets, North Beach, 771 7020, www. sfai.edu). His *The Making of a Fresco Showing the Building of San Francisco* was his first truly public piece in the US, and it drew vast crowds to its unveiling. It was significant in that it portrayed not the standard neo-classical Roman hero figures or abstractions of various virtues in the form of nymphs and gods, but workers bent to their tasks, including a rear view of the artist himself. Evidently Rivera felt confident enough to reveal his true sympathies.

His sympathies were to become clearer still when Rivera received a commission from the New Deal's Works Progress Administration to supervise the creation of murals on **Coit Tower** (pictured). The images were so controversial that their 1934 unveiling was delayed so that an errant hammer and sickle could be erased.

Rivera's largest and most ambitious mural, T*he Pan American Unity Mural* at the **City College of San Francisco** in south San Francisco (50 Phelan Avenue, 452-5201, www.riveramural.com) is regarded as one of the finest examples of his work. Five massive panels, spanning 1,800 square feet, trace the history of the North American continent from the prehistory of Mexico on its far left, to the advance of the industrial age in the middle panel, to the shaping (or raping) of the land and the labours of various American inventors on its right.

in many aspects, it succeeds. Mains focus on fish dishes, slow-roasted meats and Mexican classics; the crowd eats them up with as much enthusiasm as it does the lounge-style atmosphere, a combination of candlelight and DJ-spun music. The bar is open until 2am.

Mama's on Washington Square

1701 Stockton Street, at Filbert Street (362 6421/www.mamas-sf.com). Bus 9X, 12, 20, 30, 39, 41, 45/cable car Powell-Mason. **Open** 8am-3pm Tue-Sun. **$**. No credit cards. **Café**. Map p95 C3 ❽

The weekend queue is part of the fun at this wildly popular North Beach mainstay. Once seated, you'll be faced with such temptations as a giant made-to-order 'm'omelette' or the Monte Cristo sandwich on home-made bread.

Mario's Bohemian Cigar Store

566 Columbus Avenue, at Union Street (362 0536). Bus 9X, 12, 20, 30, 39, 41, 45/cable car Powell-Mason. **Open** 10am-11pm daily. **$**. **Café**. Map pp95 C3 ❾

You can't buy a cigar at Mario's, nor will you be allowed to smoke one. Instead, sip a flavoured Italian soda and peruse a light menu of focaccia sandwiches and salads, own-made biscotti, beer and coffee. Mario's is always packed, so lunch may be slow in coming, but there's no more essential North Beach café.

Moose's

1652 Stockton Street, between Union & Filbert Streets (989 7800/www. mooses.com). Bus 9X, 20, 30, 39, 41, 45/cable car Powell-Mason. **Open** 5.30-10pm Mon-Sat; 10.30am-2.30pm, 5.30-10pm Sun. **$$$**. **American**. Map p95 C3 ❿

This Washington Square staple was long the haunt of local politicos and bon vivants, and it's hoped that a recent refurbishment will return its original lustre. The new, comfy-looking design brings with it a new chef and updated menu.

Rogue Ale's Public House

673 Union Street, between Powell Street & Columbus Avenue (362 7880/ www.rogue.com). Bus 9X, 20, 30, 39, 41, 45. **Open** 3pm-midnight Mon-Thur; noon-2am Fri, Sat; noon-midnight Sun. **Bar**. Map p95 C3 ⓫

Oregon microbrewery Rogue Ale's bold land grab is evidenced by this ale house, devoted to its staggering array of brews. The standard selection of ambers and lagers is supplemented by such gems as chilli-pepper-tinged Chipotle Ale.

Rosewood

732 Broadway, between Stockton & Powell Streets (951 4886/www. rosewoodbar.com). Bus 9X, 12, 20, 30, 41, 45. **Open** 5.30pm-2am Tue-Fri; 7pm-2am Sat. **Bar**. Map p95 C3 ⓬

This stylish bar boasts rosewood panelling and is furnished with low black leather benches. It hasn't been overrun, and remains one of the best places in the city to sip a cocktail while DJs spin low-key tunes.

San Francisco Brewing Company

155 Columbus Avenue, at Pacific Avenue (434 3344/www.sf brewing.com). Bus 9X, 12, 20, 30, 41, 45. **Open** noon-1.30am daily. **Bar**. Map p95 C4 ⓭

Housed in a restored 1907 saloon, this brewpub offers microbrews, pub grub and even free tours. Formerly the Andromeda Saloon, it was here that gangster 'Baby Face' Nelson was allegedly captured. It's hard to pass up the $1 brews from 4pm to 6pm and midnight to 1am.

Savoy Tivoli

1434 Grant Avenue, between Green & Union Streets (362 7023/www. savoy-tivoli.netfirms.com). Bus 9X, 12, 20, 30, 39, 41, 45. **Open** 6pm-2am Tue-Thur; 5pm-2am Fri; 3pm-2am Sat. No credit cards. **Bar**. Map p95 C3 ⓮

Opened in 1906, this long-established bar tends to get packed with Marina-ites on warm, weekend nights due to the expanse of outdoor seating out front, but when things are a bit slower it's a perfect place to grab a beer and enjoy the weather or perhaps play a few games of pool.

Spec's

12 William Saroyan Place, at Broadway & Columbus Avenue (421 4112). Bus 9X, 12, 20, 30, 41, 45. **Open** 4.30pm-2am Mon-Fri; 5pm-2am Sat, Sun. No credit cards. **Bar. Map** p95 C3 ⑮
Spec's really is the quintessential old-school San Francisco bar: one part North Beach bohemian and one part Wild West saloon, with a dash of weirdness thrown in for good measure. It's tucked away in a false alley (you'll see what we mean), with nearly every inch covered with dusty detritus from around the world.

Tommaso's Ristorante Italiano

1042 Kearny Street, at Pacific Avenue (398 9696/www.tommasosnorth beach.com). Bus 9X, 10, 12, 20, 30, 41, 45. **Open** 5-10.30pm Tue-Sat; 4-9.30pm Sun. **$$. Italian. Map** p95 C4 ⑯
Tommaso's is known city-wide for its simple Italian food, which has been served family-style in a tiny, boisterous room since 1935. The wood-fired pizzas and calzones deserve their reps and the house red is surprisingly good. No affectations, no frills and no reservations. Join the queue and keep your eyes peeled: you never know who might walk in.

Tony Nik's

1524 Stockton Street, at Green Street (693 0990). Bus 9X, 12, 20, 30, 39, 41, 45. **Open** 4pm-2am daily. **Bar. Map** p95 C3 ⑰
This venerable lounge, which is essentially a long bar with a few extra seats, opened the day after Prohibition was repealed, and keeps the old-time vibe alive thanks to Atomic Age decor and comfortably hip and friendly environs. Cocktails are a serious business here: there's always a surprise lurking behind the bar if the right mixologist is on duty.

Home brew

San Franciscans appreciate quality, and if a product is crafted locally and lovingly so much the better. And what better way to enjoy craft and quality than one pint at a time at one of the local brewpubs that have sprung up around the city, making and serving their own beer, along with great food?

The rise of the brewpub began back in 1985 when North Beach's **San Francisco Brewing Company** (p98) became one of only three brewpubs in the US and the first in San Francisco. Haight Street favourite **Magnolia Pub and Brewery** (p130) is also one of the old school, having recently celebrated its tenth anniversary. It brews excellent, unique cask ales to complement its gourmet pub grub menu. Each February Magnolia and SoMa brewpub **21st Amendment** (563 2nd Street, 369 0900) play host to Strong Beer Month, featuring such brews as Magnolia's potent 11.2% ABV Old Thunderpussy Barleywine and 21st Amendment's formidable Hendrik's Russian Imperial Espresso Stout.

Meanwhile, on the edge of the Pacific, are two brewpubs in one: **Beach Chalet** and **Park Chalet** (p142). Overlooking Ocean Beach, the Beach Chalet has the dramatic sea and sunset views. Park Chalet, facing into Golden Gate Park, opens on to an expansive lawn, perfect for lounging in the sun, sipping home-made beer surrounded by the park's verdant landscape. What could be more San Francisco?

Tosca Café

242 Columbus Avenue, between Broadway & Pacific Avenue (986 9651). Bus 9X, 12, 20, 30, 41, 45. **Open** 5pm-2am Mon-Sat; 7pm-2am Sun. No credit cards.

Café. Map p95 C4 ⑱

Formica-topped tables, massive copper espresso machines, Caruso warbling from an ancient jukebox… bars with interiors this lush deserve to double as movie sets. The house speciality, a blend of coffee, steamed milk and brandy, really packs a punch.

Vesuvio

255 Columbus Avenue, between Broadway & Pacific Avenue (362 3370/www.vesuvio.com). Bus 9X, 12, 20, 30, 41, 45. **Open** 6am-2am daily.

Bar. Map p95 C4 ⑲

A funky old saloon with a stained-glass façade, Vesuvio preserves the flavour of the bars of an earlier era. It's next to the famous City Lights bookshop, and its walls are covered with Beat memorabilia.

Shopping

City Lights

261 Columbus Avenue, at Jack Kerouac Alley, between Broadway & Pacific Avenue (362 8193/www.citylights.com). Bus 12, 15, 30, 41, 45. **Open** 10am-midnight daily. **Map** p95 C3 ⑳

The legacy of Beat anti-authoritarianism lives on in this publishing company and bookshop, co-founded by poet Lawrence Ferlinghetti in 1953. Be sure to head upstairs to the Poetry Annex, where books by the Beats sit beside contemporary small-press works and the photocopied ravings of 'shroom-addled hippies, raging punks and DIY indie voices. Readings here are real events.

Graffeo Coffee Roasting Company

735 Columbus Avenue, between Filbert & Greenwhich Streets (1-800 222 6250/ 986 2429). Bus 15, 30, 39, 41, 45/ cable car Powell-Mason. **Open** 9am-6pm Mon-Fri; 9am-5pm Sat. **Map** p95 B3 ㉑

Cafe Trieste p96

If you're awake, you'll smell it. This San Francisco institution stocks fresh coffee from various plantations around the world, roasting its beans right on the premises.

Macchiarini Creative Design

1453 Grant Avenue, between Green & Union Streets (982 2229/www.ma creativedesign.com). Bus 12, 15, 30, 41, 45. **Open** 10am-6pm Tue-Sat; also by appointment. **Map** p95 C3 ㉒

Three generations of the Macchiarini family have been crafting African-inspired jewellery for more than 70 years. They also do custom wedding rings, sculpture and calligraphy. So old-school they even have a set of North Beach steps named after them.

Ooma

1422 Grant Avenue, between Green & Union Streets (627 6963). Bus 15, 30, 39, 41, 45. **Open** 11am-7pm Tue-Sat; noon-5pm Sun. **Map** p95 C3 ㉓

The name stands for 'Objects of My Affection'; owners Glenda and Jessica have a fine eye for the latest local designer threads, making it all but impossible to leave empty-handed. 'Flirty' pretty much sums up the whimsical fashions on offer.

Arts & entertainment

Bimbo's 365 Club

1025 Columbus Avenue, at Chestnut Street (474 0365/www.bimbos365 club.com). Bus 10, 20, 30/cable car Powell-Mason. **Box office** 10am-4pm Mon-Fri. **Tickets** $15-$50. No credit cards. **Map** p95 B2 🟤

This old venue has been nicely preserved, with a mermaid theme running throughout. Rita Hayworth once worked the boards as a dancer, but these days you're more likely to see Prefuse 73 spinning vinyl, or touring acts such as Sharon Jones & the Dap-Kings working up the crowd.

Beach Blanket Babylon

Club Fugazi, 678 Green Street, between Columbus Avenue & Powell Street (421 4222/www.beachblanketbabylon.com). Bus 9X, 12, 20, 30, 41, 45/cable car Powell-Mason. **Tickets** $25-$78. **Map** p95 C3 🟤

The longest-running musical revue in theatrical history, *Beach Blanket Babylon* sells its formulaic blend of songs, puns and outrageous headgear with such irresistible conviction that it's become an institution. This queer eye on the straight world will celebrate its 35th year in 2009.

Jazz at Pearl's

256 Columbus Avenue, between Broadway & Pacific Avenue (291 8255/www.jazzatpearls.com). Bus 9X, 12, 30, 41, 45. **Open** from 7.30pm daily. *Shows* 8pm, 10pm daily. **Admission** $10-$25. **Map** p95 C3 🟤

This intimate venue is the last jazz house left standing in North Beach, once the home for a hoppin' mid-century scene. It's a great little place. Singer Kim Nalley and husband Steve Sheraton bought the club in 2003 and now book acts such as Pete Escovedo, Sonny Fortune and Marcus Shelby.

Saloon

1232 Grant Avenue, at Columbus Avenue (989 7666). Bus 12, 15, 30, 41, 45. **Open** noon-2am daily. *Shows* 9pm Mon-Thur; 4pm Fri-Sun. **Admission** free-$5. No credit cards. **Map** p95 C3 🟤

A beer hall that scandalised the neighbourhood when it was established back in 1861 (it's now the oldest continuously operating bar in all of San Francisco), the Saloon remains a no-nonsense, rough-edged joint with a busy, bluesy calendar.

Fisherman's Wharf

Jefferson Street, the wharf's main drag, is a fairly undignified spectacle. At the eastern end, Pier 39 is a sprawling prefab array of seafront shops, attractions and arcade games patently designed to separate you from your money. Luckily, crowds of sea lions barking and belching on nearby pontoons provide a natural respite. There's more to enjoy to the west. The shores of **Aquatic Park** offer one of the best strolls in the city, with a panorama of the Golden Gate Bridge and Alcatraz. The **Golden Gate Promenade** begins here, continuing for three miles west along the shoreline to Fort Point.

Sights & museums

Alcatraz

Alcatraz Island, San Francisco Bay (www.nps.gov/alcatraz). Alcatraz Cruises ferry from Pier 39, Embarcadero (981 7625/www.alcatraz cruises.com). Streetcar F/bus 9X, 10, 39, 47. **Tickets** (incl audio guide) $24.50-$31.50; $15.75-$29.25 reductions. **Map** p95 C2 🟤

Despite being in operation as a federal prison for less than 30 years, Alcatraz remains fixed in the popular imagination as the ultimate penal colony. Today, its ominous prison buildings are no longer used (its last inmates left in 1963), but the craggy outcrop, now a National Park, lures over a million visitors each year. The audio tour of the facility, which features actual interviews from former prisoners and guards, is powerful, chilling and evocative, and the buildings retain an eerie and fascinating appeal. Capacity on the tours is limited; it's best to book ahead.

Hyde Street Pier

At the foot of Hyde Street (561 7000/ www. maritime.org). Streetcar F/bus 10, 19, 20, 30, 47/ cable car Powell-Hyde. **Open** 9.30am-4.30pm daily. **Admission** free ($5 for vessels). No credit cards. **Map** p95 A2 ㉙
The historic vessels permanently docked here would be typical of the ships that would have been common in the area in the 19th and early 20th centuries. Along with the San Francisco Maritime Museum (below), the set-up is the highlight of what is officially designated as the San Francisco Maritime National Historic Park. The lovely visitors' centre, at the corner of Jefferson and Hyde Streets (June-Sept 9.30am-7pm daily; Oct-May 9.30am-5pm daily), contains a fascinating series of displays on the area's seafaring history. For more on the park, call 447 5000 or visit www.nps.gov/safr.

San Francisco Maritime Museum

900 Beach Street, at Polk Street (561 7100/www.maritime.org). Streetcar F/ bus 10, 19, 20, 30, 47/cable car Powell-Hyde. **Admission** free. **Map** p95 A2 ㉚
Such is the art deco beauty of this building, closed for restoration until 2009, that you almost fail to notice its resemblance to a cruiseliner marooned on shore. Those with a yen for maritime lore will enjoy the cache of models, interactive displays, oral histories and exhibits. The renovation also promises to restore the fantastic Atlantis murals by Hilaire Hiler.

USS Pampanito

Pier 45 (775 1943/www.maritime.org). Streetcar F/bus 10, 19, 30, 47/cable car Powell-Hyde. **Open** Mid Oct-late May 9am-6pm Mon-Thur, Sun; 9am-8pm Fri,

Sat. *Late May-mid Oct* 9am-8pm Mon, Tue, Thur-Sun; 9am-6pm Wed. **Admission** $9; $3-$5 reductions; $20 family. **Map** p95 A1 ㉛
The *Pampanito* is a World War II, Balao-class Fleet submarine with an impressive record: it made six patrols in the Pacific at the height of the war, sinking six Japanese ships and damaging four others. The vessel has been restored to look much as it would have in its prime in 1945.

Eating & drinking

Alioto's

8 Fisherman's Wharf, at Taylor & Jefferson Streets (673 0183/www. aliotos.com). Streetcar F to Pier 39/ bus 9X, 10, 20, 30, 39, 47/cable car Powell-Mason. **Open** 11am-11pm daily. **$$$$.** **Map** p95 B1 ㉜
Alioto's began as a sidewalk stand serving crab and shrimp cocktails to passers-by. Now, more than eight decades later, it's a hugely popular restaurant with amazing views of the Bay. The kitchen turns out decent (if pricey) seafood, as well as fish-centred Sicilian specialities. The wine list is outstanding.

Anas Mandara

981 Beach Street, at Polk Street (771 6800/www.anamandara.com). Streetcar F to Fisherman's Wharf/bus 10, 19, 20, 30, 47/cable car Powell-Hyde. **Open** 11.30am-2pm, 5.30-9.30pm Mon-Thur; 11.30am-2pm, 5.30-10.30pm Fri; 5.30-10.30pm Sat; 5.30-9.30pm Sun. **$$$$.** **Asian**. **Map** p95 A2 ㉝
The room is beautiful, with soaring ceilings and a staircase that sweeps you to a chic lounge, and the sumptuous and beautifully presented dishes are enriched with the aromas and flavours of Vietnam. The Cham Bar has live jazz from Thursday to Saturday.

Boudin Sourdough Bakery & Café

2890 Taylor Street, at Jefferson Street (928 1849/www.boudinbakery.com). Streetcar F to Pier 39/bus 9X, 10, 20, 30, 39, 47/cable car Powell-Mason.

Fisherman's Wharf

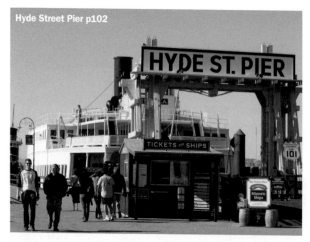
Hyde Street Pier p102

Open *Café* 8am-9pm Mon-Thur, Sun; 8am-10pm Fri, Sat. *Bistro* 11.30am-10pm Mon-Thur, Sun; 11.30am-10.30pm Fri, Sat. **$$$** (restaurant); **$** (café). **Map** p95 B2 ㉞
Locals brag that sourdough bread was invented here, and the Boudin family have baked their bread from the same mother dough since 1849. The flagship store, a relaxing alternative to ear-busting crab and seafood stands along the Wharf, offers delights as sourdough pizzas and clam chowder served in a hollowed-out sourdough bowl.

Blue Mermaid
Argonaut Hotel, 471 Jefferson Street, at Hyde Street (771 2222/www.blue mermaidsf.com). Streetcar F to Fisherman's Wharf/bus 10, 19, 20, 30, 47/cable car Powell-Hyde. **Open** 7am-9pm Mon-Thur, Sun; 7am-10pm Fri, Sat. **$$$**. **Fish**. **Map** p95 A2 ㉟
Designed to recall the history of the working wharf (don't miss the excellent on-site museum), this rustic-looking restaurant is set into the corner of the Argonaut Hotel. The menu is perfect for San Francisco's fogged-in days, with hearty chowders spooned up from large cauldrons. There's also a kids' menu: it's a top choice for families.

Gary Danko
800 North Point Street, at Hyde Street (749 2060/www.garydanko.com). Streetcar F to Fisherman's Wharf/bus 10, 19, 20, 30, 47/cable car Powell-Hyde. **Open** 5.30-10pm daily. **$$$$**. **American**. **Map** p95 A2 ㊱
Superstar chef Danko's fine-dining restaurant near the wharf is fabulous – and fabulously understated. The best way to expereince his dexterity and genius is via the tasting menues, which change seasonally but might include seared foie gras with caramelised red onions as a starter, beef tenderloin with king trumpet mushrooms as a main, and farmhouse cheeses to finish. A more casual adventure can be had at the bar. Reservations are essential and can be hard to come by.

Arts & leisure

Blazing Saddles
2715 Hyde Street, at North Point Street (202 8888/www.blazing saddles.com). Metro F to Fisherman's Wharf/bus 10, 19, 30, 47/cable car Powell-Hyde. **Open** from 8am daily. **Rates** $7-$9/hr or $28-$48/day. **Map** p95 A2 ㊲

Bikes are rented to those with a yen for cycling the eight miles from Fisherman's Wharf over the Golden Gate Bridge to Sausalito. Guided tours are also offered.

Russian Hill

Today, Russian Hill is a quiet, residential and pricey neighbourhood roughly bordered by Larkin and North Point Streets, Columbus Avenue, Powell Street and Pacific Avenue. Its most notorious landmark is the world's 'crookedest' (and no doubt most photographed) thoroughfare: **Lombard Street**, which snakes steeply down from Hyde Street to Leavenworth, packing nine hairpin bends into one brick-paved and over-landscaped block.

Sights & museums

San Francisco Art Institute

800 Chestnut Street, between Leavenworth & Jones Streets (771 7020/www.sanfranciscoart.edu). Bus 10, 20, 30, 47/cable car Powell-Hyde or Powell-Mason. **Open** *Diego Rivera Gallery* 8am-7pm daily. *Walter McBean Gallery* 11am-6pm Tue-Sat. **Admission** free. No credit cards. **Map** p95 B2 ㊳

Most people visit this prestigious art school to see Diego Rivera's mural *The Making of a Fresco*, one of various works he completed in San Francisco in the 1930s. If you're worn out from climbing all those hills, have a rest in the pretty open-air courtyard, or grab a snack in the cafeteria and soak up the views. See box p97.

Eating & drinking

La Boulange de Polk

2310 Polk Street, at Green Street (345 1107/www.baybread.com). Bus 12, 19, 47, 49, 76/cable car Powell-Hyde. **Open** 7am-6.30pm Tue-Sat; 7am-6pm Sun. **$**. **Café**. **Map** p95 A3 ㊴

In the style of a Parisian boulangerie, this café serves beautiful pastries and tasty fresh-baked bread. The best spot to watch a morning unfold is from one of the inviting pavement tables, but they can be difficult to acquire.

La Folie

2316 Polk Street, between Union & Green Streets (776 5577/www.la folie.com). Bus 12, 19, 47, 49, 76/cable car Powell-Hyde. **Open** 5.30-10.30pm Mon-Sat. **$$$$**. **French**. **Map** p95 A3 ㊵

If you want to find out why chef Roland Passot enjoys a passionate following, opt for the five-course discovery menu ($90) and sample his ever-changing selection of classic French fare, prepared with seasonally fresh ingredients. The Provençal decor and attentive staff add to the charm. The adjoining Green Room is a good option for intimate dining.

Pesce

2227 Polk Street, between Green & Vallejo Streets (928 8025/www.pesce sf.com). Bus 12, 19, 47, 49, 76/cable car Powell-Hyde. **Open** 5-10pm Mon-Thur; 5-11pm Fri; noon-4pm, 5-11pm Sat; noon-10pm Sun. **$$**. **Fish**. **Map** p95 A4 ㊶

Modest and comfortable, Pesce proves that fabulous seafood doesn't have to be fancy or expensive, making it wildly popular with those lucky enough to live nearby. Starters include excellent mussels, cod cakes and calamari; main courses tend to be Italian.

Sushi Groove

1916 Hyde Street, between Union & Green Streets (440 1905). Bus 41, 45/cable car Powell-Hyde. **Open** 5.30-9.30pm daily. **$$**. **Japanese**. **Map** p95 A3 ㊷

If you don't mind sitting elbow to elbow in a dining room that's roughly the size of a postage stamp, join the stylish clientele at this creative Japanese sushi restaurant. The decor is postmodern, the mood music is loungy and the original rolls and salads are mostly very good. The impressive saké selection alone is worth the trip.

Mission mural

The Mission & the Castro

The heady cultural mix of the Mission and Castro makes for a very San Franciscan kind of melting pot. Here, rainbow-swathed muscle shirt boutiques rub shoulders with beautiful Victorian homes, and temples to pristine gastronomy give way to burritos the size of babies' arms. These enclaves of all things queer, yuppie, hip and Latino provide a colourful snapshot of the city's remarkably diverse charm.

The Mission

The Mission today is the centre of Latin culture in San Francisco. Mission Street between 14th and Cesar Chavez Streets is the area's main drag. Along here, the scents and sights are plentiful: the mix of sidewalk sausage stands, bootleg DVD vendors, dollar stores and *taquerías* colourfully paints the strip of one of the city's tightest ethnic communities. Murals are everywhere in this neighbourhood and a crucial part of its identity. **Balmy Alley**, just off 24th Street, is covered with striking examples. The historical highlight of the area is San Francisco's oldest building, the **Mission Dolores.**

Walk a couple of blocks west to the shopper's paradise that is **Valencia Street**, lined with boutiques, and you'll see evidence of the area's other main occupants: San Francisco's creative classes.

Sights & museums

Balmy Alley
Between 24th & 25th Streets. Bart 24th Street. **Map** p109 E5 ❶
The walls of this alley of 24th Street are covered with colourful murals depicting political issues and cultural heroes.

Mission Cultural Center for Latino Arts
2868 Mission Street, at 25th Street (821 1155/www.missioncultural center.org). BART 24th Street. **Open** hours vary. **Map** p109 E5 ❷
The centre is home to a theatre and a gallery displaying works by under-the-radar local artists. It's also a great resource for the area's public art.

Mission Dolores
3321 16th Street, at Dolores Street (621 8203/www.missiondolores.org). BART 16th Street/Metro J to Church/bus 22. **Open** 9am-5pm daily. **Admission** $3-$5. **Map** p108 C3 ❸
Founded by a tiny band of Spanish missionaries and soldiers in 1776, and completed 15 years later, Mission Dolores is the oldest structure in the city. The building was originally called the Misión San Francisco de Asis (after St Francis of Assisi), and provided the town with its name. Although the original mission became an expansive outpost, housing over 4,000 monks and converts, today only the tiny old church remains. The adobe structure, constructed from 16,000 earthen bricks and 4ft (1.2m) thick, survived the 1906 and 1989 earthquakes unscathed, while the new church next door crumbled. Small wonder that the cool, dim interior looks and feels authentic: almost everything about it is original, from the redwood logs holding up the roof to the ornate altars brought from Mexico centuries ago.

A small museum on the mission premises offers volunteer-led tours, and the picturesque, flower-filled cemetery contains the remains of California's first governor and the city's first mayor, as well as assorted Spanish settlers and the mass grave of 5,000

Costanoan Indians who died in their service. Film buffs may recall that in Hitchcock's *Vertigo*, an entranced Kim Novak led Jimmy Stewart to the gravestone of the mysterious Carlotta Valdes in this very cemetery.

Precita Eyes Mural Arts & Visitor Center
2981 24th Street (285 2287/www. precitaeyes.org). **Open** 10am-5pm Mon-Fri; 10am-4pm Sat; noon-4pm. **Map** p109 E5 ❹
The vivid public art that graces the area's buildings and alleys is here largely thanks to the vision of one woman, Susan Cervantes, founder of Precita Eyes. Its shop carries mural T-shirts, mural maps and mural postcards. For the best overview, Precita Eyes runs walking tours: the Mission Trail Mural Walk runs every Saturday and Sunday at 1.30pm ($12); other slightly shorter walks are held at 11am on weekends.

Eating & drinking

500 Club
500 Guerrero Street, at 17th Street (861 2500). BART 16th Street Mission/bus 14, 22, 26, 33, 49. **Open** 3pm-2am Mon-Fri; 1pm-2am Sat, Sun. No credit cards. **Bar**. **Map** p109 D3 ❺
The 500 Club is everybody's favourite dive. Cavernous booths, a punk jukebox, a pool table and cheap, stiff drinks keep the place brimming with an incredibly varied crowd. Pull up a stool at the long, long bar and don't make any plans to leave.

Atlas Café
3049 20th Street, at Alabama Street (648 1047/www.atlascafe.net). Bus 9, 27, 33. **Open** 6.30am-9pm Mon-Wed; 6.30am-10pm Thur; 8am-9pm Sat; 8am-8pm Sun. $. No credit cards. **Café**. **Map** p109 F4 ❻
One of the outer Mission's best hangouts, with people lining up for fresh breakfast pastries in the morning and settling into just-roasted lattes for the afternoon and evening. A daily list of

The Mission & the Castro

A McAllister Street   B   Alamo Square   Painted Ladies   C Grove Street

1

MASONIC AVENUE
CENTRAL AVENUE

© Copyright Time Out Group 2008

0   500 m
0   500 yds

DIVISADERO STREET

FELL STREET

OAK STREET

Panhandle

OAK STREET

PAGE STREET

HAIGHT-ASHBURY

HAIGHT STREET

HAIGHT STREET

WALLER STREET

LOWER HAIGHT

HERMANN STREET

2

ASHBURY STREET

MASONIC AVENUE

DELMAR STREET

FREDERICK STREET

WALLER STREET

Buena Vista Park

BUENA VISTA AVENUE WEST

TERRACE EAST
BUENA VISTA AVENUE

ALPINE

Duboce Park

DUBOCE AVENUE

Muni Metro
Duboce & Noe

UCSF Davies

CHURCH STREET

63

14th STREET   NOE STREET   SANCHEZ STREET

73
69
60   67
61   57
75   59
71

Muni Metro
Church

MARKET STREET

DOLORES STREET

HENRY STREET

15th STREET

Corona Heights Park

ROOSEVELT WAY

MUSEUM WAY

STATES STREET

BEAVER STREET

16th STREET

Mission Dolores

3

CLIFFORD TERRACE

UPPER TERRACE

ROOSEVELT

Randall Museum

CASTRO STREET

72
52
58   74

POND STREET   SANCHEZ STREET   CHURCH STREET

3

17th STREET

Muni Metro
Castro

MARKET STREET   CASTRO

69   76
55   56
54

NOE STREET

18th STREET   SANCHEZ STREET

Muni Metro
Church & 18th St

CORBETT AVENUE

18th STREET

Eureka Valley Recreation Centre

DOUGLASS STREET

EUREKA STREET

COLLINGWOOD STREET

CASTRO STREET

65 64
70   59

HARTFORD STREET

66

HANCOCK STREET

Missio
Dolore
Park

4

MARKET STREET

CORWIN STREET

19th STREET

19th STREET

CUMBERLAND STREET

TWIN PEAKS BLVD

DIAMOND STREET

20th STREET

20th STREET

LIBERTY STREET

CHURCH STREET

ROMAIN ST

21st STREET

CASTRO STREET

NOE STREET

HILL STREET

CORBETT AVENUE

GRAND VIEW AVENUE

22nd STREET

CHURCH STREET

CHATTANOOGA STREET

BURNETT AVENUE

5

MARKET STREET

DOUGLASS STREET

ALVARADO STREET

23rd ST

Twin Peaks Park

Noe Valley Playground

24th ST

SANCHEZ STREET

Muni Metro
Church & 24th St

108 Time Out Shortlist | San Francisco

D FRANKLIN ST Symphony Hall MARKET STREET E SO 8th STREET F

HAYES VALLEY

1

① Sights & museums
① Eating & drinking
① Shopping
① Nightlife
① Arts & leisure

US 101 CENTRAL SKYWAY

2

BART 16th St

16th STREET

Franklin Square

17th STREET

POTRERO AVENUE

3

MISSION

Mission Playground

Coronado Playground

21st STREET

4

Precita Eyes Mural Arts & Visitors Center

BART 24th St

5

POTRERO AVENUE

Airline flights are one of the biggest producers of the global warming gas CO_2. But with **The CarbonNeutral Company** you can make your travel a little greener.

Go to **www.carbonneutral.com** to calculate your flight emissions then 'neutralise' them through international projects which save exactly the same amount of carbon dioxide.

Contact us at **shop@carbonneutral.com** or call into the office on **0870 199 99 88** for more details.

CarbonNeutral®flights

grilled sandwiches includes many vegetarian specialities, and there are also soups and salads. There's music (usually bluegrass or country) on Thursday evenings. On nice days, try for a sunny seat on the patio at the back.

Andalu

3198 16th Street, at Guerrero Street (621 2211/www.andalusf.com). BART 16th Street/bus 14, 26, 33, 49. **Open** 5.30-9.30pm Mon-Tue; 5.30-10.30pm Wed, Thur; 5.30-11.30pm Fri; 10.30am-2.30pm, 5.30-11.30pm Sat; 10.30am-2.30pm, 5.30-9.30pm. **$. International**. Map p109 D3 **7**

This spacious and inviting room is anchored by a long bar at the back – it's a great spot when you're waiting for a table. Items on the tapas-style menu are given an inventive twist, with such surprises as miso-glazed sea bass and ricotta-stuffed grilled aubergine. Save room for the fresh doughnuts.

Beauty Bar

2299 Mission Street, at 19th Street (285 0323/www.beautybar.com). BART 16th Street/bus 14, 22, 26, 33, 49. **Open** 5pm-2am Mon-Fri; 7pm-2am Sat, Sun. **Bar**. Map p109 D4 **8**

This little cocktail bar, modelled after its sister bar in New York (and there are now bars in other cities too), is decorated with bric-a-brac salvaged from a Long Island hair salon. Instead of a couch, curl up on a Naugahyde salon chair, with hairdryer still attached. On Thursday to Saturday evenings, buy a $10 cocktail and get a free manicure.

Dalva

3121 16th Street, between Mission & Guerrero Streets (252 7740). BART 16th Street/bus 14, 22, 26, 33, 49. **Open** 4pm-2am daily. No credit cards. **Bar**. Map p109 D3 **9**

An unspoiled oasis of cool in the manic Mission bar scene, Dalva worships good music. The jukebox, named Orpheus, carries a wonderfully diverse array of sounds, from Cuban music to tiki kitsch. When it's not on, DJs spin drum 'n' bass, jazz, soul, funk, salsa and other odds and sods.

Delfina

3621 18th Street, between Dolores & Guerrero Streets (552 4055/ www.delfinasf.com). BART 16th Street Mission/Metro to Church & 18th Street/bus 14, 26, 33, 49. **Open** 5.30-10pm Mon-Thur, Sun; 5.30-11pm Fri, Sat. **$$$. American**. Map p109 D3 **10**

Chef/owner Craig Stoll favours simplicity over whimsy, and tradition over fashion. Yet his food is never ordinary: fresh pasta, fish and braised meats on the daily-changing menu all burst with flavour. Stoll's casual Pizzeria Delfina, with fab thin-crust pizzas, is next door.

Doc's Clock

2575 Mission Street, at 22nd Street (824 3627). BART 24th Street Mission/ bus 12, 14, 26, 48, 49, 67. **Open** 6pm-2am Mon-Sat; 8pm-2am Sun. No credit cards. **Bar**. Map p109 E4 **11**

This place was formerly a total dive had refit a while back. The mahogany bar was buffed up, the booze selection expanded, and the CD changer now spits out anything from Air to Sufjan Stevens.

Foreign Cinema

2534 Mission Street, between 21st & 22nd Streets (648 7600/www.foreign cinema.com). BART 24th Street Mission/ bus 14, 26, 48, 49, 67. **Open** 6-10pm Mon-Thur; 6-11pm Fri; 11am-11pm Sat; 11am-10pm (until 9pm winter) Sun. *Bar & gallery* until 2am daily. **$$$. International**. Map p109 D4 **12**

Now one of the stalwarts of Mission dining, this restaurant is dominated by the screen on one side of the outdoor courtyard dining room, on which classic foreign films are projected; there are speakers at each table if you want to listen. But the focus is still the food: frequently changing, classically rooted Mediterranean favourites and a massive range of stellar oysters.

Kilowatt

3160 16th Street, between Valencia & Guerrero Streets (861 2595/www.bar bell.com/kilowatt). BART 16th Street/ bus 14, 22, 26, 33, 49. **Open** 4.30pm-2am Mon-Fri; 1pm-2am Sat, Sun. No credit cards. **Bar**. Map p109 D3 **13**

Mission Dolores p107

Does what a solid bar should, with reasonable prices, generous drink pours, a good selection of beers, top-notch jukebox, pool tables, dartboards and comfortable booths. For a meal of champions, grab a lamb shawarma from Truly Mediterranean across the street, return to the bar and order one of its mean bloody marys.

Lexington Club

3464 19th Street, at Lexington Street (863 2052/ www.lexingtonclub.com). BART to 16th Street Mission/bus 14, 26, 33, 49. **Open** 5pm-2am Mon-Thur; 3pm-2am Fri-Sun. No credit cards. **Bar**. **Map** p109 D4 ⓮

A legendary lesbian-owned, lesbian-operated bar, where 'every night is ladies' night'. Primarily for the younger set, it has a pool table and full bar; crimson walls and church-pew seating give the place a ready-for-anything atmosphere. There's no dancing, but theme nights include Sister Spit's rowdy performances, and Sunday L Word parties.

Limón

524 Valencia Street, at 16th Street (252 0918/www.limon-sf.com). BART 16th Street Mission/bus 14, 22, 26, 33, 49, 53. **Open** 5.30-10.30pm Mon; 11.30am-3pm, 5.30-10.30pm Tue-Thur; 11.30am-3pm, 5.30-11pm Fri; noon-11pm Sat; noon-10pm Sun. **$$$**. **International**. **Map** p109 D3 ⓯

One of just a handful of San Francisco eateries serving – and glamourising – Peruvian food, this chic, packed, low-lit hotspot serves the traditional dishes of this South American country inventively infused with Chinese and Japanese influences. Zesty sangria and other speciality Latin-inspired cocktails complement the food.

Luna Park

694 Valencia Street, at 18th Street (553 8584/www.lunaparksf.com). BART 16th Street Mission/Metro to Church & 18th Street/bus 14, 26, 33, 49. **Open** 11.30am-2.30pm, 5.30-10.30pm Mon-Thur; 11.30am-2.30pm, 5.30-11.30pm Fri; 11.30am-11.30pm Sat; 11.30am-10pm Sun. **$$**. **American**. **Map** p109 D3 ⓰

The notion of serving no-nonsense food at decent prices in a place where people want to linger has been a successful one. That Luna Park is tiny doesn't deter locals from queuing; a vibrant lounge bar catches the spillover. Expect

space features edgy design, with conversation-starters in each of three areas: a bar, a lounge and a bottle-service room. The menu has nicely presented renditions of Japanese small plates, as well as fresh sushi and sashimi. A list of more than 120 whiskies is a big plus.

Pauline's Pizza

260 Valencia Street, between Brosnan & 14th Streets (552 2050/www. paulinespizza.com). BART 16th Street Mission/ Metro to Church/bus 14, 22, 26, 33, 49, 53. **Open** 5-10pm Tue-Sat. **$$**. **Pizza**. **Map** p109 D2 ⑲
Pauline's inventive thin-crust pies all come with top-quality ingredients: roasted peppers, perhaps, or goat's cheese, edible flowers or exotic vegetables. The pesto pizza (basil and pesto are baked into the crust) is justly renowned.

Range

842 Valencia Street, at 22nd Street (282 8283/www. rangesf.com). BART 24th Street Mission/Metro to Church & 24th Street/bus 14, 26, 48, 49, 67. **Open** 5.30-10pm Mon-Thur, Sun; 5.30-11pm Fri, Sat. **$$$**. **American**. **Map** 109 D4 ⑳
Run by husband and wife Phil and Cameron West, Range is a big hit. The concise and constantly changing menu never fails to have something on it that you want to eat – wild-nettle stuffed pasta with lemon and goat cheese, or slow-cooked lamb shoulder with parsnip purée. The meyer lemon pudding cake will make you weep.

Slow Club

2501 Mariposa Street, at Hampshire Street (241 9390/www.slowclub.com). Bus 9, 22, 27, 33, 53. **Open** 8-11am, 11.30am-2.30pm, 6.30-10pm Mon-Thur; 8-11am, 11.30am-2.30pm, 6.30-11pm Fri; 10am-2.30pm, 6.30-11pm Sat; 10am-2.30pm Sun. **$$**. **American**. **Map** p109 F3 ㉑
With its remote location and hideaway vibe, this is a true locals' hangout. Slow Club's understated charm makes it one of the coolest restaurants in town. Typical mains include pan-roasted

a selection of hearty dishes, including flatiron steak and fries, and earthy stomach-fillers such as breaded pork cutlet stuffed with mushrooms and cheese.

Medjool Sky Terrace

2522 Mission Street, between 21st & 22nd Streets (550 9055/www.medjool sf.com). BART 24th Street Mission/bus 12, 14, 26, 48, 49, 67. **Open** 5-10pm Mon-Wed; 4pm-midnight Thur; 4pm-1.30am Fri; 2pm-1.30am Sat; noon-10pm Sun. **Bar**. **Map** p109 D4 ⑰
This two-building complex, topped by a massive roof deck, contains a restaurant, a café and an excellent hostel. Weather permitting, the deck is the primary draw. Sip cocktails, and scoff scaled-down, lighter fare from the restaurant's menu while taking in some of the Mission's best views.

Nihon

1779 Folsom Street, at 14th Street (552 4400/www. nihon-sf.com). BART 16th Street/bus 9, 12, 14, 22, 33, 49, 53. **Open** 5.30pm-midnight Mon-Sat. *Bar* until 2am. **$$**. **Japanese**. **Map** p109 E2 ⑱
With its emphasis on scene and style, this sushi lounge has given this out-of-the-way location a bit of life. The

chicken and braised beef shank. There are no reservations, but you can wait in the cosy bar area. The weekend brunch is a winner.

St Francis Fountain

2801 24th Street, at York Street (826 4200). Bus 9, 27, 33, 48. **Open** 8am-10pm daily. **$. Diner.** **Map** p109 F5 ㉒
An almost classical link from old Mission to new, this ancient soda fountain has been given a new lease of life in recent years thanks to the attention lavished on it by its new owners. The menu offers a few nods to the 21st century, but it's mainly a wonderfully retro experience, from the Formica tabletops to the magnificent mac and cheese and ice-cream sodas.

Ti Couz Creperie

3108 16th Street, between Valencia & Guerrero Streets (252 7373). BART 16th Street Mission/bus 14, 22, 26, 33, 49, 53. **Open** 11am-11pm Mon, Fri; 5-11pm Tue-Thur; 10am-11pm Sat, Sun. **$. French.** **Map** p109 D3 ㉓
The classic Breton buckwheat galettes (savoury) and crêpes (sweet) are cooked

captivatingly before your eyes. All kinds of urbanites pop in to try more than 100 fillings, from smoked salmon to lemon and brown sugar. Next door, Ti Couz Two has seafood and a full bar.

Zeitgeist

199 Valencia Street, at Duboce Avenue (255 7505). BART to 16th Street Mission/Metro to Van Ness/streetcar F/bus 26, 49. **Open** 9am-2am daily. No credit cards. **Bar.** **Map** p109 D2 ㉔
One of the hippest and most mellow bars in town, popular with bikers (Hondas rather than Harleys), bike messengers and people from every walk of alternative life. On sunny evenings, it's hard to find a seat at the benches and tables in the giant beer-garden-meets-junkyard back patio.

Shopping

Adobe Bookshop

3166 16th Street, at Albion Street (864 3936/http://adobebooks back roomgallery.blogspot.com). BART 16th Street/bus 14, 26, 33, 49. **Open** 11am-midnight daily. **Map** p109 D3 ㉕

Foreign Cinema p111

Woe is the book buyer hoping to find exactly what he or she is looking for at Adobe. But those itching for a genuine taste of today's SF bohemia must stop by. Survey the hopelessly chaotic shelves, pile into an ancient armchair to talk up a random poet or painter, or check out the artwork in the tiny exhibition space.

Aquarius Records

1055 Valencia Street, between 21st & 22nd Streets (647 2272/www. aquariusrecords.org). BART 24th Street/bus 14, 26, 48, 49, 67. **Open** 10am-9pm Mon-Wed; 10am-10pm Thur-Sun. Map p109 D4 ❷⑥
This splendid little neighbourhood record store could be classed as a boutique, were the staff not so wonderfully lacking in pretension (tiny handwritten notes attached to numerous CD covers reveal their enthusiasm). Expect carefully curated selections and rarities covering everything from art rock to sludge metal.

Candystore

3153 16th Street, between Albion & Guerrero Streets (863 8143/ www.candystore-sf.com). BART 16th Street/bus 14, 26, 33, 49. **Open** noon-7pm Mon-Sat; noon-6pm Sun. **Map** p109 D3 ❷⑦
Sweet stuff for trendy young women with an eye for whimsy: patterned wallets, new-wave slingbacks and gold danglers brush up against puffed sleeve hoodie-jackets, airy dresses and striped separates.

Curiosity Shoppe

855 Valencia Street, at 20th Street (839 6404/www.curiosity shoppe online.com). BART 16th Street/ bus 14, 26, 33, 49. **Open** 11am-7pm Wed-Sat; noon-6pm Sun. **Map** p109 D4 ❷⑧
Owners Lauren Smith and Derek Fagerstrom set up the Curiosity Shoppe to showcase their obsession with the gorgeous and strange. Pick up a kit to make a duct tape wallet or radio receiver for that crafty chum – or simply buy a sweet charm necklace.

Five & Diamond

510 Valencia Street, at 16th Street (255 9747/www.fiveand diamond.com). BART 16th Street/bus 14, 26, 33, 49. **Open** noon-8pm Mon-Thur; noon-9pm Fri-Sun. Map p109 D3 ❷⑨
Phoebe Minona Durland and Leighton Kelly – 'Nomadic artists', Yard Dogs Road Show burlesque/vaudeville performers, and designers – showcase their upscale piercing line here, along with wild and stunning jewellery. You can hop in the chair and acquire some skin art from tattoo artist Phil Milic.

Hideo Wakamatsu

563 Valencia Street, at 17th Street (255 3029/www.hideostore.com). BART 16th Street/bus 14, 26, 33, 49. **Open** noon-7pm Mon, Tue, Thur-Sat; noon-6pm Sun. **Map** p109 D3 ❸⓪
The designs of these bags are extremely well considered, the construction and materials are impeccable, and the prices are, well, sky high. Still, considering how passionate its fans are, it's no wonder Hideo Wakamatsu has gone from a cult name at Flight 001 to a stand-alone boutique.

Laku

1089 Valencia Street, between 21st & 22nd Streets (695 1462). BART 24th Street/bus 14, 26, 48, 49, 67. **Open** 11.30am-6.30pm Tue-Sat; noon-5pm Sun. **Map** p109 D4 ❸①
Exquisite, intricate little slippers and coats, sewn by Laku's owner from velvet and shantung silk on a machine in the back of the shop. For baby royalty.

Little Otsu

849 Valencia Street, between 19th & 20th Streets (255 7900/www. little otsu.com). BART 16th Street/bus 14, 26, 33, 49. **Open** 11.30am-7.30pm Wed-Sun. **Map** p109 D4 ❸②
Vegan principles in this artful, airy space translate as cute, recycled-paper cards (as well as diaries, calendars and books) printed with soy-based inks.

Minnie Wilde

3266 21st Street, at Valencia Street (642 9453, www.minniewilde.com). BART 24th Street/bus 14, 26, 48,

49, 67. **Open** noon-7pm Mon-Fri; 11am-7pm Sat; 11am-5pm Sun. **Map** p109 D4 ③

Terri Olson dreams up kicky knicker-bockers, sexy secretary frocks and par-ticularly adorable outerwear in the form of capelets and 'ca-ponchos' at this one of a kind shop.

Monument

572 Valencia Street, at 19th Street (861 9800/www.monument.1st dibs.com). BART 16th Street/bus 14, 26, 33, 49. **Open** noon-6pm Mon-Thur, Sun; noon-7pm Fri, Sat. **Map** p109 D4 ③

Mad glam mid-century modern makes its last glittery stand here. Take in the sensual lines of the sofas and the high drama of the mirrored cabinets.

Needles & Pens

3253 16th Street, at Guerrero Street (255 1534/www.needles-pens.com). BART 16th Street/bus 14, 26, 33, 49. **Open** noon-7pm daily. **Map** p109 D3 ③

This epicentre of DIY culture in Mission combined with gallery space trades in 'zines, bric-a-brac and hand-embellished T-shirts. A great place to pick up a polemical print by your local anarchist.

Painted Bird

1201A Guerrero Street, at 24th Street (401 7027/www.paintedbird.org). BART 24th Street/bus 14, 26, 33, 49. **Open** 11am-8pm daily. **Map** p109 D5 ③

Cooler than cool and extremely well priced, this brilliantly edited vintage outpost has become a must-shop for hipsters in search of granny sundresses, glam disco bags, flash but cute jew-ellery and styling shoes and boots from the 1980s, '70s and earlier eras.

Schauplatz

791 Valencia Street, between 18th & 19th Streets (864 5665). BART 16th Street/bus 14, 26, 33, 49. **Open** 1-7pm daily. **Map** p109 D4 ③

The second-hand gear on offer here, mixed with new clothing, is more art-fully collated than elsewhere in the Mission. In German, Schauplatz means 'showplace'; the name makes sense

Medjool Sky Terrace p113

when you spy Italian sunglasses, intri-cately beaded Moroccan mules or a Swedish policeman's leather jacket.

Ritmo Latino

2401 Mission Street, at 20th Street (824 8556). BART 16th Street/bus 14, 26, 33, 49. **Open** 10am-9.30pm daily. **Map** p109 D4 ③

If you look outside, you'll find hand-prints of Latin stars like Celia Cruz and Ricky Martin. Within, friendly staff can guide you to their recorded works, or to mariachi music, conjuntos or whatever rhythm you fancy. The store has expanded its wares of late into lifestyle products such as clothing.

Tartine Bakery

600 Guerrero Street, between 18th & 19th Streets (487 2600/www.tartine bakery.com). Metro to Church & 18th/bus 33. **Open** 8am-7pm Mon; 7.30am-7pm Tue, Wed; 7.30am-8pm Thur, Fri; 8am-8pm Sat; 9am-8pm Sun. **Map** p109 E4 ③

Probably the best bakery in San Francisco, Tartine triggers queues and makes foodies swoon over the hot-pressed sandwiches (on housemade French bread), brioche bread pudding, pastries, cakes and croissants.

Therapy

545 Valencia Street, between 16th & 17th Streets (865 0981). BART 16th Street/bus 14, 26, 33, 49. **Open** 11.30am-10pm Mon-Thur; 11am-10.30pm Fri; 10.30am-10.30pm Sat; 10.30am-9pm Sun. **Credit** AmEx, DC, MC, V. **Map** p109 D3 ⓸⓪

This hipster central stocks cute earrings and hair clips, stationery and undefinable gifts, as well as women's and men's clothing. For furniture and homewares, check out its other shop a few doors down.

Nightlife

Amnesia

853 Valencia Street, between 19th & 20th Streets (970 0012). Bus 14, 26, 49. **Open** 6pm-2am daily. **Admission** free-$8. No credit cards. **Map** p109 D4 41

Amnesia draws a diverse, friendly, multi-ethnic crowd, and the DJ spins suitably eclectic sounds. With a nice selection of Belgian brews and friendly staff to boot, the patrons at the bar are as likely to be neighbourhood regulars as they are curious tourists checking out the action.

NEW Mighty

119 Utah Street, at 15th Street (626 7001/ www.mighty119.com). Bus 9, 9X, 14X, 22, 53. **Open** 10pm-4am Thur-Sat. **Admission** free-$15. No credit cards. **Map** p109 F2 42

The slick interior and flawless sound system led *URB* magazine to name Mighty the 'Best New Club in America', but the place has also received plenty of accolades from San Franciscans. Indeed, it's such a well-tuned space that Austin DJ D:Fuse recorded his People_3 live set here.

Pink

2925 16th Street, between S Van Ness Avenue & Capp Street (431 8889/ www.pinksf.com). BART 16th Street Mission/bus 14, 22, 33, 49. **Open** 10pm-2am Tue-Sun. **Admission** varies. **Map** p109 E3 43

A favourite spot for fans of DJ culture, Pink is a narrow bar with a small dancefloor, uncomfortably crowded during the weekend. Although the drinks prices might seem to cater to the upper echelon, music is still the club's focus; the venue frequently hosts international DJs with very little fanfare.

Arts & leisure

12 Galaxies

2565 Mission Street, at 21st Street (970 9777/www.12galaxies.com). BART 24th Street Mission/bus 14, 26, 48, 49, 67. **Open** show nights only. *Shows* 9pm, nights vary. **Admission** $5-$25. No credit cards. **Map** p109 D4 44

The sightlines are all swell at 12 Galaxies: check out the live music from the shining, retro-style bar, hunker down in a shadowy seat by the stage, or look down from the second-floor mezzanine. The likes of Alejandro Escovedo, DJ Logic, Railroad Earth, Lightning Bolt, Deerhunter and Black Dice have all graced the stage.

Brava! For Women in the Arts

Theatre Center, 2789 24th Street, at York Street (641 7657/box office 647 2822/www.brava.org). BART 24th Street/bus 9, 27, 33, 48. **Tickets** free-$50. **Map** p109 F5 45

Housed in an old vaudeville theatre, Brava is one of few theatres that specialise in work by women of colour and lesbian playwrights.

Dark Room

2263 Mission Street, between 18th & 19th Streets (401 7987/tickets 1-800 838 3006/www. darkroom sf.com). BART 16th Street Mission/ bus 14, 22, 33, 49, 53. **Tickets** $5-$20. **Map** p109 D4 46

This funky black box theatre space knows what it likes. And if you revel in an unabashed embrace of pop culture detritus, then the chances are you'll like it too. Recent programming included a revival of *Clue: The Play* and *Creepshow Live* (a Halloween treat). Additionally a comedy showcase and music venue, the Dark Room also sports a regular bad movie night.

Elbo Room

647 Valencia Street, between 17th & 18th Streets (552 7788/www. elbo.com). BART 16th Street Mission/ bus 14, 26, 33, 49. **Open** 5pm-2am daily. Shows 9pm or 10pm daily. **Admission** free-$10. No credit cards. **Map** p109 D3 ㊼

Although the Elbo has been commandeered by yuppies, you'll still hear good music. You're likely to hear jazz, pure funk, soul or Latin jazz in the open-raftered space upstairs, but also hip hop, hard rock, metal and random whacked-out experimentalism. On Sundays, it's the legendary Dub Mission DJ night.

Intersection for the Arts

446 Valencia Street, between 15th & 16th Streets (information 626 2787/box office 626 3311/www.the intersection.org). BART 16th Street/ bus 14, 22, 26, 33, 49, 53. **Tickets** $9-$25. **Map** p109 D3 ㊽

The oldest alternative space in San Francisco, Intersection offers a community-conscious array of artistic undertakings including powerhouse theatre, combining the talents of resident company Campo Santo with visiting playwrights such as Naomi Iizuka and John Steppling. The small theatre isn't hugely comfortable – there are only folding chairs – but performances are intense. There's also a great art gallery upstairs.

Make-Out Room

3225 22nd Street, between Mission & Valencia Streets (647 2888/www.make outroom.com). BART 24th Street Mission/bus 14, 26, 48, 49, 67. **Open** 6pm-2am daily. Shows usually 9pm daily. **Admission** $5-$10. No credit cards. **Map** p109 D5 ㊾

One of the best places in town to see smallish bands, the Make-Out Room attracts a laid-back, alternative, youthful crowd on its weekend live music nights. The decor lives up to the name: there's a bearskin rug on one wall and a stag's head on another with a rainbow of bras strung from the antlers.

St Francis Fountain p114

Marsh

1062 Valencia Street, at 22nd Street (information 826 5750/tickets 1-800 838 3006/www.themarsh.org). BART 24th Street/bus 14, 26, 49, 67. **Tickets** $8-$35. **Map** p109 D5 ⑩

The Marsh works hard to present new works, especially solo fare, priding itself on allowing performers to take risks. At the same time, the atmosphere around its two stages and adjacent café is mellow and inviting.

Project Artaud Theater

450 Florida Street, between 17th & Mariposa Streets (626 4370/ www.artaud.org). Bus 22, 27, 33, 53. **Tickets** $5-$30. **Map** p109 E3 ⑪

The non-profit Project Artaud Theater offers new works, often boundary-pushing and hybrid in character, and including everything from one-person plays and modern dance to outspoken aerial circus theatre like local artist-activist Keith Hennessey's recent *Sol Niger*. Two other member theatres share parts of the block-long structure: the Traveling Jewish Theatre and the Theater of Yugen/Noh Space.

Roxie New College Film Center & Little Roxie

3117 16th Street, between Valencia & Guerrero Streets (863 1087/ www.roxie.com). BART 16th Street/ bus 14, 22, 26, 33, 49, 53. **Tickets** $9; $5-$6 reductions. No credit cards. **Map** p109 D3 ⑫

World premières of cutting-edge documentaries, classic films noirs and '60s horror flicks are only a taste of the impressive range of films screened at the Roxie. Next door's Little Roxie has a great projection set-up, a terrific sound system and a programme of stuff too weird even for its wacky parent to show. Both theatres are a bit down at heel, but the gritty atmosphere just adds to the funkiness.

Theatre Rhinoceros

2926 16th Street, between Mission Street & South Van Ness Avenue (861 5079/www.therhino.org). BART to 16th Street Mission/bus 14, 22, 26, 33, 49, 53. **Tickets** $15-$30. **Map** p109 E3 ⑬

Billing itself as the 'world's oldest continually producing, professional queer theatre', Rhino creates theatre that is genuinely inviting rather than self-segregating. Its productions comprise comedy, reinterpreted classics, original drama and the occasional musical.

The Castro

Bordered by Market, Diamond, 20th and Church Streets, the Castro is an international gay mecca. Being gay is the norm here; straights are tolerated, but they're the minority. In **Castro Street**, a rainbow-flag-festooned stretch of trendy shops and see-and-be-seen cafés and bars, most of them gay-owned, a predominantly male populace enjoys a hard-won social and political influence. A huge rainbow flag hangs over **Harvey Milk Plaza**, named for the activist who, in 1977, became San Francisco's city supervisor and the first

SAN FRANCISCO BY AREA

The art of shopping

An increasingly entrepreneurial spirit among San Francisco artists has resulted in a noticeable trend among some of the newer galleries: shops doing double duty as art galleries.

In the Mission, the **Curiosity Shoppe** (p115) carries a range of locally produced – well – curiosities, and also features a small monthly exhibition. Be sure to check out the apothecary cabinet next to the front window for a collection of small items ranging in price from five cents to a dollar. Next door, visit the outlet of printer **Little Otsu** (p116) for 'zines, comics, cards and crafts. On 16th Street, there's a monthly art show in the tiny back room at **Adobe Books** (p115). Across the street, **Needles and Pens** (p117) sells handmade clothes, 'zines and curates a regularly rotated art show on the store's back wall.

Over in the Upper Haight, **Giant Robot** (p132) is both a Japanese goods and t-shirt shop and a very small art gallery. **Park Life** (220 Clement Street, Richmond, 386 7275, www.parklifestore.com) sells similar products and also hosts a monthly art exhibition.

South of Market, visit **Electric Works** (130 8th Street, 626 5496, www.sfelectricworks.com) for its lovingly restored 1940s office decor, it gorgeous art exhibits and the kookiest collection of gifts you can imagine in the cubby cabinets behind the front desk.

openly gay elected official in the US, but was assassinated the following year.

For a great view of the Castro from above, get lunch to go and wander up to **Corona Heights** – walk all the way up 16th Street to Flint Street, then take a right; the bare red rock of Corona will loom overhead.

Eating & drinking

440 Castro

440 Castro Street, at 18th Street (621 8732/www.daddysbar.com). Metro to Castro/streetcar F/bus 24, 33, 35, 37. **Open** noon-2am daily. No credit cards. **Bar**. Map p108 B4 54

Formerly Daddy's, the Castro's reigning leather bar, 440 Castro has reinvented itself as a moderately swanky lounge but hasn't quite managed to shake off its preening he-man past. The crowd is an odd mix of old-school cruisers and youthful fans of hard techno, but the drinks specials are just right to smooth out the rougher edges.

Badlands

4121 18th Street, at Castro Street (626 9320/www. sfbadlands.com). Metro to Castro/streetcar F/bus 24, 33, 35, 37. **Open** 2pm-2am daily. No credit cards. **Bar**. Map p108 B4 55

Young gay suburbanites drenched in scent and sporting the latest in designer label knock-offs flock to this flashy video bar, which boasts one of the few dancefloors in the Castro. The music ranges from popular hip hop to early 1990s diva favourites, and the queue outside on weekends is often a scene of its own.

Bar on Castro

456 Castro Street, between 18th & Market Streets (626 7220/ www.thebarsf.com). Metro to Castro/ streetcar F/bus 24, 33, 35, 37. **Open** 4pm-2am Mon-Fri; 2pm-2am Sat, Sun. No credit cards. **Bar**. Map p108 B3 56

A heaving sweatbox crammed with a multitude of pretty boys bumping and grinding to thumping dance tunes. After-work crowds tend to congregate during the week for the two-for-one happy hour (daily until 8pm).

Chow

215 Church Street, at Market Street (552 2469/www.chowfoodbar.com). Metro to Church/streetcar F/bus 22, 37. **Open** 7am-11pm Mon-Thur; 7am-midnight Fri; 8am-midnight Sat; 8am-11pm Sun. **$$. American. Map** p108 C2 ⑰

Chow serves hugely popular, well-priced, straight-ahead American fare. The menu ranges widely, from the likes of roast chicken and burgers to Asian noodles, and the kitchen succeeds at most of things it attempts. The staff are pally, and the portions huge. What more could you want?

NEW Frisée

2367 Market Street, between Castro & Noe Streets (588 1616/www.frisee restaurant.com). Metro to Castro/ streetcar F/bus 24, 33, 35, 37. **Open** 5.30-10am Mon-Thur; 10.30-3pm, 5,30-11pm Fri-Sun. **$$. American. Map** p108 B3 ⑱

Frisée resembles an old-fashioned subway car, with curved ceilings, plenty of red velvet, and tables for two. Its organic/sustainable menu majors in healthful main-course salads at lunchtime; in the evenings chicken chowder and grilled fish (line-cut ahi, Canadian salmon) are among the highlights. The wine list is eco-friendly too.

Harvey's

500 Castro Street, at 18th Street (431 4278/ www.harveyssf.com). Metro to Castro/streetcar F/bus 24, 33, 35, 37. **Open** 11am-2am Mon-Fri; 9am-2am Sat, Sun. **Bar. Map** p108 B4 ⑲

The site of an infamous brawl with cops during the 1979 White Night riot that followed the lenient sentencing of Dan White, assassin of Harvey Milk, this bar-restaurant – named after Harvey Milk – is usually pervaded by a spirit of bonhomie. Saturdays host a mixed bag of drag and musical performances.

Home

2100 Market Street, at Church Street (503 0333/www.home-sf.com). Metro to Church/streetcar F/bus 22, 37. **Open** 5-10pm Mon-Thur; 5-11pm Fri; 10am-2pm, 5-11pm Sat, Sun. **$$. American. Map** p108 C2 ⑳

This sceney restaurant has big-city atmosphere but small-town comfort. Food comes as generous portions of well-prepared classic American fare. Roast chicken and meatloaf are right at home alongside seafood specialities and vegetable spring rolls. At weekend brunch, there's a make-your-own Bloody Mary bar.

Lucky 13

2140 Market Street, between Church & Sanchez Streets (487 1313). Metro to Church/streetcar F/bus 22, 37. **Open** 4pm-2am Mon-Thur; 2pm-2am Fri-Sun. No credit cards. **Bar. Map** p108 C2 ㉑

Dark, spacious and always busy, Lucky 13 has long been a favourite with those who crave the aura of a punk/biker bar without the perceived risk. There's pinball, pool and foosball, but the main entertainments are people-watching and choosing from one of the best German beer selections in the Bay Area.

NEW Jet

2348 Market Street, between Castro & Noe Streets (www.jetsf.com). Metro to Castro/streetcar F/bus 24, 33, 35, 37. **Open** 5pm-2am Mon-Fri; 3pm-2am Sat, Sun. No credit cards. **Bar. Map** p108 B3 ㉒

Opulently appointed, complete with leather-padded walls, a mirrored bar and a pink double bed, this pricey new joint appeals to the Bay Area's finely dressed Latin, hip hop and rock fans who like a little sparkle with their swizzle. A small dancefloor beckons with swaggering beats and raised go-go booths.

Mecca

2029 Market Street, between Dolores & 14th Streets (621 7000/www.sf mecca.com). Metro to Church/bus 22,

37. **Open** 5-10pm Tue-Wed; 5pm-midnight Thur-Sat; 11am-3.30pm Sun. **$$$. American.** Map p108 C2 ⑥③

Always in harmony with the surroundings, the food at this big, bustling and unswervingly fashionable restaurant remains one of the best bets in the Castro. Highlights might include the likes of confit of pork shoulder or prosciutto-wrapped tuna. Back at the bar, the mood gets ever looser as the cocktails flow and the DJ works his platters.

Midnight Sun

4067 18th Street, at Hartford Street (861 4186/www.midnightsunsf.com). Metro to Castro/streetcar F/bus 24, 33, 35, 37. **Open** 2pm-2am Mon-Fri; 1pm-2am Sat, Sun. No credit cards. **Bar.** Map p108 B4 ⑥④

The big draw at Midnight Sun is video – that is, classic and contemporary music cross-cut with comedy clips, *The Sopranos* or *Sex and the City*. There are two-for-one cocktails during the week (2-7pm), and weekends are a boy fest.

Mix

4086 18th Street, at Hartford Street (431 8616/ www.sfmixbar.com). Metro to Castro/streetcar F/bus 24, 33, 35, 37. **Open** 6am-2am daily. No credit cards. **Bar.** Map p108 B4 ⑥⑤

This rough-and-ready sports bar is a haven for queer jocks and those who adore them. Fans pack the place to root for the '49ers, and sunny weekends see the back patio grilling up burgers and hot dogs. The windows face 18th Street, which is perfect for ogling.

Moby Dick's

4049 18th Street, at Hartford Street (861 1199/www.mobydicksf.com). Metro to Castro/streetcar F/bus 24, 33, 35, 37. **Open** 2pm-2am Mon-Fri; noon-2am Sat, Sun. No credit cards. **Bar.** Map p108 B4 ⑥⑥

A true neighbourhood bar, Moby Dick's is exactly as it has been since the 1980s. It's popular with pool players (despite the fact that there's only one table) and pinball addicts (there are four machines at the back), but big windows and a prime Castro location afford ample cruising potential too.

Pilsners Inn

225 Church Street, at Market Street (621 7058). Metro to Church/streetcar F/bus 22, 37. **Open** 10am-2am daily. No credit cards. **Bar.** Map p108 C2 ⑥⑦

It all happens here, especially on the heated back patio. The Pilsner is a local favourite among youngish beauty boys, who like to play pool, pinball and computer games, or chat over the sounds of the retro jukebox. There's a wide choice of draft beers.

Transfer

198 Church Street, at Market Street (861 7499). Metro to Church/streetcar F/bus 22, 37. **Open** 5pm-2am daily. No credit cards. **Bar.** Map p108 C2 ⑥⑧

An indie, electro and underground dance music fiesta for all orientations and sexual persuasions. Although relatively small, this former lesbian biker bar has become the top dancefloor hotspot for youthful scenemakers who are willing to get a few sweat stains on their unique apparel. Party programming changes nightly.

Twin Peaks Tavern

401 Castro Street, at Market Street (864 9470/www.twinpeaks tavern.com). Metro to Castro/streetcar F/bus 24, 33, 35, 37. **Open** noon-2am Mon-Wed; 8am-2am Thur-Sun. No credit cards. **Bar.** Map p108 B3 ⑥⑨

Billing itself as 'the Gateway to the Castro', the snug Twin Peaks Tavern was one of the first gay bars in the United States to brave the public gaze with street-level windows. Nowadays, its habitués are mostly older, and come to enjoy a quiet chat, good music and even a game of cards. The lovely antique bar serves everything except bottled beer.

Shopping

Citizen Clothing

536 Castro Street, between 18th & 19th Streets (575 3560/www.bodyclothing.com). Metro to

Halloween in Castro

Castro/bus 4, 33, 35, 37. **Open** 10am-8pm Mon-Sat; 11am-7pm Sun. **Map** p108 B4 **70**
Citizen is all about upscale utilitarian chic: Scotch & Soda, Ben Sherman and Fred Perry appear alongside Ted Baker, Jack Spade and Gucci accessories. Boys seeking something a bit more sporty head up the street to sibling establishment Body (450 Castro Street, 575 3562).

Crossroads Trading Co
2123 Market Street, at Church Streets, (552 8740/www.crossroads trading.com). Metro to Church/bus 22, 37. **Open** 11am-8pm Mon-Sat; noon-7pm Sun. **Map** p108 C2 **71**
People who still haven't got over that 1980s retro thing should pop into the Market and Haight Street branches of this favourite local chain; the Fillmore location is best for jeans, dresses and designer and vintage pieces.

Medium Rare Records
2310 Market Street, at 16th Street (255 7273). Metro to Castro/bus 24, 33, 35, 37. **Open** 11am-9pm Mon-Thur, Sun; 11am-10pm Fri, Sat. **Map** p108 B3 **72**
A lovingly assembled collection of CDs and DVDs is crammed into the tiny space here. The range available meanders wildly across the decades and genres, with everything from disco to dance, vocal standards to show tunes. You never know what you might unearth.

Nightlife

Amber
718 14th Street, between Belcher & Church Streets (626 7827). Metro to Church/streetcar F/bus 22, 37. **Open** 6pm-2am Mon-Fri; 7pm-2am Sat, Sun. **Admission** varies. No credit cards. **Map** p108 C2 **73**
Known to locals as the unofficial straight bar of gay Castro, but the real draw – apart from the diverse crowd, underground tunes and cosy atmosphere – is the lax smoking rules. Smoking is illegal in bars, btu Amber slipped through a loophole in the law as it's owned by the staff.

The Café
2369 Market Street, at Castro Street (861 3846/www.cafesf.com). Metro to Castro/streetcar F/bus 24, 33, 35, 37. **Open** 3pm-2am daily. **Admission** varies. No credit cards. **Map** p108 B3 **74**
There's dancing every night at the Café, the Castro's largest and most

Minnie Wilde p116

popular club. Once the area's only women's bar, it now mainly attracts boys from outlying areas, but lasses show up during the day, on weeknights and (especially) on Sunday afternoons. The music blends house, hip hop and salsa. There are two bars, a dancefloor and a patio, plus pinball, pool and computer games.

Arts & leisure

Café du Nord/ Swedish American Hall

2170 Market Street, between Church & Sanchez Streets, Castro (861 5016/ www.cafedunord.com). Metro to Church/streetcar F/bus 22, 37. **Open** 1hr before show-2am. *Shows* times vary, daily. **Admission** $10-$35. **Map** p108 C3 ⑦⑤
Several San Francisco nightspots carry the feel of a Prohibition-era speakeasy, but none captures the spirit quite as well as the Café du Nord. Mind you, it's hardly surprising: it actually was one.

The subterranean front room, which hosts cultured alternative acts, has red velvet walls and a 40ft mahogany bar that bustles with scenesters. The likes of Cat Power, Joanna Newsom, Bert Jansch and Jenny Lewis have played the quaint, larger Swedish American Hall upstairs.

Castro Theatre

429 Castro Street, at Market Street, Castro (621 6120/www.thecastro theatre.com). Metro to Castro/streetcar F/bus 24, 33, 35, 37. **Tickets** $9; $6 reductions. No credit cards. **Map** p108 B3 ⑦⑥
One of San Francisco's finest and best-loved repertory cinemas, this art deco movie palace was built in 1922. It was listed as a registered historical building 55 years later, thus ensuring proper protection for its structure. These days it's a dream space of classical murals and rare old film posters, with ceilings that shimmer with gold and films introduced to the strains of a Mighty Wurlitzer organ.

Old is the new new

San Franciso's vibrant vintage clothing scene: an idyll of Summer of Love, blossom-splashed grooviness and '70s-era *Ice Storm* suburban suavitude for some retro-fashionistas, it is considered far too pricey by others, who insist that the best riches are salvaged at rock-bottom prices at the city's thrift stores.

For those who would rather have their throwback fashion filtered by discerning, style-conscious eyes, SF's vintage boutiques are a goldmine. The coolest – and amazingly, the best priced – has to be the Mission's **Painted Bird** (p117), a sunny outpost that's always blasting the hippest stoner metal or electro in town, with a refined, fun rock 'n' roll style to match: look for sprigged '70s fairy-princess sundresses, '80s-esque striped sweaters and T's and tooled and patchwork leather bags.

Further up the price spectrum, but no less hep, are the '60s- and '70s-oriented **Ver Unica** (p140) in Hayes Valley – picture a Francophile *Belle du Jour* style mixed with rich hippie embroidered coats, funky leather belts, and graphic copper jewellery – and **Static** in the Haight (p132), which is fixated on Gucci handbags, both real and knockoff; tough jackets; jeans; and cowboy boots.

Haight-Ashbury also boasts a slew of other retro reliables: the all-class **La Rosa Vintage** (1147 Haight Street, 668-3744), with its fabulous collection of men's mid-century suits; the more poppy **Held Over** (1543 Haight Street, 864-0818) with vintage concert T-shirts; the cavernous **Wasteland** (p132) with just about anything

rockin'; resale shops **Buffalo Exchange** (p132) and **Crossroads Trading Company** (p132); and the '60s and '70s cool, yet costumey and unpretentious **Aaardvark's** (1501 Haight Street, 621-3141).

Worth visiting in the vintage-focused Mission: the crammed **Schauplatz** (791 Valencia Street, 864 5665) with its splashy array of sundresses; and the glammy **Idol Vintage** (3162 16th Street, 255 9959), with its delectable array of folkloric vests, tennis sweaters, and '80s-era boots.

Meanwhile, those hardliners who find digging a challenge will want to paw through tatty castoffs to pluck out the occasional gem at the **Goodwill** and **Salvation Army** stores that stud the town (the former at Van Ness and Mission and the latter at 25th Street and Valencia are the biggest and best), or try their luck at the ginormous **Thrift Town** (2101 Mission Street, 861-1132, www.thrifttown.com).

Buena Vista Park

The Haight & Around

Mention the words 'Haight-Ashbury', or even just 'the Haight', and members of a certain generation will either sigh with a nostalgic longing or groan in exasperation, depending on their political persuasion and/or their psychological or physical proximity to 1967's legendary Summer of Love. However, once the crowds had tuned out, turned off and dropped back in again, the neighbourhood resumed duty as one of the most liveable and vibrant areas of San Francisco.

Bordering the Haight, the Western Addition has alternately been the heart of the West Coast jazz scene and the centre of its Japanese community, while Hayes Valley has emerged as an enclave of considerable hipness.

The Haight

The stretch of Haight Street that sits between Masonic and Stanyan Streets, known both as **Haight-Ashbury** and **Upper Haight**, makes for a lively scene on weekends and warm-weather days. Stores hawk new age and eastern esoterica, edgy clothing, high-fashion shoes and mountains of records and CDs. At the corner of Haight Street and Central Avenue is the aptly named, beautifully wooded **Buena Vista Park**, the oldest designated park in the city.

Just a few blocks from Haight-Asbury, the cosy enclave of **Cole Valley** is a different world altogether: low-key, smart and upscale. The businesses here are all clustered around a two-block area of Cole and Carl Streets.

While Upper Haight still clings dreamily to its political past, the young, the disenchanted and the progressive have migrated down the hill to **Lower Haight**, Hipper and harsher than its neighbour, the area centres around Haight Street between Divisadero and Octavia Streets.

Eating & drinking

Alembic

1725 Haight Street, between Cole & Shrader Streets (666 0822/www. alembicbar.com). Metro to Cole & Carl/bus 7, 33, 37, 43, 71. **Open** 4pm-midnight Mon-Thur; noon-midnight Fri-Sun. Bar until 2am daily. **$$**.
American. Map p128 A4 ❶
The Haight has no shortage of excellent drinking holes, but few possess the panache of this whisky-fuelled destination. The food menu is spare but pretty good, consisting of hits like the housemade saké gravlax, spätzle and spiced lamb burger. It's matched with a head-spinning array of boutique beers, Scottish single malts, American whiskies and even rare ryes.

Eos Restaurant

901 Cole Street, at Carl Street (566 3063/www.eossf.com). Metro to Carl & Cole/bus 6, 37, 43. **Open** 5.30-10pm Mon-Thur, Sun; 5.30-11pm Fri, Sat. **$$**.
Asian. Map p128 B5 ❷
The best of East-West fusion, served in a comfortably spare, highly designed restaurant. Classically trained chef/owner Arnold Eric Wong produces dishes such as tea-smoked peking duck and tamarind chilli-glazed spare ribs, backed up by one of the Bay Area's best wine lists. The same menu is served in the wine bar next door (101 Carl Street).

Grind Café

783 Haight Street, at Scott Street (864 0955/www. thegrindcafe.com). Bus 6, 7, 24, 71. **Open** 7am-8pm Mon-Fri; 7am-6pm Sat; 8am-6pm Sun. **$**. **Café. Map** p129 D4 ❸

This casual café is populated by too-cool-for-school denizens of the Lower Haight. The best eats are the vegetable-packed omelettes and stacks of pancakes. The open-air patio welcomes dog owners and the occasional cigarette.

Hobson's Choice

1601 Haight Street, at Clayton Street (621 5859/ www.hobsonschoice.com). Metro to Cole & Carl/bus 6, 7, 33, 37, 43, 71. **Open** 2pm-2am Mon-Fri; noon-2am Sat, Sun. **Bar. Map** p128 B4 ❹
At this 'Victorian punch bar' (the owners' description), bartenders ladle out tall glasses of tasty rum punch; the menu boasts more than 70 kinds of rum. Fresh, grilled kebabs from the neighbouring Asqew Grill are great to soak up the booze as it settles in the bellies of the collegiate-cum-jam-band set that fills the place.

Kate's Kitchen

471 Haight Street, between Fillmore & Webster Streets (626 3984). Bus 6, 7, 22, 71. **Open** 8am-2.45pm Mon-Fri; 8.30am-3.45pm Sat, Sun. **$**. No credit cards. **Diner. Map** p129 D4 ❺
A buzzing spot that's an excellent choice when you've got a mountain of Sunday papers to wade through at your leisure. Ease into the day with the assistance of a giant bowl of granola, a huge omelette or the signature dish of hush puppies (drop pancakes made of cornmeal).

Mad Dog in the Fog

530 Haight Street, between Fillmore & Steiner Streets (626 7279). Metro to Duboce & Church/ bus 6, 7, 22, 71. **Open** 3pm-midnight Mon; 11am-2am Tue; 3pm-2am Wed-Fri; 10am-2pm Sat; 10am-midnight Sun. No credit cards. **Bar. Map** p129 D4 ❻
Anglophiles and expats pack the Mad Dog for pub quizzes and football broadcasts (it opens early at weekends for English Premiership matches). Strong selections of 20 beers on tap and another 30 in bottles back up the menu of pub grub, which includes English breakfasts.

The Haight & Around

PRESIDIO HEIGHTS

PACIFIC HEIGHTS

WEST PACIFIC AVE   JACKSON   STREET   WASHINGTON   STREET   Alta Plaza Park

CHERRY   JORDAN   WALNUT   LAUREL   PRESIDIO   LYON   BAKER   CLAY   STREET

COMMONWEALTH   AVENUE   SPRUCE   LOCUST   MAPLE   CALIFORNIA   STREET   PINE   STREET

EUCLID   AVENUE   LAUREL   PINE   STREET

FARRER   HEATHER AVE   ALPINE   BUSH   STREET   UCSF Medical Center

Laurel Hill Playground   SUTTER   Street   Kaiser Medical Center

GEARY   BOULEVARD   POST   STREET

O'FARRELL STREET

Columbarium   ANZA ST   TERRA VISTA AVE   ELLIS   SCOTT

ROSSI AVE   ANZA   STREET   ANZA VISTA AVENUE   ST JOSEPH'S STREET   EDDY

Rossi Playground   University of San Francisco   TURK   STREET   McAllister   STREET   27

TURK   STREET   FULTON   STREET   GROVE   STREE

University of San Francisco   GOLDEN GATE AVENUE

McALLISTER STREET   FULTON   STREET   DIVISADERO   28

VILLARD ST NORTH   St Mary's Medical Center   GROVE   STREET   LYON   STREET   BAKER   STREET   BRODERICK   STREET   DIVISADERO ST

HAYES   STREET   Panhandle

McLaren Lodge   FELL   STREET   BUENA VISTA

STANYAN ST   OAK   STREET   MASONIC   AVENUE   CENTRAL   AVENUE

Sharon Meadow   PAGE   STREET   HAIGHT ASHBURY   16   14 19   8

HAIGHT   STREET   21 22   BELVEDERE ST   13 4   17   Buena Vista Park

23   20   25   1

Children's Playground   15   18   WALLER   STREET   COLE   STREET   BUENA VISTA   TERRACE EAST

Kezar Pavilion   COLE VALLEY   DOWNEY   DELMAR   ASHBURY   BUENA VISTA AVE WEST   BUENA VISTA   TERRACE WEST

FREDERICK   STREET   Muni Metro   Carl & Cole   11th AVE

CARL   Carl & Cole   STREET   CLAYTON   STREET   Corona Height Park

2

Kezar   PARNASSUS   AVENUE   UPPER TERRACE   ROOSEVELT   WAY   STATES STREET   MUSEUM WAY   Randall Museum

UCSF Medical Center   CLIFFORD TERRACE

© Copyright Time Out Group 2008

0   500 m
0   500 yds

Haight Street p126

Madrone Lounge

500 Divisadero Street, at Fell Street (241 0202/ www.madronelounge.com). Bus 21, 24. **Open** 2pm-midnight Mon, Sun; 2pm-2am Tue-Sat. **Bar.** **Map** p128 C4 ❼

A funky lounge and gallery whose beautifully restored Victorian exterior brought joy to the neighbours when it was revived from almost total dilapidation. Inside, draught beers, a speciality cocktail list and a bar menu keeps patrons happy and occupied while digging DJs, independent film screenings or live music.

Magnolia

1398 Haight Street, at Masonic Avenue (864 7468/www.magnoliapub.com). Bus 6, 7, 33, 37, 43, 71. **Open** noon-1am Mon-Thur; noon-1am Fri; 10am-1am Sat; 10am-11pm Sun. **Bar.** **Map** p128 B4 ❽

This brewpub's decor plays up to its history: built in 1903, it was a focal point of hippie culture in the 1960s, before being taken over by quasi-legendary local dessert maven Magnolia Thunderpussy, after whom it's now

named. A solid bar menu complements the own-brewed beer selection, which includes some cask ales.

Noc Noc

557 Haight Street, between Fillmore & Steiner Streets (861 5811/www.noc nocs.com). Metro to Duboce & Church/ bus 6, 7, 22, 71. **Open** 5pm-2am daily. **Bar.** **Map** p129 D4 ❾

The decor here has been described as post-apocalyptic industrial, and the whole place has a peculiarly organic Gaudi feel to it. Always plunged in near darkness and with a mellow chill-room vibe, Noc Noc tends to attract a multi-ethnic lot.

RNM

598 Haight Street, at Steiner Street (551 7900/www.rnmrestaurant.com). Bus 6, 7, 22, 71. **Open** 5.30-10pm Tue-Thur; 5.30-11pm Fri, Sat. **$$.** **American.** **Map** p129 D4 ❿

A slice of New York's SoHo translated for a laid-back Californian crowd. The high-style dining room (complete with massive chandelier) belies the food, which is almost entirely without pretension and mostly off-the-chart

SAN FRANCISCO BY AREA

delicious. Don't miss ahi on roasted garlic crostini or the Maine lobster with white corn risotto.

Thep Phanom

400 Waller Street, at Fillmore Street (431 2526/www.thepphanom.com).Bus 6, 7, 22, 66, 71. **Open** 5.30-10.30pm daily. **$$**. **Asian**. **Map** p129 D4 ⑪
Be sure to book in advance at Thep Phanom – and once you're there, be sure to order the *tom ka gai* (coconut chicken soup) as a starter. The 'angel wings' – fried chicken wings stuffed with glass noodles – are another universally popular choice. This place is often hailed as the best Thai restaurant in San Francisco.

Toronado

547 Haight Street, between Fillmore & Steiner Streets (863 2276/www. toronado.com). Bus 6, 7, 22, 66, 71. **Open** 11.30am-2am daily. No credit cards. **Bar**. **Map** p129 D4 ⑫
A noisy hangout and beer drinker's delight. A board posted on the wall shows the massive, ever-changing selection of draughts (which includes local brews and Belgian imports), while the blackboard behind the bar highlights bottled beer and non-alco options. Patrons are encouraged to bring in sausages from Rosamunde Sausage Grill next door.

Zam Zam

1633 Haight Street, between Clayton & Belvedere Streets (861 2545). Metro to Cole & Carl/bus 6, 7, 33, 37, 43, 71. **Open** 3pm-2am Mon-Fri; 1pm-2am Sat, Sun. No credit cards. **Bar**. **Map** p128 B4 ⑬
This tiny bar became famous under its notoriously cantankerous owner Bruno Mooshei, who waged a one-man campaign to keep it exactly as it must have been circa World War II. Mooshei died in 2000, but the place was bought by long-time patrons devoted to keeping its Casablanca aura intact. It's a great place for a pre-and/or post-cinema drink when catching a flick at the red Vic movie house just up the street.

Eos p127

Shopping

Ambiance

1458 Haight Street, between Masonic Avenue & Ashbury Stree (552 5095/ www. ambiancesf.com). Metro to Carl & Cole/bus 6, 7, 33, 43, 66, 71. **Open** 10am-7pm Mon-Sat; 11am-7pm Sun. **Map** p128 B4 ⑭
If you've got an occasion, Ambiance has the perfect ensemble for it: its glowing collection of retro-style dresses and saucy skirts is even arranged by colour for your convenience. The sales staff are beyond friendly.

Amoeba Music

1855 Haight Street, between Shrader & Stanyan Streets (831 1200/www. amoeba.com). Metro to Carl & Cole/ bus 6, 7, 33, 43, 66, 71. **Open** 10.30am-10pm Mon-Sat; 11am-9pm Sun. **Map** p128 B4 ⑮
Amoeba Music remains a mighty presence: there's every imaginable type of music, both new and used, the vast majority priced very fairly, as well as a massive DVD selection. There are free gigs, too, with some surprisingly big names.

Behind the Post Office

1510 Haight Street, between Ashbury & Clayton Streets (861 2507). Metro to Carl & Cole/bus 6, 7, 33, 43, 66, 71. **Open** 11am-7pm Mon-Thur, Sun; 11am-7.30pm Fri, Sat. **Map** p128 B4 ⑯

Space is at a premium, but this tiny boutique packs in the style with vibrant T-shirts and edgy new designers, all at moderate prices.

Buffalo Exchange

1555 Haight Street, at Clayton Street, Haight-Ashbury (431 7733/www.buffaloexchange.com). Metro to Carl & Cole/bus 6, 7, 33, 71. **Open** 11am-7pm Mon-Wed; 11am-8pm Thur-Sun. **Map** p128 B4 ⑰

Buffalo Exchange didn't achieve its lofty station as a national trade-in chain by its gentle touch: locals are used to looks of near-contempt when trying to get rid of those stone-washed Gap reverse-cut jeans. Nevertheless, the range is vast.

Giant Robot

618 Shrader Street, between Haight & Waller Streets (876 4773/www.giantrobot.com). **Open** 11.30am-8pm Mon-Fri; 11am-8pm Sat; noon-7pm Sun. **Map** p128 A5 ⑱

This innovative retailer, which spun off the 'zine of the same name and has inspired other area boutiques/galleries such as Super 7 (1628 Post Street, Western Addition, 409 4700) and Park Life (220 Clement Street, Richmond, 386 7275), specialises in Asian-American pop in all its incarnations: fine art, toys, illustration, T-shirts, anime artefacts, art books and ephemera. Be sure to check out the affordable art in the gallery space.

Shoe Biz

1446 Haight Street, between Ashbury Street & Masonic Avenue (864 0990/www. shoebizsf.com). Metro to Carl & Cole/bus 6, 7, 33, 43, 66, 71. **Open** 11am-7pm Mon-Sat; noon-6pm Sun. **Map** p128 B4 ⑲

Whether you need a spike heel or a hot-pink pointy-toed flat, Shoe Biz adds a bit of punky glamour to current trends. Trainer addicts should head for Shoe Biz II at no.1553 for racks of rare Pumas, Adidas and New Balance.

Static

1764 Haight Street, between Shrader & Cole Streets, Haight-Ashbury (422 0046/www.staticvintage.com). **Open** noon-7pm Mon-Thur, Sun; noon-8pm Fri, Sat. **Map** p128 A4 ⑳

'Vintage for the modern' is the hallmark of this boutique with a distinct high-'70s, rocker-tough and California-cool sensibility. Read: used denim and leather, Gucci bags, worn-soft T-shirts and boots.

Villains

1672 Haight Street, between Clayton & Cole Streets (626 5939). Metro to Carl & Cole/bus 6, 7, 33, 43, 66, 71. **Open** 11am-7pm daily. **Map** p128 B4 ㉑

Villains sells a mix of cropped trousers, experimental fabrics and trendy ensembles for men and women that scream 'I party!' Next door is a great selection of covetable shoes, from Schmoove to spiked heels straight out of a Joan Jett video.

Wasteland

1660 Haight Street, between Clayton & Cole Streets, Haight-Ashbury (863 3150). Metro to Carl & Cole/bus 6, 7, 33, 43, 66, 71. **Open** 11am-8pm Mon-Sat; noon-7pm Sun. **Map** p128 B4 ㉒

Possibly the most popular used clothier in town, Wasteland sells second-hand clothing with history, including a rich supply of vintage costume jewellery, fancy gowns and worn-in leather jackets.

Nightlife

Milk DJ Bar & Lounge

1840 Haight Street, between Shrader & Stanyan Streets (387 6455/www.milk sf.com). Bus 6, 7, 33, 43, 71. **Open** 9pm-2am daily. **Admission** free-$10. **Map** p128 A4 ㉓

For years, the Haight-Ashbury district was ground zero for the city's rock scene, but these days hip hop is

Wine bars reborn

San Franciscans have always loved wine – after all, some great wines are produced within hours of the city. But there's a new way to enjoy this bounty: excellent wine bars are popping up throughout the city, places where wine lovers can nibble on local cheeses and charcuterie and browse long lists of wines, local and foreign, familiar and unfamiliar. What distinguishes these places, or the people who work in them, is expertise and an enthusiasm, both of which staff are eager to share with neophytes as well as long-term wine-lovers.

Hotel Biron

The acclaimed **London Wine Bar** (415 Sansome Street at Sacramento Street, 788 4811), has the distinction of being the nation's first wine bar – established during the first great era of the wine bar, the 1970s (it opened in 1974). It offers 40-50 wines by the glass and has won Wine Spectator's Award of Excellence every year since 1982.

For a homier atmosphere, there are places like **Hidden Vine** (620 Post Street, between Taylor and Trader Vic Alley, 674 3567, www.thehiddenvine.com), where the basement location and sitting-room atmosphere are a welcome respite from the bustle of Union Square just blocks away, and **Hotel Biron** (45 Rose Street, at Market Street, 703 0403, www.hotelbiron.com), hidden away down an alley. Here drinkers can enjoy 35 wines by the glass and 80 by the bottle, while checking out the works of local artists that adorn the walls. If you're in the area and want a

contrast, the lively, flashier **Cav** (1666 Market Street; 437 1770, www.cavwinebar.com), with more than 300 bottles and 40 wines by the glass, is just around the block.

Where regeneration goes, wine bars follow in this city. Out in the Dogpatch neighbourhood near Mission Bay is **Yield Wine Bar** (2490 Third Street; 401 8984, www.yieldsf.com). Serving only organic and biodynamic wines, it is blazing a trail for the predicted invasion of biotech workers poised to take over the new Third Avenue Light Rail corridor.

If simply drinking wine isn't enough, you can make your own at **CrushPad** (2573 Third Street; 864 4232/www.crushpadwine.com). Here winemaking experts guide customers through the 10-18 month process of creating wine ready to drink. Prices start at $4,400 (you have to buy enough for a whole barrel, after all).

creeping in and proving itself a Haight Street mainstay, due in no small part to Milk's hip hop- and R&B-friendly bookers. Flash modern decor and a decent-sized dancefloor characterise the space, while big-name guests such as DJ Shadow have been known to drop in at events put on by True Skool and Future Primitive Sound.

Underground SF

424 Haight Street, between Fillmore & Webster Streets (www.underground sf.com). Bus 6, 7, 22, 71. **Open** 9pm-2am daily. **Admission** free-$10. **Map** p129 D4 ㉔

On a somewhat sketchy stretch of the Lower Haight, the club formerly known as the Top is little more than a converted dive with a smallish dancefloor. But it has a deserved reputation as a centre for turntable culture, and has become a favourite spot with more discerning queers who love disco-funk but hate ABBA.

Arts & leisure

Red Vic

1727 Haight Street, at Cole Street, Haight-Ashbury (668 3994/www.redvic moviehouse.com). Bus 6, 7, 33, 43, 66, 71. **Tickets** $8.50; $5-$6.50 reductions. No credit cards. **Map** p128 A4 ㉕

Old sofas, popcorn in wooden bowls with butter and brewer's yeast, and a choice of films ranging from revivals to the best current movies make you feel right at home here.

The Western Addition

The Western addition was not only the city's first suburb, but also its first multicultural neighbourhood. Mapped out in the 1860s to accommodate the post-Gold Rush population boom, the area was home to a thriving Jewish community from the 1890s, and later to Japanese- and African-Americans. Today it still has a very distinct character. Gentrification is creeping in,

but slowly, and the area's shopping remains mostly chain-free.

The **Fillmore District** was a mecca for jazz and blues musicians in the 1940s and '50s. However, the locale was declared a slum by the San Francisco Redevelopment Agency in the 1960s and torn apart under the guise of urban renewal. Luckily, new life is being slowly and steadily breathed into the area.

Eating & drinking

NEW 1300 On Fillmore

1300 Fillmore Street, at Eddy Street (771 7100/ www.1300fillmore.com). Bus 22, 31, 38. **Open** 5.30-11pm Mon, Sun; 5.30pm-1am Tue-Sat. *Bar from 4.30pm daily.* **$$$. American.** **Map** p129 D2 ㉖

Along with Yoshi's (below), 1300 on Fillmore is a welcome addition to the area. The Southern-influenced fare is anchored in classics: fried chicken, barbecued shrimp with grits, and mac and cheese. The room has a lounge-club atmosphere, with big leather chairs and classic jazz streaming through the air.

Café Abir

1300 Fulton Street, at Divisadero Street (567 6503). Bus 5, 21, 24. **Open** 6am-12.30am daily. **$.** No credit cards. **Café. Map** p128 C3 ㉗

This hip, laid-back café is always popular, and the friendly staff and well-chosen house music mean it's as much about nightlife as morning life. An organic grocery store, a bar, a coffee roastery and an international newsstand supplement the large café. Choose from the freshly made sandwiches and deli salads, or just get a bagel to accompany your latte.

NEW Nopa

560 Divisadero Street , at Hayes Street (864 8643/www.nopasf.com). Bus 5, 21, 24. **Open** 6pm-1am (bar open 5pm) daily. **$$. Italian. Map** p128 C3 ㉘

One of the hottest restaurants in town, Nopa's attractions include the wood-fired oven, and the late hours – unusual in a city where many kitchens pack up at 10pm. Italian- and Med-inspired ('urban rustic') dishes show an inventive use of ingredients. The interior is spacious, with high wood beams; the ambience is pleasantly casual.

NEW Yoshi's

1330 Fillmore Street, at Eddy Street (655 5600/ www.yoshis.com/sf). Bus 22, 31, 38. **Open** *5.30-10.30pm Mon-Wed; 5.30-11pm Thur-Sat; 5-10pm Sun. Bar & lounge 5pm-1am Mon-Sat; 5pm-midnight Sun.* **$$$$.** **Asian.** **Map** p129 D2 ㉓

The calendar of jazz performers is the main attraction at this new branch of the famous East Bay jazz club, but the extensive menu of sushi and other Japanese specialities doesn't disappoint. Book in advance and arrive early to enjoy dinner before moving in to the theatre for the show. Alternatively, you can dine before the later show and reserve seats through your server.

Shopping

Harputs

1527 Fillmore Street, at Geary Boulevard (923 9300/www.harputs. com). Bus 2, 3, 4, 22, 38. **Open** *11am-7pm Mon-Sat; noon-6pm Sun.* **Map** p129 D2 ㉚

The Harputs family has been supplying the 'hood with kicks since 1978. These days you'll still find rare Adidas, Nike, Converse and Royal Elastics, as well as sportswear. Amble next door (no.1525) to check out the more upscale designs, with Martin Margiela footwear, as well as Yohji Yamamoto's Y-3 line for Adidas, at Harputs Market (922 9644).

Nightlife

Madrone Lounge

500 Divisadero Street, at Fell Street (241 0202/www.madronelounge.com). Bus 21, 24. **Open** *2pm-2am daily.* **Admission** *free-$5.* **Map** p128 C4 ㉛

This cosy room on the edge of the Lower Haight, which also functions as a cutting-edge art gallery, draws its share of students from the nearby USF

and UCSF campuses for its regular happy hours and laid-back vibe. It's tiny, so when local bands notify USF's college radio station (KUSF 90.3 FM) of their concerts here, they have little trouble filling the joint.

Arts & leisure

Boom Boom Room

1601 Fillmore Street, at Geary Boulevard, Fillmore (673 8000/www. boomboomblues.com). Bus 2, 3, 4, 22, 38. **Open** *4pm-2am Tue-Sun.* **Shows** *9pm Tue-Sun.* **Admission** *$5-$20.* **Map** p129 D2 ㉜

Formerly Jack's Bar, an SF fixture for more than 50 years, the Boom Boom Room has been remade as a classy version of a blues joint: John Lee Hooker named the club after his signature song and, until his death in 2001, held court up front. These days, the venue attracts solid blues, roots, funk, R&B and groove-oriented acts, with an occasional surprise rock star dropping in.

Fillmore Auditorium

1805 Geary Boulevard, at Fillmore Street, Fillmore (24hr hotline 346 6000/www.thefillmore.com). Bus 2, 3, 4, 22, 38. **Box office** *10am-4pm Sun; also 7.30-10pm show nights.* **Tickets** *$20-$50.* **Map** p129 D2 ㉝

The 1,200-capacity Fillmore was built in 1912, but is better known as the venue in which Bill Graham launched his rock-promotion empire. The performers who play the gorgeous room tend to be on the verge of making it massive.

Independent

628 Divisadero Street, at Hayes Street, (771 1421/www.the independentsf.com). Bus 21, 24. **Box office** *11am-6pm Mon-Fri; 1hr before show.* **Tickets** *$10-$25.* **Map** p128 C3 ㉞

New owners have given this venerable black box the makeover it deserved, with work that included the installation of a stellar sound and light system. The calendar is filled with a mix of touring rock, pop, metal, rap, jazz, Americana, jam and otherwise undefinable offerings such as Madlib, Sunn 0))), the Boredoms, Fiery Furnaces, High on Fire and Lyrics Born.

Rasselas Jazz

1534 Fillmore Street, at Geary Boulevard, Fillmore (346 8696/www.rasselasjazzclub.com). Bus 2, 3, 4, 22, 38. **Open** 6pm-midnight Mon-Thur, Sun; 5pm-2am Fri, Sat. *Shows* usually 9pm Mon-Thur, Sun; 6pm, 9pm Fri, Sat. **Admission** usually 2 drink minimum. **Map** p129 D2 ㉟

Designed to be an anchor of the Fillmore Jazz Preservation District, Rasselas suffers from unadventurous programming, yet still manages to draw lively crowds at weekends. The decor – high ceilings, bachelor-pad furniture and a crackling fireplace behind the band – is suggestive of a 1960s playboy den.

Japantown

Devastated by the internment of Japanese-Americans during World War II, the community is now home to only a tiny percentage of the city's 12,000 Japanese-Americans. At the heart of Japantown is the **Japan Center**, a mostly underground maze of shops, restaurants and unique businesses that cater to Japanese residents.

Sights & museums

Cathedral of St Mary of the Assumption

1111 Gough Street, at Geary Boulevard (567 2020/www.stmarycathedralsf.org). Bus 2, 3, 4, 38. **Open** 6.45am-4pm Mon-Fri, Sun; 6.45am-5.30pm Sat. **Admission** free. **Map** p129 E2 ㊱

Dominating the skyline, the exterior of this 1970 cathedral is stark, a flowing, sculptural structure reaching 198ft (60m) into the sky. The four corner pylons were designed to support millions of pounds of pressure and extend 90ft (27m) down to the bedrock beneath the church. Inside, the staggering structure of the cupola is revealed in 1,500 triangular coffers, in over 128 sizes, meant to distribute the weight of the roof. Large corner windows allow views of the city.

Eating & drinking

Mifune

Japan Center, 1737 Post Street, between Webster & Buchanan Streets (922 0337/www.mifune.com). Bus 2, 3, 4, 22, 38. **Open** 11am-9.30pm daily. **$$**. **Asian**. **Map** p129 D2 ㊲

Good for kids and vegetarians, you'll find the lowly noodle prepared in at least 30 different ways here. Orders come quickly, and the food is that appealing combination: inexpensive and delicious.

O Izakaya Lounge

Hotel Kabuki, 1625 Post Street, at Laguna Street (614 5431/ www.jdvhotels.com/dining). Bus 2, 3, 4, 38. **Open** 6.30-10.30am, 5-10pm Mon-Fri; 7am-3pm, 5-10pm Sat, Sun. *Bar* 5pm-1am daily. **$$$**. **Asian**. **Map** p129 E2 ㊳

This combination *izakaya* house and Japanese sports bar is a bit bizarre at first glance. But the oddball vibe is all part of the charm, and it has quickly caught on with a hipster crowd and curious onlookers as well as with fans of the very good food from chef Nicolaus Balla. The menu features small plates of traditional Japanese cuisine prepared with fresh local ingredients. There are more than 20 different sakes on offer .

Seoul Garden

22 Peace Plaza, Geary Boulevard, at Laguna Street (563 7664/www.seoulgardenbbq.com). Bus 2, 3, 4, 38. **Open** 11.30am-10.30pm daily. **$$**. **Asian**. **Map** p129 E2 ㊴

Seoul Garden is a good choice when all the Japanese eateries are too crowded (which is often the case), here you grill marinated beef at your table while nibbling at the myriad little dishes that make up Korean cuisine.

Retail revolution

True Sake p140

Hayes Valley has undergone a retail renaissance in the last few years, booming to the point that finding a place to park – on streets once rife with smash-and-grab auto break-ins rather than smashing shopping finds – has become something of a sport.

Clothes by young designers, unique footwear, high-end luggage, upmarket vintage, artisanal chocolates, even sake (**True Sake**, p140): you can find all these and more on the main strip of Hayes Street. Targeting young women at various shopping phases of their lives is **Alla Prima Fine Lingerie** (p139), which specialises in date-worthy lacey underthings as well as glamorous swimsuits, while **Honey Ryder** (No.564, 255-6858) caters to the '70s-tinged disco belle. The cool young mother set will ooh and aah over the pricey, fashiony children's clothing at **Fiddlesticks'** (No.508, 565 0508, www.shop fiddlesticks.com) – and want to snap up sweetly embellished babygros at its nearby sister store **Lavish** (No.540, 565 0540,

www.shoplavish.com), which specialises in gifts, bags and infant wear. Further up Hayes, **Cotton Sheep** (p139) focuses on exquisite Japanese-made organic cotton clothing for children and women.

It's also worth venturing off Hayes Street down Gough Street for more unusual finds: the punkily DIY sewing store **Stitch Lounge** (No.182, 431 3739, www.stitch lounge.com); **Rose and Radish** (No.460, 864 4988, www.rose andradish.com), a '(modern) folk' design gallery that host new curated shows every few months.

On a leafy swathe of Octavia Boulevard, look for splashy mod felt rugs at **Peace Industry** (No. 539, 255-9940, www.peace industry.com); sporty, vintage-flavoured women's fashion by San Francisco designers **Lemon Twist** (No.537, 558-9699, www.lemontwist.net) and an always intriguing compendium of clothing, jewellery and accessories by local makers at **Rag Coop** (No.541, 621 7718, wwww.ragsf.com).

Zam Zam p131

Hayes Valley

Hayes Valley, just west of the Civic Center, was literally overshadowed by the Central Freeway for years. However, when the 1989 earthquake all but destroyed the roadway, it also hurried the transformation of the area from drug- and prostitution-riddled slum to what is perhaps the hippest urban shopping area in town. See box p137.

Eating & drinking

Absinthe

398 Hayes Street, at Gough Street (551 1590/www.absinthe.com). BART & Metro to Civic Center/ Metro to Van Ness/bus 5, 21, 47, 49 & Market Street routes. **Open** 11.30am-midnight Tue-Fri; 11am-midnight Sat; 11am-10.30pm Sun. *Bar* until 2am Fri, Sat. **$$$**. **French**. **Map** p129 E3 ⑩
The spirit of bohemian France is reborn in San Francisco as this boisterous brasserie. The French menu lists reliable favourites, including excellent coq au vin and cassoulet. Try the seafood platter to start. The bar – thanks to a change in the law – now offers genuine absinthe too.

Citizen Cake

399 Grove Street, at Gough Street (861 2228/www.citizencake.com). BART & Metro to Civic Center/ Metro to Van Ness/bus 5, 21, 47, 49 & Market Street routes. **Open** 8am-10pm Tue-Fri; 10am-10pm Sat; 10am-5pm Sun. **$$$**. **Café**. **Map** p129 E3 ⑪
Quite possibly the trendiest place for dessert in town, this recently remodelled café sells gorgeous sweet things to a crowd of well-dressed and good-looking patrons. As wonderful as the cakes and pies are, the excellent – if slightly pricey – lunch and dinner menus are also worth exploring. For a small on-the-go bite, try Citizen Cupcake next door.

Destino

1815 Market Street, between Guerrero & Valencia Streets (552 4451/www. destinosf.com). Metro to Van Ness/bus 6, 7, 26, 71. **Open** 5-10pm Mon-Thur; 5-11pm Fri-Sat; 5-10pm Sun. **$$**. **Latin American**. **Map** p129 E4 ⑫
This casual, fun restaurant serves specialities from Central and South America in a lively neighbourhood setting. The theme is small plates meant for sharing, but à la carte options are also available. Empanadas, ceviches and other indigenous dishes are all given a robust, flavourful treatment.

EspetuS

1686 Market Street, at Gough Street (552 8792/www.espetus.com). Metro to Van Ness/bus 6, 7, 26, 47, 49, 71. **Open** 11.30am-3pm, 5-10pm Mon-Thur; 11.30am-3pm, 5-11pm Fri; noon-3pm, 5-11pm Sat; noon-3pm, 4-9pm Sun. **$$$**. **Latin American**. **Map** p129 F4 ⑬
An impressive take on the increasingly popular *churrascaría*, EspetuS is San Francisco's first Brazilian-style steakhouse. Servers cruise through the restaurant wielding skewers laden

with straight-from-the-fire pork, steak, shrimp and lamb, awaiting your request; this is indicated by displaying a green chip while red indicates a full stop. All the while, the evocative strummings of Brazilian jazz unfurl in the background.

Hotel Biron

45 Rose Street, between Market & Gough Streets (703 0403/www.hotel biron.com). Metro to Van Ness/ streetcar F/bus 6, 7, 26, 71. **Open** 5pm-2am daily. **Bar**. **Map** p129 F4 ㊹
The wine bar in this charming and unpretentious hotel has a list boasting 80 wines by the bottle and 35 or so by the glass, plus a selection of beers and a small but appealing menu of cheeses, caviar and olives. It's a great, low-key place for drinkers who like to be able to talk.

Jade Bar

650 Gough Street, at McAllister Street (869 1900/www.jadebar.com). Bus 5, 21, 47, 49. **Open** 5pm-2am Mon-Sat; 8pm-2am Sun. **Bar**. **Map** p129 E3 ㊺
Restaurateur Greg Medow calls his lounge 'three bars in one', thanks to the distinct personality of each of its three modest floors. Signature cocktails go down easy in the shag-shod loft; the stylish main- floor bar comes with orchids in highlighted nooks; and a 20ft (6m) waterfall trickles into the basement lounge. Male patrons will appreciate being able to keep an eye on their drink even while in the gents, thanks to a one-way mirror that overlooks the bar.

Shopping

African Outlet

524 Octavia Street, between Hayes & Grove Streets (864 3576). Bus 21, 47, 49. **Open** 10.30am-7pm daily. **Map** p129 E3 ㊻
This gorgeous jumble of tribal artefacts and antiques – brilliantly coloured textiles, jewellery and beads, sculpture, fetishes, and ceremonial masks – has been gathered by a Nigerian expat and his wife, who

delight in explaining their pieces. to interested customers. The only drawback is that you may have trouble hearing them over the blasting reggae.

Alabaster

597 Hayes Street, at Laguna Street (558 0482/www.alabaster sf.com). Bus 21. **Open** 11am-6pm Mon-Wed; 11am-7pm Thur-Sat; noon-5pm Sun. **Map** p129 E3 ㊼
The elegant Alabaster not only looks beautiful, but sells beautiful things: there's alabaster, of course, in the form of urns and lamps, but also a variety of little boxes, Buddhas, vintage globes and even framed exotic butterflies and beetles.

Alla Prima Fine Lingerie

539 Hayes Street, between Laguna & Octavia Streets (864 8180/www.alla primalingerie.com). Bus 21, 47, 49. **Open** 11am-7pm Mon-Sat; noon-5pm Sun. **Map** p129 E3 ㊽
Known for its thorough fittings and sky-high designer offerings, Alla Prima specialises in everything from Dolce & Gabbana bras and La Perla delicacies to sublime swimsuits and thigh-high fishnets.

Cotton Sheep

573 Hayes Street, between Laguna & Octavia Streets (621 5546). Bus 16, 21, 47, 49. **Open** 11am-7pm Mon-Sat; 11am-6pm Sun. **Map** p129 E3 ㊾
Organic cotton garments, designed and manufactured in Japan, rule the roost at Cotton Sheep. Finger the utterly sweet children's hoodies or the truly unusual toddlers' socks shaped like Godzilla heads.

Dark Garden

321 Linden Street, between Octavia & Gough Streets (431 7684/www.dark garden.net). Bus 21, 47, 49. **Open** 1-7pm Mon-Sat. **Map** p129 E3 ㊿
Autumn Carey-Adamme's métier is bespoke fabric corsets. Select style, fabric and colour and, by the magic of 12 individual measurements, she'll create a custom-fit garment. The off-the-rack models are seductive, and the bridal corsets remain hugely popular.

Flight 001

525 Hayes Street, between Laguna & Octavia Streets (487 1001/www. flight001.com). Bus 21, 47, 49. **Open** 11am-7pm Mon-Sat; 11am-6pm Sun. **Map** p129 E3 ⑤①

If it's important that you travel in style, Flight 001 is the place to go. Streamlined like a jet airliner, the store sells beautiful modern designs, from Japanese metal suitcases to gorgeous accessories.

Get Lost Travel Books, Maps & Gear

1825 Market Street, at Pearl Street, Hayes Valley (437 0529/www.getlost books.com). Metro to Van Ness/bus 26. **Open** 10am-7pm Mon-Fri; 10am-6pm Sat; 11am-5pm Sun. **Map** p129 E4 ⑤②

This excellent enterprise offers a compelling assortment of travel guides and literature, plus various other bits and pieces to help you on your way (maps, accessories and the like).

Grooves Vinyl Attractions

1797 Market Street, between Pearl & McCoppin Streets (436 9933). Metro to Van Ness/bus 26. **Open** 11am-7pm daily. **Map** p129 E4 ⑤③

Vinyl heaven – at least if your tastes don't run far beyond the 1970s. The store is packed with oddities and curios, including tons of old soundtracks, comedy records and sets by forgotten '70s crooners.

Lavish

540 Hayes Street, at Octavia Street (565 0540/www.shoplavish.com). Bus 21, 47, 49. **Open** 11am-7pm Mon-Sat; 11am-6pm Sun. **Map** p129 E3 ⑤④

Gorgeous letterpress cards, charming print bags, delicate jewellery and oodles of whimsical baby clothes make this a must-stop on the way to a girlie soirée or baby shower.

MAC (Modern Appealing Clothing)

387 Grove Street, between Franklin & Gough Streets (863 3011). Bus 16, 21, 47, 49. **Open** 11am-7pm Mon-Sat; noon-6pm Sun. **Map** p129 E3 ⑤⑤

Belgian designers as well as local creatives get the treatment they deserve in this brother and sister owned boutique that resembles a chic pied-à-terre. Men, in particular, who are willing to open their wallets wide will discover great items by Martin Margiela, Dries Van Noten and AF Vandevorst, in addition to Raf Simons for Jil Sander.

True Sake

560 Hayes Street, between Laguna & Octavia Streets (355 9555/www. truesake.com). Bus 21, 47, 49. **Open** noon-7pm Mon-Sat; 11am-6pm Sun. **Map** p129 E3 ⑤⑥

A beautiful and elegant place, this is the first US shop devoted entirely to saké. Owner Beau Timken is every bit as helpful and knowledgeable about the rice-fermented beverage as you might hope, even suggesting food pairings for your purchase.

Ver Unica

437B Hayes Street, between Gough & Octavia Streets (431 0688/www.ver-unica.com). Bus 21, 47, 49. **Open** 11am-7pm Mon-Sat; noon-6pm Sun. **Map** p129 E3 ⑤⑦

Ver Unica is where people with a proper pay cheque go to buy second-hand: it sells unique retro finds, not cast-offs crammed together on dusty shelves. It now stocks men's clothing too.

Arts & leisure

Rickshaw Stop

155 Fell Street, at Franklin Street (861 2011/www.rickshawstop.com). Metro to Van Ness/bus 21, 47, 49 & Market Street routes. **Open** 7pm-2am Wed-Sat. *Shows* times vary. **Admission** $5-$10. No credit cards. **Map** p129 F3 ⑥③

Doing its best to fill a sparse strip near Civic Center, the Rickshaw taps a cool collegiate/rec-room vibe with its crash-pad decor of mod plastic loungers, foosball table and odalisque-via-Target lighting. Come for the laid-back hipster ambience and low-priced snack menu, but stay for hep local and touring bands and hot, hard-edged electro and mash-up DJs.

De Young Museum p142

Golden Gate Park

Roughly three miles in length and half a mile wide, Golden Gate Park is one of the largest man-made parks in the world and a testament to human dominion over nature – or, put another way, a gargantuan project that introduced non-native species and used vast resources in ways that would never have been approved in modern-day San Francisco.

The ambitious task of creating this pastoral loveliness – a thousand acres of landscaped gardens, forests and meadows – from barren sand dunes began in 1870. The park's public debut occurred in 1894, when more than 1.3 million people visited for the Midwinter International Exposition. The six-month fair filled more than 100 temporary buildings. Two still remain: the **Japanese Tea Garden** and the **Music Concourse**. As the park's fame spread, horticulturalists from all over the world sent in seeds and cuttings. Today, a rose garden, a Shakespeare garden, a tulip garden and a rhododendron dell are among hundreds of living delights.

Sampling all the park's attractions, from the natural ones to the **de Young Museum** and **California Academy of Sciences**, would take days, but one way to see it in a single afternoon is to stroll all the way from the entrance of the park along the footpaths beside John F Kennedy Drive, the park's main east–west artery, to **Ocean Beach**. It takes a few hours if you stop along the way, but your reward will be the crashing waves of the Pacific. Indeed, if you join the throngs of locals biking, walking, jogging and in-line skating along JFK Drive on a Sunday afternoon, when the road is closed to traffic, you'll soon understand why the Golden Gate Park is known as San Francisco's backyard.

In 2007, the 1887 Children's Playground was completely overhauled and renamed the **Koret Children's Quarter**. It is now a whimsical interactive tribute to the Bay Area landscape, featuring a treehouse village, climbing wave walls, sea caves, tidepools, spinning cattails, and an enormous climbing net with a lookout perch.

Information about the park is available from the headquarters in **McLaren Lodge**.

Sights & museums

NEW **California Academy of Sciences**
55 Concourse Drive (321 8000/ www.calacademy.org). Bus 5, 44. Map p143 E1 **❶**
See box p145.

Conservatory of Flowers
John F Kennedy Drive (666 7001). **Open** 9am-4.30pm Tue-Sun. **Admission** $5; $1.50-$3 reductions. Map p143 F1 **❷**

Opened in 1879, this is the oldest glass-and-wood Victorian greenhouse in the western hemisphere, home to nearly 2,000 plant species, displayed in five 'galleries', with a focus on tropical habitats. Between March to November hosts of butterflies make a living demonstration of plant pollination in action in the Butterfly Zone.

De Young Museum
50 Hagiwara Tea Garden Drive (863 3330/www.deyoungmuseum.org). Bus 5, 44. **Open** 9.30am-5.15pm Tue-Thur, Sat, Sun; 9.30am-8.45pm Fri. **Admission** $10; $6-$7 reductions; free under-12s. Map p143 E1 **❸**

The most prominent feature of this controversial future-primitive building, designed by Herzog & de Meuron, is the massive tower that emerges from the surrounding canopy of trees – a structure at once overwhelming and electrifying. The exterior walls are all made from patterned copper designed to take on the colour of the surrounding greenery as they oxidise.

Along with its vast collections of American art from the 17th to 20th centuries, the museum showcases works from New Guinea and the Oceania, as well as contemporary crafts and textiles. There's also an excellent store and café with outdoor seating. However, with

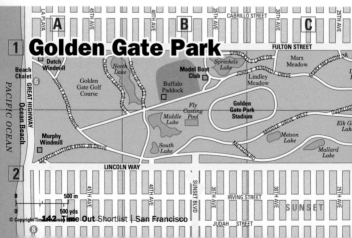

© Copyright Time Out Group

commanding views over the park, the soaring observation tower is worth the trip alone. The courtyard, café, store, sculpture garden and tower can be entered without paying the entrance fee.

Japanese Tea Garden

Martin Luther King Drive (752 1171). **Open** *Garden* 8.30am-5.30pm daily. *Tea house* 8.30am-5.15pm daily. **Admission** $3.50 **Map** p143 E1 ④

This landmark garden – ironically the spot where the Chinese fortune cookie is said to have been invented – delights visitors with its steep bridges, bonsai trees, huge bronze Buddha and outdoor tearoom with kimono-clad servers.

Strybing Arboretum & Botanical Garden

Ninth Avenue and Lincoln Way (661 1316/www.strybing.org). **Open** 8am-4.30pm Mon-Fri; 10am-5pm Sat, Sun. *Guided walks* 1.30pm daily. **Admission** free. **Map** p143 E2 ⑤

The arboretum and garden are home to some 7,000 species from diverse climates. There's a fragrant garden designed for the visually impaired and an appealing Japanese moon-viewing garden. The John Muir nature trail focuses on local flora. Other gardens have plants from regions including southwestern Australia, New Zealand and the Mediterranean.

Eating & drinking

Beach Chalet & Park Chalet

1000 Great Highway (visitor centre 751 2766/restaurant 386 8439/www.beach chalet.com). Bus 5, 18. **Open** *Visitor centre & Beach Chalet* 9am-10.30pm daily. *Park Chalet* noon-10.30pm daily. **$$$ American**. **Map** p142 A1 ⑥

A perfect spot for sunset cocktails, the Beach Chalet, a historic Willis Polk-designed building on the coast, is home to a fine restaurant and brewpub. The ground-floor walls are awash in frescoes by Lucien Labaudt depicting notable San Franciscans, among them sculptor Benny Bufano and John McLaren. The views of the ocean from upstairs are stupendous.

The newer Park Chalet, an extension that faces Golden Gate Park, lacks the views of the Beach Chalet. However, the more mellow atmosphere makes it ideal for whiling away a sunny afternoon in one of the Adirondack chairs arrayed around the lush and beautifully landscaped lawns, or cooling off with a beer after a walk along Ocean Beach. Adirondack chairs arrayed around the lush and beautifully landscaped lawns, or cooling off with a beer after a walk along Ocean Beach.

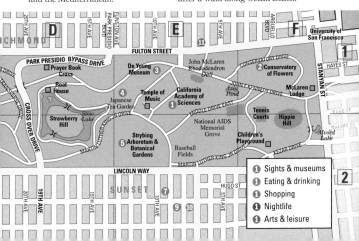

Ebisu

1283 9th Avenue, between Irving Street & Lincoln Way (566 1770/www.ebisu sushi.com). Metro to Judah & 9th/bus 6, 43, 44, 66. **Open** 11.30am-2pm, 5-10pm Mon-Thur; 11.30am-2pm, 5-11pm Thur, Fri; 11.30am-11pm Sat. **$$.**
Asian. Map p143 E2 **7**

Some say this is the best sushi in town – and so there's often a wait for a table. Put your name on the list and get a drink at the bar with a light heart, because you're going to enjoy house specialities like the 'pink Cadillac' (salmon sushi roll) and seafood salad. Or, you can happily forgo it for the traditional Japanese cooked food.

Java Beach Café

1396 La Playa Boulevard, at Judah Street (665 5282/www.javabeachcafe. com). Metro to Ocean Beach/bus 18. **Open** 5.30am-11pm Mon-Fri; 6am-11pm Sat, Sun. **$. Café**. Map p142 A2 **8**

A funky and civilised café, with the wetsuits and grand Pacific views making it feel a bit like LA's Hermosa Beach. Surfers, cyclists and others pop in for a sandwich, some soup or a pastry.

PJ's Oyster Bed

737 Irving Street, between 8th & 9th Avenues (566 7775/www.pjsoyster bed.com). Metro to Judah & 9th/bus 6, 43, 44, 66. **Open** 5-10pm Tue-Thur, Sun; 5-11pm Fri, Sat. **$$. American**. Map p143 E2 **9**

There's a bit of New Orleans fun in this friendly seafood restaurant, which makes some of San Francisco's freshest and most authentic Cajun food. The seafood is displayed on ice, with oysters shucked to order, and portions are generous. It's always packed.

Tart to Tart

641 Irving Street, between 7th & 8th Avenues (504 7068). Metro to Judah & 9th/bus 6, 43, 44, 66. **Open** 6am-1am Mon-Thur, Sun; 6am-2am Fri, Sat. **$.**
Café. Map p143 E2 **10**

There are few late-night options around in the park, perhaps because residents are mainly families. No matter: at Tart to Tart you can get freshly made cookies and cakes, above-average salads and sandwiches, and more tarts than you could comfortably sample over the course of a month.

Arts & leisure

Golden Gate Park Skate & Bike

3038 Fulton Street, between 6th & 7th Avenues (668 1117). Bus 5, 21, 31, 44. **Open** 10am-5pm Mon-Fri; 10am-5.30pm Sat, Sun. **Rates** *Bikes* $5/hr or $25/day. *Skates* $5/hr or $20/day. **Map** p143 E1 **11**

Bikes, rollerskates and in-line skates are all available for rent (helmet and knee and elbow pads included).

Ocean Beach p142

Natural science

Set to open in autumn 2008, the new California Academy of Sciences complex, across from the de Young Museum in Golden Gate Park, promises to be the jewel in the crown of San Francisco's museums.

The 12 original buildings of the 152-year-old institution were taken apart and reused as part of the new $484-million construction. Its design reflects a radical breadth of vision, and the results are nothing short of spectacular.

Take the roof. It is 197,000 square feet of green 'living roof', shaped to look like rolling hills and containing 1.7 million native plants. Absorbing two million gallons of water annually, the vegetation will keep the building 10 degrees cooler than would a standard roof, while also insulating it, thus saving energy and cutting costs.

Inside is a living rainforest, a 210,000-gallon aquarium with 1,500 species of living coral, a swamp complete with giant turtles and a rare albino alligator, and some 20 million specimens and 38,000 live animals from around the globe.

The four-storey rainforest's 90-foot-tall spiralling walkway is open to free-flying birds and butterflies, and visitors will be able to walk from the top of the forest canopy down to its very root system. A glass elevator takes visitors further below to a 25-foot-long submarine tunnel to view live anacondas, piranhas and giant catfish.

The structure also contains a digital planetarium which can broadcast live NASA feeds on its 75-foot screen. It is also able to produce images where the viewer seems to travel through space in an experience that has been described as 'like Google Earth but for the galaxy'.

More state-of-the-art computer technology will allow museum staff to update exhibits to respond to current events, and dozens of channels of audio content will teach visitors about particular animals or exhibits.

Marina Green p153

Pacific Heights to Golden Gate Bridge

If there's one classic San Francisco view – in a city with a multitude – it is the vista across the Bay from Pacific Heights and the northern waterfront. What sets this view apart is the presence of the iconic Golden Gate Bridge. However, the wealthy had already staked their claim to these hills long before its contruction began in 1933.

The area covered in this chapter spans Bush Street to the Bay and from Van Ness Avenue to the Presidio, and it has much to offer beyond the engineering marvel that grabs all the attention. The Pacific Heights mansions overlook some of the most beautiful coastline in the United States, while the vast expanses of wooded trails and cliffs in the former military base of the Presidio run up against the well-scrubbed opulence of the Marina.

Pacific Heights

True to its name, Pacific Heights peers over the Pacific from on high, its mansions home to the cream of San Francisco's high society for generations. The eastern edge of the neighbourhood contains some beautiful Victorian houses. The blue-and-white **Octagon House** is perhaps the most famous, but there are also rich pickings to the south: the **Haas-Lilienthal House**, for example, which offers visitors a rare chance to see inside a grand old Queen Anne.

Sights & museums

Haas-Lilienthal House

2007 Franklin Street, between Washington & Jackson Streets (441 3000/www.sfheritage.org/ house.html). Bus 1, 12, 27, 47, 49, 76. **Open** noon-3pm Wed, Sat; 11am-4pm Sun. **Admission** $8; $5 reductions. **Map** p149 E4 ➊

Built in 1886 by Bavarian immigrant William Haas, this 28-room house has elaborate wooden gables and a circular tower, marking it as being in the Queen Anne style. Fully restored and filled with period furniture, it also has photos documenting its history and that of the family that lived in it until 1972.

Octagon House

2645 Gough Street, at Union Street (441 7512). Bus 41, 45. **Open** noon-3pm 2nd & 4th Thur, 2nd Sun of mth. **Admission** free. **Map** p149 E3 ➋

The 1861 Octagon House is home to the small Museum of Colonial and Federal Decorative Arts, but is most notable as one of two surviving examples of eight-sided homes in San Francisco. Across the nation, 700 such houses were built in the belief that

they improved their occupants' health by letting in more natural light.

Eating & drinking

Ella's

500 Presidio Avenue, at California Street (441 5669/www.ellassan francisco.com). Bus 1, 2, 3, 4, 43. **Open** 7am-3pm Mon-Fri; 8.30am-2pm Sat, Sun. **$**. **American**. **Map** p148 B5 ➌

This stylish and neighbourly corner restaurant is famed for its weekend brunch. Favourites include the chicken hash with eggs and toast, and the potato scramble, prepared with a frequently changing list of fresh ingredients. The thick, perfectly crisped French toast is superb.

Florio

1915 Fillmore Street, between Bush & Pine Streets (775 4300/www.florio sf.com). Bus 1, 2, 3, 4, 22. **Open** 5.30-10pm Mon, Tue, Sun; 5.30-11pm Wed-Sat. **$$**. **French**. **Map** p149 D5 ➍

A quintessential local bistro, with just the right degree of refinement. Dark wood and white tablecloths set the tone for the French-inspired robust

Octagon House

Pacific Heights

© Copyright Time Out Group 2008

0   500 m

0   500 yds

Wave
Organ

Golden Gate
Yacht Club

YACHT ROAD

Marina
Small Craft
Harbor

Golden Gate Promenade

Marina

Parking

MASON STREET

MARINA BOULEVARD

MARINA
GATE

DOYLE DRIVE

RICHARDSON

Exploratorium

22

Palace of
Fine Arts

23

JEFFERSON STREET

BEACH STREET

NORTH POINT STREET

BAY STREET

FRANCISCO STREET

CHESTNUT STREET

GREENWICH STREET

MARINA

CASA

RICO

CERVANTES

CAPRA WAY

AVILA STREET

PIERCE STREET

SCOTT STREET

26

DIVISADERO STREET

24

101 LOMBARD

101

LINCOLN BOULEVARD

GORGAS AVENUE

EDIE ROAD

GIRARD RD

LINCOLN BLVD

GORGAS
GATE

AVENUE

Letterman
Digital Arts
Center

LETTERMAN DRIVE

LOMBARD
GATE

17

LOMBARD STREET

36

Cow Hollow
Playground

GREENWICH STREET

FILBERT STREET

UNION STREET

GREEN STREET

VALLEJO STREET

BROADWAY

BRODERICK STREET

SCOTT STREET

PACIFIC AVENUE

JULIUS ROAD

MONTGOMERY STREET

GRAHAM STREET

MESA STREET

FUNSTON AVENUE

Main Post

35

BARNARD ROAD

MACARTHUR

BARNARD ROAD

KOBACA AVE

i

Visitor
Centre

DUARY

PORTOLA

SIMONDS
LOOP

SHAFTER RD

PRESIDIO BOULEVARD

Presidio

See
p155

WEST BROADWAY

PRESIDIO
GATE

Julius Kahn
Playground

WEST PACIFIC AVENUE

JACKSON STREET

LYON STREET

BAKER STREET

WASHINGTON STREET

11

CLAY STREET

PRESIDIO HEIGHTS

SUELLO BLVD
GATE

CHERRY STREET

MAPLE STREET

SPRUCE STREET

LOCUST STREET

LAUREL STREET

WALNUT STREET

PRESIDIO AVENUE

SACRAMENTO STREET

ARGUELLO BOULEVARD

8

CALIFORNIA STREET

3 6

CALIFORNIA STREET

PINE STREET

BUSH STREET

SUTTER STREET

EUCLID AVENUE

SPRUCE STREET

HEATHER AVE

IRIS AVENUE

MANZANITA AVE

COLLINS ST

LAUREL STREET

Laurel Hill
Playground

POST STREET

Kaiser Medical
Center

D   E   Municipal
Pier

F

Hyde Street
Pier   Fisherman's
Wharf

Aquatic
Park

National
Maritime
Museum

The Cannery

1

The
Anchorage

MARINA GREEN DRIVE

Green

MARINA BLVD

25   21   30
  31
A   B   C   D

Fort Mason
Center

Cable
Car

Ghirardelli
Square

Russian
Hill Park

San Francisco
Art Institute

BEACH STREET

Great
Meadow

Hostel

MACARTHUR AVENUE

2

Lombard
Street

NORTH POINT STREET

BAY   STREET

RUSSIAN

BAY   STREET

FRANCISCO   STREET

Moscone
Playground

CHESTNUT   STREET

MAGNOLIA   STREET

LOMBARD   STREET

HILL

STREET

MOULTON   STREET

COW HOLLOW

18

GREENWICH   STREET

FILBERT   STREET

UNION   STREET

BROADWAY

3

20

PIXLEY

16

19

Octagon
House

2

101

7

GREEN   STREET

VALLEJO   STREET

POLK

GULCH

PACIFIC

HEIGHTS

PACIFIC   AVENUE

Haas-Lilienthal
House

1

JACKSON   STREET

CLAY   STREET

4

WASHINGTON   STREET

SACRAMENTO

Alta Plaza
Park

14

California Pacific
Medical Center

Lafayette
Park

VAN

NESS

Cable
Car

SACRAMENTO   STREET

AUSTIN   STREET

13
12

5

CALIFORNIA   STREET

AVENUE

FERN   ST

PINE   STREET

4
9
10

15

BUSH   STREET

5

JAPANTOWN

UCSF
Medical
Center

Peace
Plaza

Japan Center

FILLMORE

Hamilton Recreation
Center

GEARY   EXPRESSWAY

Kimbell
Playground

Cathedral of St Mary
of the Assumption

• Sights & museums
• Eating & drinking
• Shopping
• Nightlife
• Arts & leisure

rural cooking. The ribeye steak-frites and the Tuscan seafood stew are always soul-warming.

Fresca

2114 Fillmore Street, at California Street (447 2668/ www.frescasf.com). Bus 1, 3, 22. **Open** 11am-3pm, 5-10pm Mon-Thur; 11am-3pm, 5-11pm Fri, Sat; 11am-3pm, 5-9pm Sun. **$$$**. **Peruvian**. Map p149 D4 ⑤

Fresca claims to have San Francisco's only ceviche bar, but has a broader menu than you might expect. Try tangy halibut ceviche or flambéed pisco prawns to start, followed by grilled rib-eye with fries and plantains or sweet soy-roasted trout. The space can be very loud and tables are crammed together, but the quality of the Peruvian food makes up for any discomfort.

G Bar

Laurel Inn, 488 Presidio Avenue, between Sacramento & California Streets (409 4227/www.gbarsf.com). Bus 1, 2, 3, 4, 43. **Open** 6pm-midnight Mon, Tue; 6pm-2am Wed-Fri; 7pm-2am Sat. **Bar**. Map p148 B5 ⑥

If you're saddened that San Francisco doesn't look like Los Angeles, head to the bar at the Laurel Inn: once this place was a nondescript motel; now, the bar has been revamped a neo-1950s look and bachelor-pad atmosphere.

Harris'

2100 Van Ness Avenue, at Pacific Avenue (673 1888/www.harris restaurant.com). Bus 12, 27, 47, 49, 76. **Open** 5.30-9.30pm Mon-Fri; 5-10pm Sat; 5-9pm Sun. **$$$$**. **American**. Map p149 F3 ⑦

One of San Francisco's steakhouse standbys, Harris' offers classy old-style dining, with big steaks, big martinis, and big bills.

NEW Spruce

3640 Sacramento Street, at Spruce Street (931 5100/www.sprucesf.com). Bus 1, 3, 4, 33, 43. **Open** 11.30am-11pm Mon-Fri; 5-11pm Sat, Sun. **$$$**. **American**. Map p148 B5 ⑧

This handsome restaurant has managed to set the city abuzz, and the scarcity of available reservations shouldn't put you off trying to experience chef Mark Sullivan's approach to fresh, inventive cooking. Specialities of lobster and steak and other extravagances make the point that this is a place of comfort and style. A lounge, a takeout area and a formal dining room coexist peacefully.

SPQR

1911 Fillmore Street, between Bush & Pine Streets (771 7779/www.spqr sf.com). Bus 1, 2, 3, 4, 22. **Open** 11.30am-2.30pm, 5.30-10pm Mon-Wed, Sun; 10.30am-2.30pm, 5.30-11pm Thur-Sat. **$$**. **Italian**. Map p149 D5 ⑨

In this small, spare, one-room dining space, the spirit of Roman cuisine shines through. Dishes are rustic, unadorned and incredibly flavourful. The toughest part is getting a table – no reservations are accepted, but browsing the excellent by-the-glass wine list will help pass the time.

Shopping

Erica Tanov

2408 Fillmore Street, between Jackson & Washington Streets (674 1228/ www.ericatanov.com). Bus 3, 12, 22, 24. **Open** 11am-6pm Mon-Sat; 11am-5pm Sun. **Map** p148 C4 ❿

Antique fabrics are the highlight at Erica Tanov – and they're multitasking in the form of gossamer party dresses, bed linens, delicate lingerie and imported sweaters.

Brown Eyed Girl

2999 Washington Street, at Broderick Street (409 0214/www.shopbrown eyedgirl.com). Bus 1, 3, 22. **Open** 11am-7pm Mon-Sat; noon-5pm Sun. **Map** p148 C4 ⓫

Housed in a renovated Victorian, and strewn with comfy sofas, this pastel-hued shop for moneyed 20-year-olds has designer denim and an endless array of pricey clingy tees.

Gallery of Jewels

2115 Fillmore Street, between California & Sacramento Streets (771 5099/www.galleryofjewels.com). Bus 1, 2, 3, 4, 12, 24. **Open** 10.30am-6.30pm Mon-Sat; 11am-6pm Sun. **Map** p149 D4 ⓬

Peruse local creations of silver and semi-precious stones, as well as funky beads and antique bracelets. Designs run from fresh and modern to mumsy.

Jonathan Adler

2133 Fillmore Street, at Sacramento Streets (563 9500/www.jonathan adler.com). Bus 2, 3, 4, 22, 38. **Open** 11am-7pm Mon-Wed; 10am-7pm Thur-Sat; noon-6pm Sun. **Map** p149 D4 ⓭

Everything that New York designer Jonathan Adler touches becomes utterly groovy in a very *Ice Storm* kind of way: his animal figurines, pillows, pottery and furnishings all scream 'Let the key party begin!'

Brown Eyed Girl

Nest

*2300 Fillmore Street, at Clay Street
(292 6199). Bus 1, 3, 12, 22, 24.* **Open**
10.30am-6.30pm Mon-Sat; 11am-6pm
Sun. **Map** p149 D4 ⑭

A nest in the magpie sense, this
Parisian bohemia-inspired shop is a
beguiling compilation of tin jack-in-the-
boxes, gauzy Chinese lanterns, wood-
cuts, glassware, French jewellery and
some adorable kids' clothes.

Zinc Details

*1905 Fillmore Street, between Bush
& Pine Streets, (776 2100/www.zinc
details.com). Bus 2, 3, 4, 22, 38.* **Open**
11am-7pm Mon-Sat; noon-6pm Sun.
Map p149 D5 ⑮

Fun, funky and often fabulous contemporary design by Artemide, Le Klint,
Marimekko, Vitra and other European
and Japanese makers can be found in
this forward-thinking, jam-packed
emporium of rugs, lighting, tables,
glassware, furniture, textiles and vases.

Cow Hollow

From Pacific Heights, it's only a
few bloks downhill towards Cow
Hollow, Once a dairy pasture, the
neighbourhood is still serene, but
its grazers are now of the well-
heeled, two-legged kind. The
activity is centred on Union Street
between Broderick and Buchanan
Streets, a chic and bijou stretch of
bars, restaurants and boutiques.

Eating & drinking

Betelnut

*2030 Union Street, between Webster &
Buchanan Streets (929 8855/www.betel
nutrestaurant.com). Bus 22, 41, 45.*
Open 11.30am-11pm Mon-Thur, Sun;
11am-midnight Fri, Sat. **$$. Asian**.
Map p149 D3 ⑯

This cool-looking restaurant has man-
aged to retain its popularity by com-
bining a relatively exotic South Pacific
concept and consistent execution. The
menu is made for grazing. The best bet
is to keep ordering small plates (tea-
smoked duck, braised short ribs,
papaya salad) until either your waist-
line or your credit card goes pop.

Liverpool Lil's

*2942 Lyon Street, between Lombard
& Greenwich Streets (921 6664/www.
liverpoollils.com). Bus 28, 41, 43, 45,
76.* **Open** 11am-1am Mon; 11am-2am
Tue-Fri; 10am-2am Sat; 10am-1am
Sun. **Bar**. **Map** p148 B3 ⑰

The façade looks like it's made out of
driftwood, and the main decorative
touches are old sports photos and
paintings of jazz greats. No matter: this
is the Marina's least pretentious bar.
There's a considerable pub menu too.

Matrix

*3138 Fillmore Street, between Filbert
& Greenwich Streets (www.
matrixfillmore.com). Bus 22, 28, 43,
76.* **Open** 5.30pm-2am daily. **Bar**.
Map p149 D3 ⑱

At the original Matrix, you might have
seen Hunter S Thompson sucking LSD
off a stranger's sleeve, or the Grateful
Dead playing an impromptu set. But
these days the Matrix draws label-con-
scious fashionistas and financiers who
sip from the pricey cocktail menu at
what is really a high-style pick-up joint.

Mauna Loa

*3009 Fillmore Street, at Union Street
(563 5137). Bus 22, 28, 41, 43, 45,
76.* **Open** 2pm-2am Mon-Fri; noon-
2am Sat, Sun. No credit cards. **Bar**.
Map p149 D3 ⑲

Originally opened by a Hawaiian in the
late 1950s, Mauna Loa has morphed into
perhaps the only bar in the Marina that
could be considered divey. A pool table,
foosball and Pop-A-Shot entertain
patrons, but at weekends it's tough to
manoeuvre your cue through the crush.

PlumpJack Café

*3127 Fillmore Street, between
Greenwich & Filbert Streets (563 4755/
www.plumpjack.com). Bus 22, 28, 41,
43, 45, 76.* **Open** 11.30am-2pm, 5.30-
10pm Mon-Fri; 5.30-10pm Sat, Sun.
$$$. American. **Map** p149 D3 ⑳

The great success of PlumpJack Wines
inspired the opening of this high-

The Presidio p156

profile, special-occasion eaterie. A blend of new ideas and old money (co-owner Gavin Newsom is the city's mayor), it produces outstanding California cuisine, with a penchant for interesting seafood and Mediterranean recipes. Wines are the main attraction.

The Marina & the waterfront

In a city justifiably famous for its gay scene, the pastel-painted Marina is known for being conspicuously straight. It's also one big pick-up joint; for decades, even the local Safeway was a pulling spot, and featured in Armistead Maupin's *Tales of the City*.

A little more levity is provided at the eastern edge of the Marina waterfront. The **Fort Mason Center** started out as a US Army command post in the 1850s, and its reconditioned military buildings retain a forbidding mien, but these days they house some fine little museums and exhibitions.

The vast, sloping lawns of the **Marina Green** (Marina Boulevard, between Scott and Webster Streets) are the locals' favourite place to fly kites, jog or picnic, offering dizzying views of the Golden Gate Bridge and the Bay.

Sights & museums

Fort Mason Center
Marina Boulevard, at Buchanan Street (441 3400/ www.fortmason.org). Bus 10, 22, 28, 30, 47, 49. **Map** p149 E1 ㉑
This collection of ex-military buildings features various cultural institutions, including the Museo ItaloAmericano (Building C, 673 2200, www.museo italoamericano.org) and the airy SFMOMA Artists' Gallery (Building A, 441 4777, www.sfmoma.org), the latter selling and renting out contemporary works by northern Californians. Both museums are closed on Mondays and offer free admission on the first Wednesday of the month.

Other enterprises here include the Book Bay Bookstore (Building C, 771 1076,www.friendsandfoundation.org/bookstores.cfm), which sells rejected stock from the public library, as well as LPs and art. Over in Building D is the Magic Theatre (441 8822, www.magictheatre.org), which stages works by a mix of emerging and established playwrights in its two performance spaces. Before the performance, have dinner at Greens (Building A, 771 6222,www.greens restaurant.com).

Palace of Fine Arts
Lyon Street, at Bay Street (563 6504/ www.palaceoffinearts.org). Bus 28, 30, 43, 76. **Map** p148 B2 ㉒
Local architect Bernard Maybeck's pièce de résistance, the Palace is a neoclassical domed rotunda supported by a curved colonnade topped with friezes and statues of weeping women, and flanked by a pond alive with ducks, swans and lily pads. The original building was demolished in 1964 – only the shell of the rotunda remained – then reconstructed at ten times the original cost. The Palace is currently in the final phases of a $21-million renovation that aims to create an aeration system for the Palace of Fine Arts lagoon and restore the surrounding landscape, with work due for completion in 2009. The Palace is home to the Palace of Fine Arts theatre as the Exploratorium (below).

Exploratorium
3601 Lyon Street, at Marina Boulevard, Marina (563 7337/www.exploratorium.edu). Bus 28, 30, 76. **Open** 10am-5pm Tue-Sun. **Admission** $13; $10 13-17s, discounts; $8 4-12s; free under-4s. Free 1st Wed of mth. **Map** p148 B2 ㉓
Housed in the historic Palace of Fine Arts (above), the Exploratorium has over 600 interactive exhibits about science, art and human perception. A highlight is the Tactile Dome, a geodesic hemisphere of total blackness in which you try to identify various objects; book in advance (561 0362, $16). Another highlight is the Wave

Organ, located nearby on the water's edge. Sea waves rush in underneath, pushing air up through the organ's tubes to create a symphony of eerie tones and sighs.

Eating & drinking

Bin 38
3232 Scott Street, between Lombard & Chestnut Streets (567 3838/ www.bin38.com). Bus 28, 30, 43, 76. **Open** 3pm-midnight Mon-Wed; 3pm-1am Thur-Fri; 2pm-1am Sat; 2pm-midnight Sun. **$$. American**. **Map** p148 C2 ㉔
This wine bar and small-plates restaurant is as big on atmosphere as it is on choice of tipple. The menu of Wine Country-inspired American fare is designed to be easily paired with selections from the wine and beer list. Indeed, suggestions are offered on the page – so you needn't worry if your grilled grass-fed beef tenderloin kebabs will go well with the cabernet from Napa's Spring Mountain.

Greens
Building A, Fort Mason Center, Marina Boulevard, at Buchanan Street (771 6222/www.greens restaurant.com). Bus 10, 19, 28, 30, 47, 49. **Open** 5.30-9pm Mon; noon-2.30pm, 5.30-9pm Tue-Sat; 10.30am-2pm Sun. **$$. American**. **Map** p149 E1 ㉕
Vegans and carnivores alike extol the virtues of venerable Greens, with its waterfront views of the Golden Gate Bridge and award-winning, all-vegetarian menu. An extensive wine list complements mesquite-grilled vegetables and wood-fired pizzas topped with wild mushrooms.

Grove
2250 Chestnut Street, at Avila Street (474 4843). Bus 28, 30, 43, 76. **Open** 7am-11pm Mon-Fri; 8am-11pm Sat, Sun. **$. Café**. **Map** p148 C2 ㉖
A true outpost of café culture in Pacific Heights. As well as coffee, beer, wine and comfort food (lasagne, chicken pot pie), patrons can enjoy a game of chess and backgammon.

The Presidio &
Golden Gate Bridge

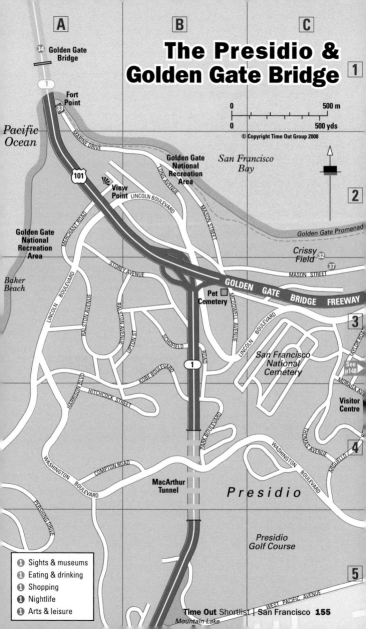

A **B** **C**

1

0   500 m
0   500 yds

© Copyright Time Out Group 2008

2

Golden Gate
Bridge

Fort
Point

Pacific
Ocean

MARINE DRIVE

Golden Gate
National
Recreation
Area

San Francisco
Bay

View
Point

LINCOLN BOULEVARD

LINCE AVENUE

MASON STREET

Golden Gate Promenad

Golden Gate
National
Recreation
Area

Crissy
Field

Baker
Beach

STOREY AVENUE

MASON STREET

3

GOLDEN GATE BRIDGE FREEWAY

Pet
Cemetery

MERCHANT ROAD

RALSTON AVENUE

RALSTON AVENUE

LINCOLN

SCHOFIELD

KOBE BOULEVARD

LINCOLN BOULEVARD

LINCOLN BOULEVARD

MCDOWELL AVENUE

RUAD

San Francisco
National
Cemetery

MORAGA AVE

See
p148

Visitor
Centre

4

HARRISON BLVD

HITCHCOCK STREET

PARK BOULEVARD

WASHINGTON BOULEVARD

ARGUELLO

HINAN AVENUE

WASHINGTON BOULEVARD

COMPTON ROAD

MacArthur
Tunnel

Presidio

5

PERSHING DRIVE

Presidio
Golf Course

Sights & museums
Eating & drinking
Shopping
Nightlife
Arts & leisure

WEST PACIFIC AVENUE

Mountain Lake

Isa

*3324 Steiner Street, between Chestnut
& Lombard Streets (567 9588/www.isa
restaurant.com). Bus 22, 28, 30, 43,
76.* **Open** *5.30-10pm Mon-Thur; 5.30-
10.30pm Fri, Sat.* **$$**. **International**.
Map p149 D2 ㉗

Expect such interesting fare as roast
mussels with shallots and white wine,
or hanger steak with tarragon mustard
and roast garlic potatoes from the
tapas-like menu at Isa. Cosy, with a
secluded back patio, it is winningly
free of Marina affectations.

Los Hermanos

*2026 Chestnut Street, at Fillmore
Street (921 5790). Bus 22, 28, 30,
43, 76.* **Open** *10.30am-9.30pm Mon-
Sat.* **$**. *No credit cards.* **Latin
American**. **Map** p149 D2 ㉘

Chaotic but friendly, with people shout-
ing orders from three rows back, this
nondescript spot thinks it's in the
Mission. Expect authentic Mexican
food, including enormous, freshly
made burritos.

Shopping

Dylan

*2146 Chestnut Street, at Pierce
Street (931 8721/www.dylan
boutique.com). Bus 30.* **Open** *11am-
7.30pm Mon-Sat; 11.30am-5.30pm
Sun.* **Map** p148 C2 ㉙

This locale showcases a dizzying
spread of boutique designers: expect to
find clothing and jewellery by the likes
of Alexander Wang, Cacharel, Anna
Sui, Charlotte Ronson, Jill Stuart, J
Brand and Eugenia Kim, plus shoes
from Galliano, Stella McCartney,
Christian Lacroix, Chloé and 3.1 by
Phillip Lim.

Arts & leisure

Magic Theatre

*Building D, Fort Mason, Marina
Boulevard, at Buchanan Street (441
8822/www.magic theatre.org). Bus
10, 20, 22, 28, 30, 47, 49/cable
car Powell-Hyde.* **Tickets** *$20-$50.*
Map p149 E1 ㉚

Drawing its name from a line in
Herman Hesse's Steppenwolf, the
Magic Theatre has impressed locals
throughout its 40-year history with
stagings of groundbreaking works by
the likes of former resident playwright
Sam Shepard. The two 150-seat houses,
in premises overlooking the Golden
Gate Bridge, offer an intriguing mix of
new works by both emerging play-
wrights and leading lights.

Oceanic Society Expeditions

*Quarters 35N, Fort Mason, at Franklin
& Bay Streets(1-800 326 7491/www.
oceanic-society. org). Bus 10, 19, 28,
30, 47, 49.* **Open** *9am-5pm Mon-Fri.*
Rates *Voyages (reservations required)
$85-$105.* **Map** p149 E1 ㉛

A cut above most tourist trips – the
staff are experts in natural history and
marine life. At weekends from June to
November, a full-day trip heads 26
miles west to the Farallon Islands,
home of the largest seabird rookery in
the continental US. Along the way,
humpback whales can often be seen.
Trips to see grey whales take place the
rest of the year.

The Presidio

The Presidio is sometimes called
'the prettiest piece of real estate in
America'; it's certainly among the
most valuable. At the northern tip
of the city, overlooking the Bay,
the Pacific and the Golden Gate
Bridge, its location could hardly be
more stunning, but for centuries it
endured a workaday existence as a
military base, closed to the public.
Now completely demilitarised and
amazingly revitalised, it has
become a national park, complete
with 11 miles of hiking trails, 14
miles of bicycle routes and three
miles of beaches, and with the
more recent addition of several
fine restaurants.

A plot near the Lombard Gate,
formerly home to the Letterman

Crissy Field

Hospital, has been given over to George Lucas's Industrial Light & Magic film company, which spent $350 million developing the 24-acre plot into the **Letterman Digital Arts Center**, a state-of-the-art complex of offices, restaurants and studios.

Follow Sheridan Avenue west from the **Main Post** and you'll soon arrive at the military **San Francisco National Cemetery**. Continuing along Lincoln and taking the first right (McDowell Avenue), you'll soon stumble upon the humble **Pet Cemetery**, where servicemen buried their animals. Heading north, you will end up at the ocean and **Crissy Field**, an area preserved as pristine marshland.

Much of the rest of the Presidio is a jumble of former servicemen's quarters, now converted into private homes. Around 500 structures from the former military base remain, ranging from Civil War mansions to simple barracks. Some are utilitarian, but others,

such as Pilot's Row on Lincoln Boulevard near the Golden Gate Bridge toll plaza, are truly delightful. In between these sometimes melancholic clusters run numerous hiking and cycling paths, all marked on the maps available from the visitors' centres: the **Crissy Field Center** on Mason Boulevard; the **Visitor Center** in the old Officers' Club at the Main Post, and the **Battery East Overlook**, close to the Golden Gate Bridge.

Sights & museums

Crissy Field

North side of Presidio. Map p155 C2 ②
The large expanse of lawn and bucolic wetlands on the northern Presidio shoreline, Crissy Field has a military past, used first as a parade ground and subsequently as an airfield. It was returned to the city in the 1990s, and workers and volunteers restored it to its original state, planted with over 100,000 native plants: a pristine tidal marshland home for hundreds of migrating bird species.

Fort Point

Marine Drive, beneath Golden Gate Bridge (556 1693/www.nps.gov/fopo). Bus 28, 29. **Open** 10am-5pm Fri-Sun. **Admission** free. **Map** pp155 A1 ㉝

The spectacular brick-built Fort Point was constructed between 1853 and 1861 to protect the city from a sea attack. The assault never came; the 126 cannons remained idle, and the fort was closed in 1900. Today the four-storey, open-roofed building houses various military exhibitions; children love to scamper among the battlements and passageways. Climb on to the roof for a fabulous view of the underbelly of the Golden Gate Bridge, which was built more than seven decades after the fort was completed.

Golden Gate Bridge

921 5858, www.goldengatebridge.org. **Map** p155 A1 ㉞

Luminous symbol of San Francisco and of California itself, the Golden Gate Bridge (linking the Presidio to Marin County), may not be the longest bridge in the world, but it's among the most beautiful and may well be the most famous. Completed in 1937, it's truly immense: the towers are 746 feet (227 metres) high, the roadway runs for 1.75 miles, and enough cable was used in its construction to encircle the globe three times. However, raw statistics can't convey the sense of awe the bridge inspires, and no trip to the city is complete without walking, cycling or driving across it (drivers pay $5 for the southbound journey only).

Reputedly five times stronger than it needs to be, the bridge has survived hurricane-force winds, earthquakes and over 65 years of heavy use and abuse, without showing the slightest sign of damage. Built to flex under pressure, it can sway up to 21 feet and sag ten feet while withstanding 100mph winds, and can support the weight of bumper-to-bumper traffic across all of its six lanes at the same time as shoulder-to-shoulder pedestrians covering the walkways.

Although many San Franciscans are reluctant to discuss the bridge's status as the world's most popular suicide spot, there is something about that fact that engenders a solemn respect for the bridge both as a monument to the triumph of the human spirit and a memorial to its fragility.

Main Post

Presidio. **Map** p148 A2 ㉟

The centre of the Presidio is this complex of old buildings arrayed along parallel streets on the site of the original Spanish fort. Aside from the main visitors' centre, you'll also find two 17th-century Spanish cannons on Pershing Square, plus rows of Victorian-era military homes along Funston Avenue.

Eating & drinking

Presidio Social Club

563 Ruger Street, Building 563, at Lombard Street (885 1888/www. presidiosocialclub.com). Bus 28, 29, 41, 43, 45, 76. **Open** 5.30-11pm Mon-Sat; 4.30-9.30pm Sun. *Bar* from 5pm Mon-Sat; 4pm Sun. **$$$. American. Map** p148 B3 ㊱

Housed in wooden building – a former army barracks – in the Presidio, the Social Club makes for an atmospheric venue as night falls and the foghorn moans outside. The menu features unfussy classics of the comforting steaks and chops variety. With its large communal table, the bar is perfect for soaking up the atmosphere on misty evenings.

Shopping

Sports Basement

610 Mason Street, at Crissy Field, Presidio (437 0100/www.sports basement.com). **Open** 9am-8pm Mon-Fri; 8am-7pm Sat, Sun. **Map** p148 A2 ㊲

Size is everything at Sports Basement: this large branch includes end-of-line goods from top-tier brands (North Face, Teva, Pearl Izumi), offered at reductions of 30% to 60%.

Columbarium p160

Other Districts

Richmond

Bordering the northern edge of
Golden Gate Park, from beyond
Arguello Boulevard to the Pacific
Ocean and from Fulton to California
Streets, the largely residential
neighbourhood of Richmond is
a highly flavoured cultural mix.
Clement Street is the district's
primary commercial centre.

Sights & museums

California Palace of
the Legion of Honor

*Lincoln Park, at 34th Avenue &
Clement Street (750 3600/www.
thinker.org). Bus 1, 2, 18, 38.* **Open**
9.30am-5.15pm Tue-Sun. **Admission**
$10; $6-$7 reductions; free under-12s.
Free 1st Tue of mth.

Built as a memorial to the Californians
who died in World War I, and set in a
wooded spot overlooking the Pacific
Ocean, the Palace of the Legion of
Honor is San Francisco's most beautiful museum, its neo-classical façade
and Beaux Arts interior virtually
unchanged since it was completed in
1924. A cast of Rodin's *The Thinker*
dominates the entrance; the collection
of his work here is second only to that
of the Musée Rodin in Paris. A glass
pyramid acts as a skylight for galleries containing more than 87,000
works of art, spanning 4,000 years
but with the emphasis on European
painting and decorative art (El Greco,
Rembrandt, Monet).

Cliff House

*1090 Point Lobos Avenue, at the
Great Highway (386 3330/www.
cliffhouse.com). Bus 18, 38.*

Open *Bar/restaurant* 11.30am-3.30pm, 5-9.30pm daily. *Bistro* 9am-9.30pm Mon-Sat; 8.30am-9.30pm Sun. *Walkways* 24hrs daily. **$$**. **American**.

The current structure, completed in 2004 (previous buildings on this site were devastated by fire and the 1906 earthquake), includes an upscale restaurant and bar with floor-to-ceiling glass walls that make the most of its breathtaking Pacific views. Public walkways allow the less well-heeled to amble around the building. The whimsical camera obscura, a 19th-century optical marvel, was saved after a public outcry halted its demolition and is still accessible on the walkway; it projects an image of the outside world, including a large stretch of Ocean Beach, on to a giant parabolic screen using mirrors and lenses.

Columbarium

1 Loraine Court, off Anza Street (752 7891). Bus 31, 33, 38. **Open** 9am-5pm Mon-Fri; 10am-3pm Sat, Sun. **Admission** free.

This round domed and neo-classical rotunda is honeycombed with hundreds of niches, all of them filled with lavishly and individualistically decorated cremation urns. Some contain the remains of members of the city's first families.

Eating & drinking

Khan Toke Thai House

5937 Geary Boulevard, between 23rd & 24th Avenues (668 6654). Bus 2, 29, 38. **Open** 5-10pm daily. **$**. **Thai**.

One of the city's most attractive Thai restaurants, Khan Toke should be considered by anyone looking for an authentic experience. Slip off your shoes, sit on a low chair and enjoy fiery, colourful curries with excellent noodles and decent wines.

Mayflower

6255 Geary Boulevard, at 27th Avenue (387 8338). Bus 2, 29, 38. **Open** 11am-2.30pm, 5-10pm Mon-Fri; 10am-2.30pm, 5-10pm Sat, Sun. **$$**. **Chinese**.

Best known for its terrific mid-morning dim sum, the Mayflower also serves good seafood, fine clay-pot dishes and superb roast chicken and duck. Alongside the broad range of Cantonese options you'll find Mongolian beef, another favourite. The restaurant is large, noisy and family-friendly.

Tommy's Mexican Restaurant

5929 Geary Boulevard, between 23rd & 24th Avenues (387 4747/www.tommys mexican.com). Bus 1, 2, 29, 31, 38. **Open** noon-11pm Mon, Wed-Sun. **Bar**.

Although there is a restaurant attached to the bar, it's all about the tequila, on which Julio Bermejo, son of founder Tommy, is a global authority. Ask him for advice on which of the 240-plus varieties to sample; then sip, don't shoot. The house margarita, made with fresh Peruvian limes, agave nectar and top-shelf tequila, is a doozy.

Ton Kiang

5821 Geary Boulevard, between 22nd & 23rd Avenues (387 8273/www.ton kiang.net). Bus 2, 29, 38. **Open** 10am-10pm Mon-Thur; 10am-10.30pm Fri; 9.30am-10.30pm Sat; 9am-10pm Sun. **$$**. **Asian**.

This large restaurant's stock-in-trade is quality hakka cuisine, a style of Chinese gypsy cooking. Favourite dishes include the authentic salt-baked chicken served with a ground garlic and ginger paste. Around Chinese New Year there's a delicious seasonal menu, and dim sum is very popular on weekend mornings.

Trad'r Sam

6150 Geary Boulevard, between 25th & 26th Avenues (221 0773). Bus 1, 2, 29, 31, 38. **Open** 10am-2am daily. No credit cards. **Bar**.

A local favourite since 1939, this unabashedly traditional tiki bar serves the kind of cocktails that can only be described as dangerous. Planter's punch, mai tais, singapore slings, the ever-popular Volcano & Goldfish Bowl… there's a guaranteed hangover under every tiny umbrella.

Potrero Hill & Bernal Heights

On the outskirts of the Mission, the quiet neighbourhoods of Potrero Hill (loosely bordered by 16th Street, I-280, Cesar Chavez Avenue and Potrero Avenue) and Bernal Heights (south of the Mission) are often sunny, even when the rest of San Francisco is shrouded in fog. Home to a mix of young families, dog-walking lesbians and hipsters who have had enough of the Mission, both areas boast compact, lively commercial districts.

Eating & drinking

Mabel's Just for You Café

732 22nd Street, at 3rd Street, Potrero Hill (6473033/www.justfor youcafe.com). Metro to 20th Street/ bus 22, 48. **Open** 7.30am-3pm Mon-Fri; 8am-3pm Sat, Sun. **$**. No credit cards. **Café**.

The popularity of the original version of this dyke-run café prompted the owners to move to these bigger premises in Dogpatch, close to the Bay. The house speciality is a Cajun-style breakfast, with superb grits and fluffy pancakes.

Arts & entertainment

Bottom of the Hill

1233 17th Street, at Missouri Street, Potrero Hill (621 4455/www.bottom ofthehill.com). Bus 10, 22, 53. **Open** 8.30pm-2am Mon, Tue, Sat, Sun; 4pm-2am Wed-Fri. **Shows** usually 9pm daily. **Admission** $5-$20.

This little club, wedged among warehouses at the base of Potrero Hill, has long been a favourite with the indie-rock crowd. It features local and touring acts most nights, as well as occasional arena acts (Mars Volta, the Beastie Boys) hankering to play an intimate show. The decor is classic dive, with quirky touches.

Café Cocomo

650 Indiana Street, between 19th & Mariposa Streets (824 6910/www.cafe cocomo.com). Bus 15, 22. **Open** 9pm-midnight Mon, Wed; 10pm-2am Thur; 9m-2am Fri, Sat; 8pm-1am Sun.

A sizzling salsa hotspot, with DJs, live performances, and lots and lots of dancing. Tango Sundays and mambo nights add to the mix. On most nights there are dancing lessons before the opening hours listed.

Thee Parkside

1600 17th Street, at Wisconsin Street (252 1330/www.theeparkside.com). Bus 10, 22, 53. **Open** 2pm-2am daily. **Shows** usually 9pm. **Admission** free-$15. No credit cards.

This roadhouse started out as a lunch spot for dot-commers. When the boom went bus, Thee Parkside found new life as a rowdy joint specialising in roots, punk, country and garage rock. Things get sweaty in the main room, where the so-called 'stage' abuts the door. In the tiki patio out back, beer guzzlers heat up with a bit of ping-pong.

Thick House

1695 18th Street, at Carolina Street, Potrero Hill (401 8081/www.thick house.org). Bus 19, 53. **Tickets** vary. No credit cards.

Home of Thick Description, a leading producer of multiracial theatre, this black box theatre also hosts other worthwhile companies, with an output geared towards contemporary and cutting-edge drama.

East Bay: Berkeley

Berkeley worked hard to earn a reputation for avant-garde arts, leftist politics and marvellous food. A solid case can be made that the roots of San Francisco's high culinary standing lie here, principally at Chez Panisse, where California cuisine was born.

It remains a fascinating and wonderfully contradictory place, where gourmet eating is accepted

University of California, Berkeley

as a form of radical liberalism and Noam Chomsky always attracts standing-room-only crowds.

The **University of California** campus here, known locally just as 'Cal', and the birthplace of America's youth revolution 40 years ago, is the straw that stirs the Berkeley drink. Drop in to the Visitors' Center just outside the campus on University Avenue for maps and information on sights and tours.

Sights & museums

Berkeley Art Museum

2626 Bancroft Way, at Telegraph Avenue (1-510 642 0808/www.bampfa. berkeley.edu). BART Downtown Berkeley. **Open** 11am-5pm Wed, Fri-Sun; 11am-7pm Thur. **Admission** $8; $5 reductions; free under-12s. Free 1st Thur of mth.

Opened in 1970, this dramatic exhibition space is arranged in terraces so visitors can see the works from various vantage points. The collection's strength is 20th-century art, and there's also a good collection of Asian pieces.

Lawrence Hall of Science

Centennial Drive, nr Grizzly Peak Boulevard (1-510 642 5132/www.lhs. berkeley.edu). BART Downtown Berkeley. **Open** 10am-5pm daily. **Admission** $10; $5.50-$8 reductions; free under-3s. Perched on the hills facing the Bay, this kids' science museum has computers to explore the inside of your brain, a Young Explorers Area and a huge DNA model to scramble over. Fascinating temporary exhibits appeal to all ages. It's also a great spot for daytime views and evening stargazing. Don't miss the telescope and wind-driven organ pipes at the back.

Eating & drinking

Blake's on Telegraph

2367 Telegraph Avenue, between Durant Avenue & Channing Way (1-510 848 0886/www.blakeson telegraph.com). BART Downtown Berkeley. **Open** 11.30am-2am Mon-Sat; 11.30am-1am Sun. **Bar**.

A Berkeley institution, Blake's has grown up with the university. Three floors handle overflow crowds on days when Cal teams play, but at other times the space offers something for everyone: you may find a ska band hopping in the basement, a crowd from the local fraternity on the main floor and a mellow vibe upstairs. Each floor has its own bar.

César

1515 Shattuck Avenue, between Cedar & Vine Streets (1-510 883 0222/www.barcesar.com). BART Downtown Berkeley. **Open** noon-11pm Mon-Thur, Sun; noon-11.30pm Fri, Sat. *Bar* until midnight daily. **$$**.
Spanish.

It was pretty daring to locate César right next door to Chez Panisse, but it has more than held its own, despite the competition from the neighbours. It no doubt helps that the ambience here is very different (lively, thanks in part to the presence of a bar area), but the food, a collection of Spanish-influenced tapas made from high-quality ingredients, also impresses.

Chez Panisse

1517 Shattuck Avenue, between Cedar & Vine Streets (restaurant 1-510 548 5525/café 1-510 548 5049/www.chez panisse.com). BART Downtown Berkeley. **Open** *Restaurant sittings* (reservations required) 6-8.30pm, 8.30-9.30pm Mon-Sat. *Café* 11.30am-3pm, 5-10.30pm Mon-Thur; 11.30am-3.30pm, 5-11.30pm Fri, Sat. **$$$$** (restaurant).
American.

This is where chef/owner Alice Waters famously created California cuisine more than 35 years ago. Her modest, wood-framed restaurant still reigns supreme in Bay Area dining, serving impeccable *prix fixe* dinners downstairs in the restaurant and more casual à la carte meals in the upstairs café. Ingredients are always fresh, local, organic and of the very best quality. The excellent wine list combines French and Californian options, but you can also bring your own if you're prepared to pay the $25 corkage fee. You can (and should) book up to one month in

From plot to plate

Local. Organic. Sustainable. For virtually all of human history, these three words defined our food.

But by the mid 20th century that had changed – in much of the west at least. There was a glimmer of a backlash with the Back to Earth movement of the 1960s. And then, in 1971, Alice Waters, a young graduate of the UC Berkeley – inspired by a year in France eating food bought daily and sourced locally – started her seminal **Chez Panisse** (left). Waters always believed that food should be fresh and local, and 21st century environmental concerns have blended seamlessly with her philosophy.

Chez Panisse alumni have taken over the region. They are responsible for the renowned roast chicken at San Francisco's **Zuni** (p73), gourmet vegetarian **Greens** (p154), and hotspots **Foreign Cinema** (p111) and **Quince** (1701 Octavia Street, Pacific Heights, 775 8500, www.quincerestaurant.com).

Waters recently made news when she stopped selling bottled water; it's estimated that her restaurant used to sell 25,000 bottles annually. These days customers can get their tap water filtered, and – if they choose – carbonated. After all, with one of the best water sources on the planet – the Hetch Hetchy Reservoir, located in Yosemite National Park and fed by pure Sierra snowmelt – why would anyone want to truck, ship or fly it in from abroad?

SAN FRANCISCO BY AREA

Chez Panisse p163

advance for both the restaurant and café; a credit card deposit of $25 per person is required for the restaurant.

Jupiter

2181 Shattuck Avenue, between Allston Way & Center Street (1-510 843 8277/www.jupiterbeer.com). BART Downtown Berkeley. **Open** 11.30am-1am Mon-Thur; 11.30am-1.30am Fri; noon-1.30am Sat; 1pm-midnight Sun. **Bar**.
The copper bar, the interior walls clad in patterned tin siding, the pews, the two-storey outdoor beer garden… there's much to love about this pub even before you've thought about which of the 34 locally brewed draft beers to drink, and whether to supplement it with a pizza from the wood-fired oven. Jupiter is the creation of one of the founders of the hallowed Triple Rock (1920 Shattuck Avenue, at Hearst Avenue, 1-510 843 2739, www.triplerock.com).

Rivoli

1539 Solano Avenue, between Neilson Street & Peralta Avenue (1-510 526 2542/www.rivolirestaurant.com). Bus 18, G. **Open** 5.30-9.30pm Mon-Thur; 5.30-10pm Fri; 5-10pm Sat; 5-9pm Sun. **$$$. Italian**.

Rivoli is a charming, intimate and neighbourly Italian-inspired restaurant, run by talented chef Wendy Brucker. The menu offers simple versions of classic dishes, prepared with seasonal organic produce; although it changes every three weeks there are certain constants: the portobello mushroom fritters (a signature dish), for example, along with Caesar salad and the excellent hot fudge sundae.

Arts & entertainment

Ashkenaz Music & Dance Community Center

1317 San Pablo Street, at Gilman Street, Berkeley (1-510 525 5054/ www.ashkenaz.com). BART North Berkeley/AC Transit bus 9, 52, 72, 73. **Open/shows** times vary. **Admission** $6-$20. No credit cards.
Jam band groupies and folk fans will find plenty to love at this East Bay institution, which has been putting the groove into groovy since 1973. Known for its folk dance nights, Grateful Dead tributes and zydeco bands, the centre also serves up Western swing, African, Balkan and klezmer sounds.

Essentials

Palace Hotel p174

Hotels

One positive result of the lean years of the post 9/11 tourism slump was that it forced San Francisco's hotels to stop resting on their laurels and to start earning a fresh batch, through extensive renovations and innovations.

The Union Square area and Financial District are home to most of the city's large hotels. In addition, there are a number of smaller, more charming boutique properties run by operators who don't forsake comfort or style in the name of economy. Indeed, the city is home to three chains, each of which has established mini-empires of chic hotels. Both **Joie de Vivre** (www.jdvhospitality.com) and **Kimpton** (www.kimpton hotels.com) have garnered a reputation for attention to customer care and unexpected luxury at

reasonable prices. The more budget-oriented **Personality Hotels** (www.personalityhotels.com) has made a name for itself with clever makeovers of vintage properties.

Some of the big players have added individual appeal thanks to artful makeovers. The **JW Marriott San Francisco** (p172), for example, is transforming its stunning 18-storey, third-floor lobby into a 'great room', with bar, restaurant an d coffee kiosk. The eco-friendly **Orchard Garden Hotel** (p178), meanwhile, is the city's first hotel built to exacting 'green' specifications.

Information & prices

Prices vary wildly. From hotel to hotel, sure, but also for the same room within a single property,

ESSENTIALS

which might double in price from a dreary midwinter Tuesday to a July weekend or even during a big convention. The Financial District hotels tend to offer the best deals on Friday and Saturday nights, when the suits have gone home.

While occupancy rates (and prices) are rising, savvy travellers can still find bargain prices, even for peak travel times and dates. Many hotels offer internet-only deals and special packages; it's also worth checking reservation systems such as hotels.com, expedia.com and priceline.com, or San Francisco Reservations (1-800 677 1570, 1-510 628 4440, www.hotelres.com).

Downtown

Campton Place Hotel

340 Stockton Street, between Post & Sutter Streets, CA 94108 (1-866 332 1670/781 5555/www.campton place.com). BART & Metro to Montgomery/bus 2, 3, 4, 15, 30, 38, 45, 76 & Market Street routes/cable car Powell-Hyde or Powell-Mason. **$$$.**
Although it sits just half a block from Union Square, this refined hotel attracts a very discreet and wealthy following. It offers exceptional service, including valet-assisted packing and unpacking. Dogs are allowed to stay with their owners, and staff will even walk them. Room amenities are excellent, and there's an elegant restaurant and handsome cocktail lounge downstairs.

Clift

495 Geary Street, at Taylor Street, CA 94102 (1-800 697 1791/775 4700/www.clifthotel.com). Bus 2, 3, 4, 27, 38, 76/cable car Powell-Hyde or Powell-Mason. **$$$.**
This Schrager-Starck property is still the hippest hotel in town, and doesn't it know it. There's no denying the beauty of the public spaces – from the striking lobby to the gorgeous Redwood Room bar and classy Asia de Cuba

SHORTLIST

The best transformations
- Hotel Kabuki (p180)
- Hotel Vertigo (p177)
- Mosser (p175)

Eco-hotels
- Orchard Garden Hotel (p178)
- Triton (p170)

Unashamed, unabashed luxury
- Four Seasons (p168)
- Mandarin Oriental (p172)
- Ritz-Carlton (p178)
- St Regis (p175)

The best views
- Hotel Serrano (p170)
- Hotel Vitale (p172)
- Huntington Hotel (p177)
- Mandarin Oriental (p172)
- Westin St Francis (p175)

Old-style appeal
- Hotel Majestic (p180)
- Inn San Francisco (p179)
- Palace Hotel (p174)
- Queen Anne Hotel (p180)
- Stanyan Park Hotel (p180)

Best for art
- Hotel des Arts (p169)
- Hotel Rex (p170)

Best for children
- Hotel del Sol (p181)
- Metropolis (p170)
- Wharf Inn (p179)

A touch of Zen
- Metropolis (p170)
- Hotel Triton (p170)

Chic and contemporary
- Diva (p168)
- Hotel Triton (p170)
- Hotel des Arts (p169)
- Hotel del Sol (p181)
- Phoenix (p174)

Upmarket urban chic
- Clift (p167)
- Hotel W (p176)

ESSENTIALS

Clift p167

restaurant – but as a place to stay it does feel, whisper it, just a touch overrated. Sure, the minimalist rooms are on the right side of comfortable, with easy-on-the eye grey, tangerine and lavender decor, but standard rooms lack the 'wow' factor. Snag a heavily discounted rate on the website and it'll feel like value for money.

Diva

440 Geary Street, between Mason & Taylor Streets, CA 94102 (1-800 553 1900/885 0200/www.hotel diva.com). Bus 2, 3, 4, 27, 38, 76/cable car Powell-Hyde or Powell-Mason. **$$**.
The Diva has a dressier look these days, with new deluxe bedding, as well as designer lounges by top local artists. High tech complements the high style: there are CD players and 36in flat-screen TVs in the rooms, while the Little Divas suite for children comes with a loaned iPod Shuffle, a karaoke machine and a costume trunk. It's part of the local Personality Hotels chain.

Edwardian Inn

1668 Market Street, between Rose & Haight Streets, CA 94102 (1-888 864 8070/864 1271/www. edwardiansf hotel.com). Metro to Van Ness/bus 6, 7, 71. **$**.
This European-style hotel is one of the best bargains in the area, offering charm and tidiness for a relative song. It's close to various performing arts venues and with easy access to Market Street transport. Some rooms are small, but most offer private bathrooms (some with jetted tubs), and all are warmly appointed with good-quality bedlinens and nice touches such as freshly cut flowers.

Four Seasons

757 Market Street, between 3rd & 4th Streets, CA 94103 (1-800 819 5053/ 633 3000/www.four seasons.com). BART & Metro to Powell/bus 27, 30, 45 & Market Street routes/cable car Powell-Hyde or Powell-Mason. **$$$$**.
The sleek 36-storey Four Seasons is situated nicely on the south side of Market Street, convenient for both Union Square and SoMa. Its 277 rooms and suites, 142 residential condos, high-end shops and upscale restaurant create the feeling of a city unto itself. The design and ambience are pretty similar to other Four Seasons around the world: the amply sized rooms are sumptuously appointed. The list of onsite amenities is lengthy and all-encompassing; perhaps the jewel is the health club, with spa, pool and jacuzzi.

Galleria Park Hotel

191 Sutter Street, at Kearny Street, CA 94104 (1-800 792 9639/781 3060/ www.jdvhotels.com/galleria_park). Bus 1, 9X, 30, 31, 38, 45. **$$**.
Built in 1911, the Galleria Park was looking a bit frayed until the Joie de Vivre chain recently snapped it up and poured in $7 million of updates. Now its rooms provide pillow-top bedding with Frette linens, flat-panel TVs and DVD players, and free internet access and office supplies. The endearingly snug lobby, with its elegant art nouveau fireplace and evening wine reception, is the hotel's showcase of charm.

ESSENTIALS

Harbor Court Hotel

165 Steuart Street, between Mission & Howard Streets, CA 94105 (1-866 792 6283/882 1300/www.harbor courthotel.com). BART & Metro to Embarcadero/bus 1, 12, 20, 41 & Market Street routes. **$$**.

On the Embarcadero waterfront, Harbor Court is something of an undiscovered treat. The stylishly cosy rooms look out to San Francisco Bay and the bridge; in addition to niceties such as bathrobes and a top-notch Japanese restaurant and saké bar, guests enjoy freebies such as wireless internet access and a weekday morning in-town car service.

Hotel Adagio

550 Geary Street, between Taylor & Jones Streets, CA 94102 (1-800 228 8830/775 5000/www.thehoteladagio. com). Bus 2, 3, 4, 27, 38, 76. **$$**.

The Adagio has been in town in one incarnation or another since 1929. Its current version is the best yet: casual, mellow decor combines desery muted colours and arty photos, making it feel comfortable as well as chic and smart. Lather bathroom products, high-definition TVs and on-the-spot room service help guests feel pampered. Having the attractive, Mediterranean-flavoured Cortez as the bar-restaurant and breakfast room is another major boon.

Hotel des Arts

447 Bush Street, between Grant & Kearny Streets, CA 94108 (1-800 956 4322/956 3232/www.sfhotels arts.com). Bus 2, 3, 4, 9X, 30, 45/ cable car California. **$$**.

Once a Victorian boarding house, this small hotel has been dramatically altered by local cutting-edge artists over the last few years. An aggressive, urban aesthetic dominates (spray paint is popular). Bathrooms are on the small side, like the guest rooms – but then a two-room suite isn't much more expensive than the regular rate. Stairs are steep, and opening the windows will let in street noise, but pluses include flat-panel cable TV, mini fridge, a basic but free breakfast and complimentary wireless internet access.

Hotel Bijou

111 Mason Street, at Eddy Street, CA 94102 (771 1200/www.hotel bijou.com). BART & Metro to Powell/ bus 27, 30, 38, 45 & Market Street routes/cable car Powell-Hyde or Powell-Mason. **$$**.

If you're happy in this slightly edgy pocket of the Tenderloin, you'll appreciate this Joie de Vivre hotel's proximity to Market Street. Cinephiles will love the cleverly executed homage to 1930s movie houses: walls are covered in black and white images of old cinema marquees and local film schedules are posted on a board. Best of all, there's a mini-theatre, with real vintage cinema seating, in which guests can enjoy nightly viewings (albeit on a TV). Free pastries, coffee and tea in the morning will help you face the all-too-real world outside.

Hotel Adagio

ESSENTIALS

Hotel Metropolis

25 Mason Street, at Turk Street, CA 94102 (1-800 553 1900/775 4600/www.hotelmetropolis.com). BART & Metro to Powell/bus 27, 31 & Market Street routes/cable car Powell-Hyde. **$$**.

An oasis where Market Street turns dodgy, the Metropolis is eco-friendly yin meets mid-priced yang, with each floor colour-coded in shades of olive green (earth), taupe (wind), yellow (fire) and aquamarine (water). The compact rooms have nicely understated furnishings; a kids' suite has bunk beds, a blackboard and toys. From the tenth floor, where some rooms have balconies, there are splendid views over Potrero Hill to the Oakland hills beyond. A 'well-being room' will keep you centred.

Hotel Milano

55 5th Street, between Market & Mission Streets, CA 94103 (543 8555/www.hotelmilanosf.com). BART & Metro to Powell/bus 27, 30, 45 & Market Street routes. **$$**.

The Milano boasts some of the best-value rooms in Downtown, and one of the best locations. The neo-classical façade dates from 1913, while the guest rooms are modern, featuring Italian decor (blond wood, black accents). A two-storey fitness centre with a steam room, a sauna and a jacuzzi, plus a well-priced Thai restaurant with a bar that stays open late put this place a cut above the average.

Hotel Nikko

222 Mason Street, between Ellis & O'Farrell Streets, CA 94102 (1-800 248 3308/394 1111/www.hotelnikko sf.com). BART & Metro to Powell/bus 2, 3, 4, 15, 30, 38, 45, 76 & Market Street routes/cable car Powell-Hyde or Powell-Mason. **$$$**.

Part of the Japan Airlines hotel chain, the 25-storey Nikko is popular with Japanese visitors but welcoming to all. The rooms and suites are large, bright and reasonably attractive, furnished with Frette linens, pillow-top beds and pale furniture. Elsewhere, the design is clean, with Asian touches throughout.

There's an indoor pool that lets in light through a glass ceiling, plus a gym and a kamaburo (dry Japanese sauna).

Hotel Rex

562 Sutter Street, between Powell & Mason Streets, CA 94102 (1-800 433 4434/www.thehotelrex.com). Bus 2, 3, 4, 27, 38, 76/cable car Powell-Hyde or Powell-Mason. **$$**.

One of the city's most appealing small hotels. Twentieth-century literary salons are the inspiration. There are books scattered throughout, and walls are adorned with caricatures of writers with local ties. Literary events are often held in the back salon, and the modern business centre even has a few antique typewriters. Local artists' work decorates the guest rooms.

Hotel Serrano

405 Taylor Street, at O'Farrell Street, CA 94102 (1-866 289 6561/885 2500/www.serranohotel.com). Bus 2, 3, 4, 27, 38, 76/cable car Powell-Hyde. **$$**.

Right next door to the more lavish and expensive Monaco (p172), this 17-storey Spanish Revival building is no less decoratively daring. The lobby is in a Moorish style – jewel tones, rich dark woods and high, elaborately painted ceilings – but the rooms are cosier, with buttery yellow damask walls, cherrywood furniture and warm red striped curtains. The upper floors have good city views. Pet- and kid-friendly, the Serrano has a games library; guests are invited, at check-in, to play a round of blackjack for prizes. Ponzu, the hotel's hip Asian-fusion restaurant, is a great place for dinner.

Hotel Triton

342 Grant Avenue, between Bush & Sutter Streets, CA 94108 (1-800 800 1299/394 0500/www.hotel triton.com). Bus 2, 3, 4, 9X, 30, 38, 45, 76. **$$**.

This colourful hotel, across from the ornate Chinatown gate, succeeds in being both fun and funky. It's a leader in 'green hotel' practices. Rooms offer organic cotton bed linens and 'Earthly Beds', which are made entirely of

Hotel Metropolis

recycled materials; the seventh-storey 'Eco-Floor' has special water- and air-filtration systems and water-saving devices. Much of the joy, though, is in the design quirks: the small 'Zen Dens' have incense, books on Buddhism and daybeds, and there are celebrity suites designed by Jerry Garcia, Carlos Santana and others.

Hotel Vitale

8 Mission Street, at Embarcadero, CA 94105 (1-888 890 8688/278 3700/ www.hotelvitale.com). BART & Metro to Montgomery/bus 2, 3, 4, 31 & Market Street routes. **$$$**.

Blessed with a truly dramatic location on the Embarcadero (many of the rooms have great views of the Bay Bridge, and the spa is atop a penthouse suite), Joie de Vivre's Hotel Vitale is otherwise discreet in its stylishness. The capacious rooms are done out in pale colours, all the better to reflect the light, with super-comfortable beds and excellent amenities – including wall-mounted LCD flat-screen TVs. There's a spa on the roof.

Inn at the Opera

333 Fulton Street, between Gough & Franklin Streets, CA 94102 (1-800 325 2708/863 8400/www.innatthe opera.com). BART & Metro to Civic Center/bus 5, 21, 47, 49 & Market Street routes. **$$**.

Tagged by crooner Tony Bennett as the 'best romantic hotel I know', this charmer is popular with a culturally motivated older crowd, thanks to its handy location near the Opera House and Davies Symphony Hall. Framed portraits of composers hang on the walls, and there are sound systems in every room. Rooms are fairly hand-some and spacious, and most have kitchenettes (a continental breakfast buffet is complimentary).

JW Marriott San Francisco

500 Post Street, at Mason Street, CA 94102 (1-800 605 6568/771 8600/ www.marriott.com). Bus 2, 3, 4, 27, 38, 76/cable car Powell-Hyde or Powell-Mason. **$$$**.

The former Pan Pacific is far enough from Union Square that guests can avoid the crush, but close enough that the shops are mere steps away. The dazzling third-floor lobby, with its soaring 18-storey ceiling, is morphing in early 2008 into a 'great room' with coffee kiosk, bar and American restaurant. Rooms now include bigger flat-screen TVs, sophisticated lighting and a gold and sage palette with rich red accents.

Mandarin Oriental

222 Sansome Street, between Pine & California Streets, CA 94104 (1-800 622 0404/276 9888/www.mandarin oriental.com). Bus 1, 10, 12, 15, 41/cable car California. **$$$$**.

Few hotels in the world can boast such extraordinary views, or such decadent means of enjoying them, as the San Francisco's Mandarin Oriental. All of the rooms and suites are on the top 11 floors, affording breathtaking vistas of the city and the Bay. Rooms contain Asian artwork and plush furnishings in sumptuous, bold red and blue fab-rics, courtesy of a recent renovation that also added iPod docking stations and big flat-screen plasma TVs. All have binoculars, and some have glass-walled bathtubs beside the windows.

Monaco

501 Geary Street, at Taylor Street, CA 94102 (1-866 622 5284/292 0100/ www.monaco-sf.com). Bus 2, 3, 4, 27, 38, 76/cable car Powell-Hyde or Powell-Mason. **$$**.

Part of the Kimpton group, the Monaco is much more down to earth than its swanky neighbour, the Clift. But that doesn't mean it's boring: rooms feature striped wallpaper, huge mirrors and beds with silk canopies, and there are funky touches such as animal-print robes, iHomes and flat-screen TVs. Thoughtful extras include complimentary wi-fi, and free wine and cheese receptions every night. The location is great, but with the Grand Café and Spa Equilibrium within the hotel, you need never set foot outside the door.

Meet me under the clock

Even icons need updating now and then, and the **Westin St Francis** has been a San Francisco institution for more than 100 years. But tinkering with institutions always brings reactions, whether it be celebration or consternation.

The original 150-room building, funded by Charles Crocker, one of California's Big Four railroad magnates, opened its doors with great eclat in 1904. Scarcely two years later, the elegant rooms were in ruins, thanks to fire following the great earthquake. A bigger and better St Francis opened in 1907, the same year that the arrival of a grand 'master clock' from Austria set the stage for the decades-long tradition of lunch dates arranged with the phrase 'Meet me under the clock'.

Perhaps the most dramatic and best-known of the hotel's many changes was the addition of a 32-storey tower in 1971; its outdoor glass elevators still provide a free (if dizzying) ride to one of the city's most dazzling panoramas.

Meanwhile, the ornate lobby café has had a variety of guises over the decades: from its original look (said to be based on the Cluny Museum in Paris), it was

transformed into the dark-draped Patent Leather Bar, then into a lounge with kimono-clad waitresses. Later its original architecture was restored, with added Asian accents, for its incarnation as the plush Compass Rose, in 1980. More dramatic still, as part of a major lobby makeover in 2004, the Compass Rose became the *haute moderne* Michael Mina restaurant, and the clock was consigned to the mezzanine. In many San Franciscans' minds, the first change was akin to giving the Mona Lisa a moustache, the second was like moving her to the Louvre's broom closet.

But change has its rewards. The Michael Mina restaurant has become a culinary landmark, and the tens of millions of dollars worth of much-needed room renovations have brought a level of comfort that is anything but old-fashioned.

In late 2007 the St Francis launched another renovation project. Included was a remodelling of the main lobby by designer David Rockwell. Central to this will be the addition of a Clock Bar – and the return of the famous clock.

Omni San Francisco

*500 California Street, at Montgomery
Street, CA 94104 (1-888 444 6664/
677 9494/www.omni hotels.com). BART
& Metro to Montgomery/bus 1, 9X, 10,
12, 41/cable car California.* **$$$**.

This business-friendly hotel is fairly
new, but built into a historic structure,
with decor inspired by the 1920s and
'30s. The rooms are larger than you
might expect and are appointed with
good amenities, including upscale bath
accessories, plush robes and large work
desks. Service is exceptional.

Palace Hotel

*2 New Montgomery Street, at Market
Street, CA 94105 (1-800 325 3589/
512 1111/www.sf palace.com). BART
& Metro to Montgomery/bus 2, 3, 4,
30, 45 & Market Street routes.* **$$$**.

Famous guests are nothing new to the
Palace, which was rebuilt to magnificent effect after the 1906 quake and
thoughtfully renovated in 1991, main-
taining its unique identity with only a
few key nods to the 21st century.

Mosser

Elegantly furnished rooms and modern bathrooms are small, but ceilings
are high – and none higher than the
soaring glass of the Garden Court
restaurant, a popular breakfast destination. The large, fourth-floor lap pool
benefits from a skylight roof.

Phoenix Hotel

*601 Eddy Street, at Larkin Street, CA
94109 (1-800 248 9466/776 1380/
www.thephoenixhotel.com). BART &
Metro to Civic Center/bus 19, 31 &
Market Street routes.* **$$**.

Add funky styling to affordable rates
and parking for tour buses in a gritty
neighbourhood, then sit back and
watch the hipsters roll in. That's cer-
tainly the way things have worked
at the Phoenix. Rooms are bright
and casual, but they're not the main
draw. The adjoining Bambuddha
restaurant and cocktail lounge and
the hotel's heated pool are both pop-
ular places to lounge (and be seen
lounging); the free continental break-
fast is also served poolside.

Sir Francis Drake Hotel

*450 Powell Street, between Post &
Sutter Streets, CA 94102 (1-800
795 7129/392 7755/www.sirfrancis
drake.com). Bus 1, 2, 3, 4, 30, 31,
38, 45, 76/cable car Powell & Mason,
Powell & Hyde.* **$$**.

The grand and venerable Sir Francis
Drake , built in 1928, has had a massive refurbishment over the last few
years. Rooms have been updated to little jewel boxes of plush green, gold an
cream, with flat-screen TVs and DVD
players. The ornate lobby has been
rejigged to accommodate a delightfully inviting bar with a luxurious 1930s
design. The iconic Beefeater-costumed
doormen are still here, though.

Touchstone Hotel

*480 Geary Street, between Mason
& Taylor Streets, CA 94102 (1-800
620 5889/771 1600/www.the
touchstone.com). BART & Metro
to Powell/bus 2, 3, 4, 27, 38, 76
& Market Street routes/cable car
Powell-Hyde or Powell-Mason.* **$**.

Argonaut Hotel p178

Basic accommodation in a convenient location (it's two blocks from Union Square and virtually next door to the pricier Clift). Rooms are clean, but without frills. The Jewish deli downstairs is a local institution.

Westin St Francis

335 Powell Street, at Union Square, CA 94102 (397 7000/www.westinst francis.com). Bus 1, 2, 3, 4, 30, 31, 38, 45, 76/cable car Powell & Mason, Powell & Hyde. **$$$**.
See box p173.

SoMa & South Beach

Courtyard San Francisco Downtown

229 2nd Street, between Howard & Folsom Streets, CA 94105 (1-800 321 2211/947 0700/www.marriott.com/ courtyard). BART & Metro to Montgomery/bus 9X, 12, 30, 45, 76 & Market Street routes. **$$**.
Although it's run by Marriott, this comfortable, modern hotel with artful touches feels like a one-off. Amenities are far nicer than those of most hotels of this calibre. The recently upgraded rooms and suites include 37in flat-screen

TVs, and plenty of accessories (big desks, free internet) designed to cater to business travellers.

NEW Mosser

54 4th Street, between Market & Mission Streets (1-800 227 3804/986 4400/www.themosser.com). BART & Metro to Powell/bus 9X, 14, 30, 45, 76 and Market Street routes/cable car Powell-Hyde & Powell-Mason. **$$**.
A gem of a newly renovated hotel. A distinguished Victorian lobby leads up to light, modern rooms that are not large, but are comfortable, with clever use of space. All come with CD players. A few rooms are available without bath, hence the very reasonable charges at the lower end of the price scale.

St Regis Hotel

125 3rd Street, at Mission Street, CA 94103 (1-877 787 3447/284 4000/ www.stregis.com). BART & Metro to Montgomery/bus 9, 9X, 12, 30, 45, 76 & Market Street routes. **$$$$**.
The St Regis has redefined luxury (and how much people are willing to pay for it). Guest rooms come with butler service, limestone baths, high-end finishings and high-tech fixtures; rooms on

ESSENTIALS

Hotel Bohème p178

the sixth floor and above have the best city views. A combination of new and old construction, the high-rise property includes sprawling spa facilities with a heated indoor lap pool, the new Museum of the African Diaspora and two restaurants patronised by the city's elite, Aim and Vitrine.

W Hotel
181 3rd Street, at Howard Street, CA 94103 (1-888 625 5144/777 5300/ www.whotels.com). BART & Metro to Montgomery/bus 9X, 12, 30, 45, 76 & Market Street routes. **$$$**.
This trailblazing, chic and ever-so-slightly snooty urban hotel chain continues to expand around the country, but it hasn't yet reached the point at which hip and fashionable turns to yesterday's thing. For that, full credit goes to the design, which eschews grand flourishes in favour of a simple and unobtrusive stylishness. Immediately on entering the hotel, you'll find yourself in a buzzing lobby bar. Rooms are modern and loaded up with indulgences: CD players,

wireless keyboards, and goose-down duvets. The Bliss Spa includes manicures with movies.

Nob Hill & Chinatown

Andrews Hotel
624 Post Street, between Jones & Taylor Streets, CA 94109 (1-800 926 3739/563 6877/www.andrewshotel. com). BART & Metro to Powell/bus 2, 3, 4, 27, 38, 76/cable car Powell-Hyde or Powell-Mason. **$**.
Formerly the opulent Sultan Turkish Baths, the guest rooms here are well kept, if hardly stylish. The public spaces are considerably more charming, and Fino, the hotel's restaurant, is a decent spot. The main drawback: walls are on the thin side – but that's true of many vintage buildings.

Cornell Hotel de France
715 Bush Street, between Powell & Mason Streets, CA 94108 (1-800 232 9698/421 3154/www.cornellhotel.com). Bus 2, 3, 4, 9X, 30, 45, 76/ cable car Powell-Hyde or Powell-Mason. **$**.

One of a number of small hotels and B&Bs along Bush Street, the Cornell makes no secret of its origins: the Lamberts, who've run the Cornell for decades, are French imports. Downstairs is a restaurant, Jeanne d'Arc, serving complimentary breakfast and non-complimentary dinners; the place is a blast on Bastille Day. Rooms are attractive; the smallest ones have just a shower in the bath, but lower rates to match. Note that the whole property is non-smoking.

Executive Hotel Vintage Court

650 Bush Street, at Powell Street, CA 94108 (1-800 654 1100/392 4666/ www.executivehotels.net/vintage court). Bus 2, 3, 4, 27, 38, 76/cable car Powell-Hyde or Powell-Mason. **$$.**

Pay no attention to the deeply uninspiring name; this elegant, relaxed hotel gives guests a real taste of the Wine Country: every room is named after a Californian winery, and there are daily tastings beside the grand marble fireplace in the lobby. The penthouse Niebaum-Coppola Suite boasts views of the Bay, a jacuzzi, a wood-burning fireplace and a 1912 stained-glass window. But the best reason to bunk here is that guests get guaranteed reservations at Masa's (p133), the hotel's hard-to-access French restaurant.

Golden Gate Hotel

775 Bush Street, between Powell & Mason Streets, CA 94108 (1-800 835 1118/392 3702/www.goldengatehotel. com). Bus 2, 3, 4, 9X, 30, 45, 76/ cable car Powell-Hyde or Powell-Mason. **$.**

This Edwardian hotel is a real charmer; a little creaky in places, certainly, but generally delightful. Rooms vary in style, thanks to the presence throughout of one-of-a-kind antiques, but the majority are cosy and easy on the eye. The welcome from owners John and Renate Kenaston couldn't be warmer. Wireless internet is free. The traffic noise from busy Bush Street isn't as bad as you might expect, but light sleepers should ask for a room in the back.

Grant Plaza Hotel

465 Grant Avenue, at Pine Street, CA 94108 (1-800 472 6899/434 3883/ www.grantplaza.com). BART & Metro to Montgomery/bus 1, 2, 3, 4, 9X, 30, 45, 76/cable car California. **$.**

As long as you don't need to find somewhere to park, the Grant Plaza Hotel, located right in the middle of busy Chinatown, is an excellent deal. The immaculately clean (if rather small) rooms are hardly stacked with amenities (basically a bath, a TV, a clock radio and a phone), but it's all about the location, location, location for most people who stay here.

NEW Hotel Vertigo

940 Sutter Street, between Leavenworth & Hyde Streets, CA 94109 (1-800 553 1900/885 6800/www.personality hotels.com). Bus 2, 3, 4, 27, 38, 76. **$$.**

Part of the Personality Hotels mini chain, this striking property was undergoing a transformation at the time of writing. LA designer Thomas Schoos is responsible for its identity shift from the York to become the Hotel Vertigo, going for a bold effect with plenty of colour and bold patterns. Rooms here are larger than many in the city. The new restaurant has chef Tyler Florence at the helm.

Huntington Hotel

1075 California Street, at Taylor Street, CA 94108 (1-800 227 4683/ 474 5400/www.huntingtonhotel.com). Bus 1/cable car California, Powell-Hyde or Powell-Mason. **$$$.**

One of the truly iconic San Francisco hotels, this old-world, family-owned and -operated property exemplifies understated luxury. The hotel is perched high on Nob Hill, and features lovely, well-appointed rooms and suites, offering Irish linens, iPod clock radios and eye-popping views of the city. What could be better than a swimming pool overlooking Union Square? Of course, you'll pay for the privilege: if you have to check the rates before booking, you're probably in the wrong place. The California cable car line rattles past the front door.

ESSENTIALS

NEW Orchard Garden Hotel

466 Bush Street, between Grant & Kearny Streets, CA 94108 (1-888 717 2881/399 9807/www.theorchard gardenhotel.com). Bus 1, 2, 3, 4, 9X, 30, 31, 38, 45, 76/cable car Powell-Hyde or Powell-Market. **$$**.

Opened in 2007, the Orchard Garden was only the fourth hotel in the world to win LEED (Leadership in Energy & Environmental Design) certification, meaning it was designed to strict environmental standards. Chemical-free cleaning products are used in its energy-saving rooms, which are large by boutique hotel standards (and surprisingly quiet too); furnishings sport a pale green and light wood palette. The lobby-level restaurant relies on organic and seasonal ingredients. The fitness centre is petite, but discounted day passes are available to larger gyms; the rooftop garden beckons in fair weather.

Ritz-Carlton

600 Stockton Street, at California Street, CA 94108 (1-800 241 3333/ 296 7465/www.ritzcarlton.com). Bus 1, 9X, 30, 45/cable car California, Powell-Hyde or Powell-Mason. **$$$$**.

The Ritz-Carlton has been the choice for dignitaries and heads of state for years. Rooms and suites are sumptuously appointed, immaculately clean, stocked with luxurious treats and gadgets like 32in LCD flat-panel TVs and iPod docking stations. Amenities include an indoor spa with gym, swimming pool, whirlpool and sauna; the Dining Room, a top-class French restaurant; daily piano performances in the Lobby Lounge; and an armada of valets to meet your every need.

White Swan Inn

845 Bush Street, between Taylor & Mason Streets, CA 94108 (1-800 999 9570/775 1755/www.whiteswaninn sf.com). Bus 2, 3, 4, 27, 38, 76/cable car Powell-Hyde or Powell-Mason. **$$**.

Essentially, California's version of an English B&B. Some will find its lodgings quaint and delightful, others will take one look, throw both hands in the air, holler 'Chintz!' and run screaming from the premises. Either way, the early-evening wine receptions and the breakfast buffet with freshly baked bread are a nice touch (as are fireplaces in all the rooms) and the staff are charmers. The Petite Auberge (www. petite aubergesf.com) next door is a cheaper, country-French version of the Swan.

North Beach to Fisherman's Wharf

Argonaut

495 Jefferson Street, at Hyde Street, CA 94109 (1-866 415 0704/563 0800/ www.argonauthotel.com). Streetcar F/bus 10, 19, 20, 30, 47/cable car Powell-Hyde. **$$$**.

This beautiful luxury hotel is the best in the area by far. Located directly opposite Hyde Street Pier, the property has maritime decor and abundant nautical props. The regular rooms have all the mod cons (flat-screen TVs, Aveda products), but it's in the suites that the hotel excels itself: hot tub with a view of the ocean, tripod telescope in the lounge by the dining table. If you want a sea view, ask for a north-facing room on the third floor or above.

Hotel Bohème

444 Columbus Avenue, between Vallejo & Green Streets, CA 94133 (433 9111/ www.hotel boheme.com). Bus 9X, 12, 30, 39, 41, 45. **$$**.

The Bohème positively brims with North Beach Beat-era history. The walls are lined with smoky black and white photos of 1950s jazz luminaries, fragments of poetry turn up everywhere and you may even sleep in Allen Ginsberg's room (no.204). Rooms are pretty tiny, on the whole, but at least you're surrounded by cafés and restaurants. For quiet nights, request a room not facing bustling Columbus Avenue.

San Remo Hotel

2337 Mason Street, at Bay Street, CA 94133 (1-800 352 7366/776 8688/ www.sanremohotel.com). Bus 9X, 10, 30, 39, 47/cable car Powell-Mason. **$**.

Hotel del Sol p181

d'oeuvres every afternoon. Rates also include a decent continental breakfast.

Wharf Inn

2601 Mason Street, at Beach Street, CA 94133 (1-800 548 9918/673 7411/ www.wharfinn.com). Streetcar F/bus 9X, 10, 30, 39, 47/cable car Powell-Mason. **$$**.

This little hotel doesn't look like much from the outside. And, if we're being totally honest, it doesn't look like much from the inside, either. However, the location is perfect for those travelling with children, and the rates are decent (the free parking is a real bonus). The service is friendly, and most of the rooms – which are done out with a playful retro beach motel theme – have balconies.

The Mission & Castro

Inn San Francisco

943 S Van Ness Avenue, between 20th & 21st Streets, CA 94110 (1-800 359 0913/641 0188/www.innsf.com). BART to 24th Street Mission/bus 12, 14, 49. **$$**.

This friendly Italianate Victorian, built in 1872, invites you to sprawl about in its beautifully restored sitting rooms, rather than just admire them. You can also take advantage of the garden hot tub or the city panoramas from its rooftop if your antiques-bedecked room starts to feel a bit too cosy. All but two rooms have private baths; thick rugs and carpets help dampen the noise common to older hotels. A breakfast buffet is served until 11am.

Parker House

520 Church Street, between 17th & 18th Streets, CA 94114 (1-888 520 7275/www.parkerguesthouse .com). Metro to Castro & Church & 18th Street/bus 22, 33. **$$**.

A couple of blocks from the heart of the Castro, this smartly renovated Victorian caters to gay and lesbian travellers, but everyone is welcome. Most rooms have private baths, and all have homey, contemporary decor. On sunny days the gardens provide a nice respite from the

Although the rooms are on the small side and the spotless shower rooms are shared (there's also one bath), you would be hard-pressed to find a finer hotel in San Francisco at this price. The rooms have either brass or cast-iron beds, wicker furniture and antique armoires, but otherwise are fairly basic. Ask for a room on the upper floor facing Mason Street or, if the penthouse is free, book it: it's so lovely you'll never want to leave.

Washington Square Inn

1660 Stockton Street, between Union & Filbert Streets, CA 94133 (1-800 388 0220/981 4220/ www.wsisf.com). Bus 9X, 12, 30, 39, 41, 45. **$$**.

Close to one of San Francisco's prettiest urban parks, this is a convivial little inn, beautifully decorated with large gilt mirrors, pots of exotic orchids and lots of character. The smallish rooms are furnished with antiques and luxurious fabrics, and the modern touch of free wireless internet access. Guests are provided with tea, wine and hors bustling street scene. Continental breakfast, free internet access and a wine social are included.

The Haight & Around

Edward II Inn & Pub

3155 Scott Street, between Greenwich & Lombard Streets, CA 94123 (1-800 473 2846/922 3000/www.edward ii.com). Bus 28, 30, 43, 76. **$**.

You can choose from 26 rooms – some with shared baths – or three suites, with living rooms and whirlpool baths. Most have 'traditional British' (country house) decor. Complimentary continental breakfast and evening drinks are served in the adjoining pub. The inn's location is a little traffic-heavy, but it's near local shops and restaurants.

NEW Hotel Kabuki

1625 Post Street, at Laguna Street, CA 94115 (1-800 533 4567/922 3200/www. hotelkabuki.com). Bus 2, 3, 4, 38. **$$**.

As the Radisson Miyako, this efficient Japantown hotel was a favourite of Japanese business travellers. Its new incarnation, unveiled in late 2007, should appeal to both eastern and western sensibilities, with its sophisticated, modern Japanese design and plush American comforts. Rooms include 26in flat-panel TVs, iPod docking stations, and new marble and tile baths. Other oriental touches include Asian tea kettles in the rooms and a traditional welcome tea service.

Hotel Majestic

1500 Sutter Street, at Gough Street, CA 94109 (1-800 869 8966/441 1100/www.thehotelmajestic.com). Bus 2, 3, 4, 38. **$$**.

The Majestic is the oldest hotel in the city to have remained in continuous operation: it welcomed its first guests in 1904. Living up its name, every room in this white five-storey Edwardian has canopied four-poster beds with quilts, French Imperial and English antiques, and Gilchrist & Soames goodies. Ask to stay on an upper-floor room to avoid street noise.

Metro Hotel

319 Divisadero Street, between Oak & Page Streets, CA 94117 (861 5364/ www.metrohotelsf.com). Bus 6, 7, 22, 24, 66, 71. **$**.

The 24-room Metro is cheap, convenient and a good base for exploring neighbourhoods somewhat off the tourist track. The decor is bare-bones, the walls are a little thin, and the street-side rooms are noisy at night; all rooms have shower stalls only. Still, at these prices, complaining seems a little churlish. Request a room overlooking the back garden, which the hotel shares with an excellent French bistro.

Queen Anne Hotel

1590 Sutter Street, at Octavia Street, CA 94109 (1-800 227 3970/441 2828/www.queenanne). Bus 2, 3, 4, 38. **$$**.

Housed in a handsome old Victorian property, the Queen Anne began life as a finishing school for the city's debs, before being converted in the 1980s. Each individually decorated room contains Victorian antiques, and the lobby area is a splendid space. Continental breakfast, afternoon tea and sherry, and a weekday morning car service to Downtown are all included in the rate.

Red Victorian

1665 Haight Street, between Belvedere & Cole Streets, CA 94117 (864 1978/ www.redvic.com). Metro to Cole & Carl/bus 7, 33, 37, 43, 71. **$**.

Still basking in the Summer of Love, the hotel – a red Victorian, funnily enough – wears its hippie heart on its sleeve: wildly colourful rooms revel in names such as Flower Child and Rainbow, and there's a Peace Café downstairs. Rooms have no TVs; only six have private baths; some of the furnishings are looking rather tatty, but neatness wasn't exactly what the '60s were about. A continental breakfast is included.

Stanyan Park Hotel

750 Stanyan Street, at Waller Street, CA 94117 (751 1000/www.stanyan park.com). Metro to Cole & Carl/bus 7, 33, 37, 43, 71. **$$**.

ESSENTIALS

This beautifully maintained, three-storey Victorian building on the edge of Golden Gate Park has been accommodating travellers in fine style since 1904. The handsome rooms are filled with authentic Victorian antiques, right down to the drapes and quilts. Large groups may be attracted to the six big suites with full kitchens, dining rooms and living spaces. The rates include free Wi-Fi, breakfast and afternoon tea.

Pacific Heights to Golden Gate Bridge

Hotel Drisco

2901 Pacific Avenue, at Broderick Street, CA 94115 (1-800 634 7277/ 346 2880/www.hoteldrisco.com). Bus 3, 24, 43. **$$**.
The rooms at the Drisco pay a gentle homage to the hotel's hundred-year history: the decor is a crisp, modern update of past fashions, and the fittings as handsome and refined as the environs. There's a morning car service to the Financial District during the week, as well as a complimentary breakfast buffet, and free wine and cheese in the evenings.

Hotel Del Sol

3100 Webster Street, at Greenwich Street, CA 94123 (1-877 433 5765/ 921 5520/www.thehoteldelsol.com). Bus 28, 30, 43, 76. **$$**.
It's the splashy tropical palette that makes this 1950s motel sunny: the 47 rooms and ten suites (three with kitchenettes, two with fireplaces) are decorated with bright crayon colours. Guests can choose their own headrests from the quirky pillow library. Complimentary coffee, tea and muffins are served by the heated outdoor pool each morning. The free parking is a valuable commodity.

Jackson Court

2198 Jackson Street, at Buchanan Street, CA 94115 (929 7670/www. jacksoncourt.com). Bus 3, 12, 24. **$$**.
In calm, residential stretch of Pacific Heights, Jackson Court is built into a beautiful 19th-century brownstone mansion and is as quiet as a church. Each of the eight rooms and two suites is furnished with a soothing combination of antiques and tasteful contemporary pieces. All have private baths; some have working fireplaces. Rates include continental breakfast and afternoon tea.

Laurel Inn

444 Presidio Avenue, between California & Sacramento Streets, CA 94115 (1-800 552 8735/567 8467/www.thelaurel inn.com). Bus 1, 2, 3, 4, 43. **$$**.
A motor inn renovated in mid-century modern style a few years ago, this neighbourhood gem packs plenty of hip into a modest shell. Rooms are chicly appointed, with great bathroom amenities and modern accessories; some have kitchenettes and city views. The lobby level is home to the popular G Bar (p150). Service is excellent, and continental breakfast is included.

Marina Inn

3110 Octavia Street, at Lombard Street, CA 94123 (1-800 274 1420/ 928 1000/www.marinainn.com). Bus 28, 30, 76. **$**.
The rooms at the Marina Inn are surprisingly quiet. Spread over four storeys of this Victorian-style inn (it actually dates to 1924), they are all furnished with floral wallpaper, pine fittings and four-poster beds. Continental breakfast is included.

Union Street Inn

2229 Union Street, between Fillmore & Steiner Streets, CA 94123 (346 0424/ www.unionstreetinn.com). Bus 22, 41, 45. **$$**.
Rooms at this B&B are furnished in traditional style, with canopied or brass beds. All have private bathrooms, some with jacuzzi tubs. An extended continental breakfast can be taken in the parlour, in your room or on a terrace overlooking the hotel garden. Evening pampering is available in the form of hors d'oeuvres and cocktails, included in the room price.

ESSENTIALS

Getting Around

Airports

San Francisco International Airport (SFO)

1-650 821 8211/www.flysfo.com. SFO lies 14 miles south of the city, near US101.

If you're staying in downtown San Francisco, take the train from the **BART** station in the International terminal (accessible from all airport terminals via SFO's free Airtrain). The journey into town costs $5.15 and takes 30mins; trains leave SFO from 4am to 10.15pm.

BART is a far better option than the three SamTrans **bus** routes – the KX, the 292 and the 24-hour 397 – that serve SFO (fares range between around $1.50 and $4); the buses can take a long time to make the journey from the airport to the city.

Shuttle vans, which hold 8-12 people and offer door-to-door service, are a faster option. Shuttles operate on a walk-up basis at the airport, though you must book for your return journey. Firms running shuttle vans include Bay Shuttle (564 3400), SuperShuttle (558 8500) and American Airporter Shuttle (202 0733); the airport's website has a full list. The fare into San Francisco will be $10-$17; ask about discounted rates for two or more travellers in the same party. Vans leave regularly from the upper level of the terminal: follow the red 'passenger vans' signs outside the baggage-claim area.

Taxis run to and from SFO, though they're pricey: expect to pay around $50 plus tip, though you might be able to haggle a flat rate.

For a **limousine**, use the toll-free white courtesy phones located in the terminal to summon a car (walk-up service isn't permitted). The fare will likely be at least $60 plus tip.

Mineta San Jose International Airport (SJC)

1-408 501 7600/www.sjc.org.

Without a car, the best way to get to San Francisco from SJC is by train. Ride the Airport Flyer bus (20mins) from the airport to Santa Clara station, then take the **Caltrain** service to San Francisco station (4th & King Streets, $7.50, 90mins). Door-to-door **shuttle vans**, available on a walk-up basis, are quicker, but cost up to $90. A **taxi** will set you back $130 plus tip.

Oakland International Airport (OAK)

1-510 563 3300/www.flyoakland.com.

The **AirBART** bus shuttle links the airport to the Coliseum/Oakland Airport BART station; the ride costs $3 and takes 20-30mins. From the station, take the next Daly City or Millbrae train to San Francisco ($3.35; about 25mins to Downtown). Note: this is generally not a safe option for lone passengers at night. Instead, take one of the myriad **shuttle vans**, available on a walk-up basis, or a very expensive **taxi/limo** ride.

Public transport

San Francisco's mass-transit network is comprehensive and efficient. Buses, streetcars and cable cars are run by the San Francisco Municipal Railway, aka **Muni** (www.sfmuni.com, 701-2311) while the Bay Area Rapid Transit rail network, aka **BART** (989 2278, www.bart. gov) connects San Francisco to Oakland, Berkeley and beyond. Maps and timetables are available online, and free leaflets available at stations offer details on popular routes and services. However, Muni's system-wide Street & Transit Map, costing $3 and

ESSENTIALS

available from bookshops and drugstores, is a sound investment. Further details on Bay Area transit, including route guidance, can be found at www.511.org or www.transit.511.org, or by calling 511 from a local phone.

If you plan to travel often in the Bay Area, the **TransLink** card may help: the reuseable ticket is valid on all major transit networks, including Muni, BART and Caltrain. Tag the TransLink card when you start your journey (and, on BART, when you exit). The cost of the ride will be deducted, and any remaining value can be used on your next trip. When the card runs low, add funds at machines around the transit network. TransLink cards are available online and at shops displaying the Translink logo; for more information, see www.translink.org.

Alternatively, the **Passport**, valid for unlimited travel on all Muni vehicles (but not BART trains), is aimed at tourists. Passports are valid for one day ($11), three days ($18) and seven days ($24), and are sold at the Visitor Center (p189) or the cable car ticket booths, both downtown at Powell and Market, Ghirardelli Square at Hyde and Beach Streets, and in Fisherman's Wharf at Bay and Taylor Streets, Montgomery metro station, the TIX booth in Union Square, the SFMTA Customer Service Centre and SFO.

At $15, the weekly **Muni Pass** is cheaper than the equivalent Passport, but comes with two caveats: one, the pass only runs Monday to Sunday (seven-day Passports begin on any day of the week), and two, there's a $1 surcharge for each cable car ride. The monthly Muni Pass ($45), valid from the first of the month until three days into the following month, is also valid on the eight

BART stations within the city of San Francisco, but not beyond (so you'll have to pay extra to get to Oakland, Berkeley and SFO). Weekly and monthly passes are available at the locations listed above, with the exception of TIX.

BART

Bay Area Rapid Transit is a network of five high-speed rail lines serving San Francisco, Daly City, Colma and the East Bay. BART is of minor use for getting around San Francisco – it only has eight stops in the city – four on Market Street, two on Mission Street and two further south – but it's the best way to get to Berkeley and Oakland.

Fares vary by destination, from $1.50 to $6.60. Machines at each station dispense reusable tickets encoded with the amount of money you entered (cash and credit cards are both valid). Your fare will be deducted from this total when you end your journey, and any remaining value will be valid for future trips. You can add value to the card at all ticket machines.

Stations are marked with blue and white signs at street level. Trains run from 4am on weekdays, 6am on Saturday and 8am on Sunday, and shut down around midnight. For scheduling and other information, see www.bart.gov.

Buses

Muni's orange and white buses are the top mode of public transport in SF. Relatively cheap, they can get you to within a block or two of almost anywhere in town. Bus stops are marked by a large white rectangle on a street with a red kerb; a yellow marking on a telephone or lamp post; a bus shelter; and/or a brown and orange sign listing buses that serve that route.

ESSENTIALS

A single journey on a Muni bus is $1.50; seniors, 4-17s and the disabled pay 50¢, while under-4s travel free. Exact change is required. Free transfers, which let passengers connect with a second Muni bus or streetcar route at no extra charge, are valid for 90 minutes after the original fare was paid. (The transfer tokens serve as your ticket/receipt; ask for one when you board.)

Buses run 5am-1am during the week, 6am-1am on Saturdays and 8am-1am on Sundays. From 1am to 5am, a skeleton crew runs the Owl, nine lines on which buses run every half-hour.

Cable cars

There are 44 cable cars in San Francisco, 27 in use at peak hours, moving at top speeds of 9.5mph on three lines: California (California Street, from the Financial District to Van Ness Avenue), Powell-Mason and Powell-Hyde (both from Market Street to Fisherman's Wharf).

Lines operate from 6am to midnight daily. If you don't have a Muni pass, buy a $5 one-way ticket from the conductor (under-5s go free). Transfers are not valid. The stops are marked by pole-mounted brown signs with a cable car symbol; routes are marked on Muni bus maps.

Streetcars

The Muni Metro streetcar – or tram – is used rarely by tourists, though it's very useful. Five lines (J, K, L, M and N) run under Market Street in Downtown and above ground elsewhere; the F line runs beautiful vintage streetcars on Market Street and along the Embarcadero as far as Fisherman's Wharf. Fares are the same as on Muni's buses, and transfers are valid.

Along Market Street, Muni makes the same stops as BART; past the Civic Center, routes branch out towards the Mission, the Castro, Sunset and beyond. Lines run 5am-1am Mon-Sat; 8am-1am Sun.

Taxis

Taxi travel in San Francisco is relatively cheap, since the city is relatively small. The base fare is $3.10, with an additional charge of 45¢ per one-fifth of a mile ($2.25 a mile); there's a $2 surcharge for all rides starting at SFO.

The problem is that there simply aren't enough cabs, especially during morning and evening rush hours and sometimes late at night. If you're downtown, your best bet is to head for one of the bigger hotels; or, if you're shopping or at dinner, to ask the shop or restaurant call a cab for you.

Driving

Three words: don't do it. It's not so much that the traffic in San Francisco is bad – it's no worse (and, it should be added, not much better) than any average US city. However, the hills are hellish (remember, you're not Steve McQueen and this isn't *Bullitt*), the streetcars are a bitch and the parking is horrendous. There's very little street parking, and private garages can charge as much as $15 to $30 day.

However, if you must drive, be aware of a few things. The speed limit is 25mph; seatbelts are compulsory. Cable cars always have the right of way. When parking on hills, set the handbrake and 'kerb' the front wheels (towards the kerb if facing downhill, away if facing uphill). Always park in the direction of the traffic, and never block driveways.

Don't park at kerbs coloured white (passenger drop-off zones), blue (drivers with disabilities only), yellow (loading and unloading commercial vehicles only) or red (bus stops or fire hydrants). Green kerbs allow only ten-minute parking. And if you venture across the water, make sure you have enough cash to pay the toll ($5 for the Golden Gate Bridge and $4 for the Bay Bridge), levied on the return trip.

For information on the latest highway conditions, call the 24-hour CalTrans Highway Information Service on 511, or check online at www.dot.ca.gov.

Parking

There are garages around town, but you'll pay for the privilege of parking in them. Inquire about discounted (or 'validated') rates, but before you park, and always ask your hotel: few have their own lots, but many have an arrangement with a nearby garage or will at least be able to recommend your nearest. If you're parking during the day, look out for the few large city lots where you can plug a parking meter by the hour (keep your quarters handy).

Vehicle hire

Most big-name car-hire agencies are at or near the airport, though some have satellite locations downtown. Call around for the best rate, and book well ahead if you're planning to visit during a holiday weekend. Every firm requires a credit card and matching driver's licence; few will rent to under-25s. Prices won't include tax, liability insurance or collision damage waiver (CDW); US residents may be covered on their home policy, but foreign residents will need to buy insurance.

Alamo US: 1-800 462 5266/www.goalamo.com. UK: 0870 400 4562/www.alamo.co.uk.

Avis US: 1-800 230 4898/331 1212/www.avis.com. UK: 0844 581 0147/www.avis.co.uk.

Budget US: 1-800 527 0700/www.budget.com. UK: 0844 581 2231/www.budget.co.uk.

Dollar US: 1-800-800-5252/1-800 800 3665/www.dollar.com. UK: 0808 234 7524/www.dollar.co.uk.

Enterprise US: 1-800 261 7331/www.enterprise.com. UK: 0870 350 3000/www.enterprise.com/uk.

Hertz US: 1-800 654 3131/www.hertz.com. UK: 0870 844 8844/www.hertz.co.uk.

National US: 1-800 227 7368/www.nationalcar.com.

Thrifty US: 1-800 847 4389/www.thrifty.com. UK: 01494 751 600/0808 234 7642/www.thrifty.co.uk.

Cycling

San Francisco is a real cycling city. A grid of major cycle routes across the town is marked by oval-shaped bike-and-bridge markers. North–south routes use odd numbers; east–west routes even; full-colour signs indicate primary cross-town routes; neighbourhood routes appear in green and white. The *Yellow Pages* has a map of the routes, but you can also call the **Bicycle Information Line** on 585 2453 for details. Daunted by hills? The *San Francisco Bike Map & Walking Guide* indicates the gradients of the city's streets. It also describes two scenic routes: from Golden Gate Park south to Lake Mercel and from Golden Gate Bridge into Marin County.

You can take bicycles on BART free of charge (except during rush hour). Bike racks on the front of certain Muni buses take up to two bikes. On CalTrain, cyclists can take their bikes on cars that display yellow bike symbols. You can also stow bikes in lockers at CalTrain stations.

ESSENTIALS

Resources A-Z

Accident & emergency

For the ambulance, police or fire service, dial **911**.

Foreign visitors should always ensure they have full travel insurance: health treatment can be pricey. Call the emergency number on your insurance before seeking treatment; they'll direct you to a hospital that deals with your insurance company. There are 24hr emergency rooms at the locations listed below.

California Pacific Medical Center *Castro Street, at Duboce Avenue, Lower Haight (600 6000). Metro to Duboce & Church/bus 24, 37.*

St Francis Memorial Hospital *900 Hyde Street, between Bush & Pine Streets, Nob Hill (353 6000). Bus 1, 2, 3, 4, 27, 38, 76.*

San Francisco General Hospital *1001 Potrero Avenue, between 22nd & 23rd Streets, Potrero Hill (206 8000). Bus 9, 33, 48.*

UCSF Medical Center *505 Parnassus Avenue, between 3rd & Hillway Avenues, Sunset (476 1000). Metro to UCSF/bus 6, 43.*

Customs

International travellers go through US Customs directly after Immigration. Give the official the filled-in white form you were given on the plane.

Foreign visitors can import the following goods duty free: 200 cigarettes or 50 cigars (not Cuban; over-18s) or 2kg of smoking tobacco; one litre of wine or spirits (over-21s); and up to $100 in gifts ($800 for returning Americans). You must declare and maybe forfeit plants or foodstuffs. Check

US Customs online for details (www.cbp.gov/xp/cgov/travel). UK Customs & Excise allows returning travellers to bring in £145 worth of goods.

Dental emergencies

1-800 Dentist *1-800 336 8478/www. 1800 dentist.com.* **Open** 24hrs daily. Dental referrals.

University of the Pacific School of Dentistry *2155 Webster Street, at Sacramento Street, Pacific Heights (929 6400). Bus 1, 3, 12, 22.* **Open** 8am-5pm Mon-Fri.

Supervised dentists-in-training provide a low-cost service.

Disabled

Despite its topography, San Francisco is disabled-friendly; California is the national leader in providing facilities for the disabled. All public buildings are required by law to be wheelchair-accessible; most city buses can 'kneel' to make access easier; the majority of city street corners have ramped kerbs; and most restaurants and hotels can accommodate wheelchairs. Privileges include free parking in designated (blue) areas and in most metered spaces; display a blue and white 'parking placard' for both. Still, what a building is supposed to have and what it actually has can be different; wheelchair-bound travellers should call the Independent Living Resource Center (543 6222, www.ilrcsf.org).

Electricity

US electricity voltage is 110-120V 60-cycle AC. Except for dual-voltage, flat-pin plug shavers, foreign electrical appliances will generally need an adaptor.

Consulates

For a complete list, consult the Yellow Pages.

Australian Consulate-General *Suite 1800, 575 Market Street, at Sansome Street, CA 94105 (536 1970/ www.austemb.org). BART & Metro to Montgomery/bus 2, 3, 4, 76 & Market Street routes.*

British Consulate-General *Suite 850, 1 Sansome Street, at Market Street, CA 94104 (617 1300/www. britainusa.com/sf). BART & Metro to Montgomery/bus 2, 3, 4, 76 & Market Street routes.*

Consulate-General of Canada *Suite 1288, 580 California Street, at Kearny Street, CA 94104 (834 3180/ www.dfait-maeci.gc.ca). Bus 1, 9X,10, 12, 20, 41/cable car California.*

Consulate-General of Ireland *Suite 3350, 100 Pine Street, at Front Street, CA 94111 (392 4214/www. irelandemb.org). BART & Metro to Embarcadero/bus 1, 2, 9X,10, 14, 20, 41 & Market Street routes.*

New Zealand Consulate *Suite 700, 1 Maritime Plaza, Front Street, at Clay Street, CA 94111 (399 1255/ www.mfat.govt.nz). BART & Metro to Embarcadero/bus 1, 2, 9X,10, 14, 20, 41 & Market Street routes/ cable car California.*

ID

Even if you look 30, you'll need photo ID (preferably a driver's licence with a photo) to get into the city's bars, or to buy alcohol in a restaurant or shop.

Internet

Getting online here is very easy these days. Most hotels offer some form of in-room high-speed access for travellers with laptops; a number of hotels also provide at least one public computer.

In addition, a number of cafés and even a few bars across the city offer 'free' wireless access (you pay for your drink, but not the connection), and the city has a handful of wireless 'hotspots'; the best known is in **Union Square**. If you don't have a laptop, head to the **Main Library** (p71), which has several terminals available for free, or an internet café. For more on getting online in the city, see www.bawug.org, www.wifinder.com or www. wififreespot.com/ca.html.

Opening times

Most banks are open from 9am to 6pm Monday to Friday and from 9am to 3pm on Saturday. Shops usually open daily, closing between 6pm and 9pm during the week and on Saturdays, with earlier closing times on Sundays.

Police

Central Station *766 Vallejo Street, between Stockton & Powell Streets, North Beach (315 2400). Bus 9X, 12, 20, 30, 41, 45/cable car Powell-Mason.*

Southern Station *850 Bryant Street, between 6th & 7th Streets, SoMa (553 1373). Bus 9X, 12, 19, 27, 47.*

Post

Most post offices open from 9am to 5.30pm Monday to Friday, 9am to 2pm Saturday. All close on Sundays. Phone 1-800 275 8777 for your nearest branch.

Stamps can be bought at any post office and also at some hotel receptions, vending machines and ATMs. Stamps for postcards within the US cost 26¢; for Europe, the charge is 90¢.

Poste Restante (General Delivery) *Main Post Office, 101 Hyde Street, at Golden Gate Avenue, Civic Center (1-800 275 8777). BART &*

Metro to Civic Center/bus 5, 19, 21, 47, 49 & Market Street routes. **Open** *10am-2pm Mon-Sat.*

If you need to receive mail in San Francisco and you're not sure where you'll be staying, have the envelope addressed with your name, c/o General Delivery, San Francisco, CA 94102, USA. Mail is only kept for ten days from receipt, and you must present some photo ID to retrieve it.

Smoking

Smokers may rank as the only group of people who are not especially welcome in San Francisco. Smoking is banned in all public places, including banks, sporting arenas, theatres, offices, the lobbies of buildings, shops, restaurants, bars, and any and every form of public transport. There are many small hotels and B&Bs that don't allow you to light up anywhere inside. On the other hand, a select few bars get around the law by being owner operated, and employing no staff.

Telephones

The **area code** for San Francisco is **415**; the code for Oakland and Berkeley is **510**. All phone numbers in this guide are given as if dialled from San Francisco; hence Berkeley numbers have the 1-510 prefix, while San Francisco numbers have no prefix.

If you are dialling outside your area code, dial 1 + area code + phone number; on pay phones an operator or recording will tell you how much money to add.

For international calls, dial 011 followed by the country code. If you need operator assistance with international calls, dial 00.

Long-distance, particularly international, calls are best paid for with a rechargeable, pre-paid phonecard ($6-$35) available from vending machines and many shops. You can use your MasterCard with AT&T (1-800 225 5288) or Sprint (1-800 877 4646).

Collect calls

For collect or when using a phone card, dial 0 + area code + phone number and listen for the operator/recorded instructions. If you're completely befuddled, dial 0 and plead your case with the operator.

Public phones

Public pay phones only accept nickels, dimes and quarters, but check for a dialling tone before you start feeding in your change. Local calls usually cost 50¢, though some companies operate pay phones that charge exorbitant prices. The rate also rises steeply as the distance between callers increases (an operator or recorded message will tell you how much to add).

Mobile phones

Travellers from Europe with tri-band phones will be able to connect to networks here. Check the price of calls before you travel. Rates may be hefty and, unlike in the UK, you'll probably be charged for receiving as well as making calls. If you're going to be making a lot of calls it will probably be cheaper to rent or buy a mobile phone while you're in town – try the agency below, or check the Yellow Pages. Or you can simply get a pre-paid SIM card when you arrive.

AllCell Rentals *1-877 724/www.all cellrentals.com.* **Open** 24hrs daily.

Operator services

Operator assistance 0
Emergency (police, ambulance and fire) 911
Local and long-distance directory enquiries 411

Toll-free numbers generally start with 1-800, 1-888 or 1-877, while pricey pay-per-call lines (usually phone-sex numbers) start with 1-900.

Tickets

To avoid booking fees, call the venue's own box office or book online at its website. If you're willing to take a chance, the **TIX Bay Area** booth in Union Square (433 7827, www.tixbayarea.org) sells half-price tickets for many shows on the day of the performance. It opens at 11am Tuesday to Friday, and at 10am at weekends. Some venues sell through **Ticketmaster** (512 7770, www.ticketmaster.com). Other agencies, some of which charge quite hefty fees, include **Mr Ticket** (775 3031, www.mrticket.com) and **City Box Office** (392 4400, www.cityboxoffice.com).

Time & dates

San Francisco is on Pacific Standard Time, which is three hours behind Eastern Standard Time (New York) and eight hours behind Greenwich Mean Time (UK). Daylight Savings Time, which is almost concurrent with British Summer Time, runs from the first Sunday in April, when the clocks are rolled ahead one hour, until the last Sunday in October.

British readers should note that in the US, dates are written in the order month, day, year: thus 2.5.08 is February 5, not May 2.

Tipping

Tipping is a way of life in the US: people in service industries rely on gratuities as part of their income. In general, tip bellhops and baggage handlers should get $1-$2 a bag; tip cab drivers, waiters and waitresses, hairdressers and food delivery people 15-20 per cent of the total tab; valets $2-$3; and tip counter staff 25¢ to 10 per cent of the order, depending on its size. In restaurants, you should tip at least 15 per cent of the total bill and usually nearer 20 per cent; most restaurants will add this to the bill automatically for a table of six or more. In bars, bank on tipping around a buck a drink, especially if you want to hang around for a while.

If you get good service, leave a good tip; if you get bad service, leave little and tip the management with words.

Tourist information

San Francisco Visitor Information Center *Lower level of Hallidie Plaza, 900 Market Street, at Powell Street (391 2000/http://onlysf. sfvisitor.org). BART & Metro to Powell/bus 27, 30, 45 & Market Street routes/cable car Powell-Hyde or Powell-Mason.* **Open** 9am-5pm Mon-Fri; 9am-3pm Sat, Sun.
The visitor centre for the efficient and helpful San Francisco Convention & Visitor Bureau. There are tons of free maps, brochures and coupons, and plenty of advice is available. The number above gives access to a 24hr recorded message listing daily events and activities; you can also use it to request free information about hotels, restaurants and shopping.

What's on

The *San Francisco Chronicle* Sunday 'Datebook' section, accessible online at ww.sfge.com, has extensive listings. The *San Francisco Bay Guardian* and *San Francisco Weekly Guardian*, two weekly free sheets, also run reviews and listings. For online listings check www.bayinsider.com and ww.sfarts.org.

ESSENTIALS

Index

Sights & areas

ESSENTIALS